the limits of death

MANCHESTER
UNIVERSITY PRESS

the limits of death

between philosophy and psychoanalysis

edited by
JOANNE MORRA
MARK ROBSON
and
MARQUARD SMITH

Manchester University Press
Manchester and New York

distributed exclusively in the USA by St. Martin's Press

Published by Manchester University Press
Oxford Road, Manchester M13 9NR, UK
and Room 400, 175 Fifth Avenue, New York, NY 10010, USA
http://www.manchesteruniversitypress.co.uk

Distributed exclusively in the USA by
St. Martin's Press, Inc., 175 Fifth Avenue, New York,
NY 10010, USA

Distributed exclusively in Canada by
UBC Press, University of British Columbia, 2029 West Mall,
Vancouver, BC, Canada V6T 1Z2

British Library Cataloguing-in-Publication Data
A catalogue record for this book is available from the British Library

Library of Congress Cataloging-in-Publication Data applied for

ISBN 0 7190 5750 7 *hardback*
      0 7190 5751 5 *paperback*

First published 2000
07 06 05 04 03 02 01 00   10 9 8 7 6 5 4 3 2 1

Typeset by Special Edition Pre-press Services, London
Printed in Great Britain by
Bell & Bain Ltd, Glasgow

Contents

Part 3 Death and testimony

Contributors

BORIS BELAY is preparing a thesis (at SUNY Stony Brook and at the Université des Sciences Humaines de Strasbourg) on the disquieting effects of the secret in Bataille's politics. He has published on Bataille, Kojève, Derrida and deconstruction.

DAVE BOOTHROYD is Course Leader for Cultural Studies at the University of Teesside. He has recently published on Nietzsche, Derrida, Levinas and Irigaray.

FRED BOTTING is Professor of English at the University of Keele. He has published *Making Monstrous*, *Gothic* and *Sex, Machines, and Navels*. He has co-edited, with Scott Wilson, *Georges Bataille: A Reader* and *Georges Bataille: A Critical Reader*. They have two books forthcoming: *Holy Shit: The Tarantinian Ethics* and *Bataille*.

ELISABETH BRONFEN is Professor of English and American Studies at the University of Zurich. Her recent books include *Over Her Dead Body: Death, Femininity and the Aesthetic*, *The Knotted Subject: Hysteria and its Discontents* and *Heimlich*, a book on the construction of home in Hollywood cinema, forthcoming in English translation.

SIMON CRITCHLEY is Professor of Philosophy at the University of Essex and Directeur de Programme at the Collège International de Philosophie in Paris. He is the author of *The Ethics of Deconstruction*, *Very Little ... Almost Nothing* and *Ethics – Politics – Subjectivity*.

JONATHAN DOLLIMORE is Professor of English at the University of York. His publications include *Radical Tragedy*, *Sexual Dissidence* and *Death, Desire and Loss in Western Culture*.

ALPHONSO LINGIS is Professor of Philosophy at Pennsylvania State University. Among his many publications are *Excesses: Eros and Culture*, *Libido: The French Existential Theories*, *Phenomenological*

Explanations, Deathbound Subjectivity, The Community of Those Who Have Nothing in Common, Abuses, Foreign Bodies and *Sensation: Intelligibility in Sensibility.*

JOHN LLEWELYN has held posts of Reader in Philosophy at the University of Edinburgh and Visiting Professor at Loyola University, Chicago, and Memphis State University. His publications include *Beyond Metaphysics?, Derrida on the Threshold of Sense, The Middle Voice of Ecological Conscience, Emmanuel Levinas: The Genealogy of Ethics* and *The HypoCritical Imagination*. He has translated Françoise Dastur's *Death: An Essay on Finitude.*

SUHAIL MALIK is Course Leader for Postgraduate Critical Studies at Goldsmiths College, London. He is currently working on a project examining the digital redeployment of human experience.

JOANNE MORRA is Lecturer in Modern and Contemporary Art and Theory in the Department of Fine Art at Oxford Brookes University. She has published on modern and contemporary art and culture, including recent essays on translation and art history and on the film *The Matrix*. Currently, she is working on the figures of allegory and translation in the art practices of Pieter Bruegel and Robert Rauschenberg. She is a founder of the journal *parallax*.

GRISELDA POLLOCK is Professor of the Social and Critical Histories of Art and Director of the Centre for Cultural Studies, at the University of Leeds. Her recent publications include *Avant-Garde and Partisan Review* (with Fred Orton), *Generations and Geographies, Differencing the Canon*, and *Mary Cassatt*.

MARK ROBSON is Lecturer in English at the University of Nottingham. He has published articles on early modern literature and culture, Thomas More, women's writing, critical theory and the representation of violence. He is currently working on a book, *Rhetorics of the Early Modern*, editing the poetry of Lady Hester Pulter and putting together a collection, *Thomas More's* Utopia: *New Interdisciplinary Essays*.

NICHOLAS ROYLE is Professor of English at the University of Sussex. His books include *Telepathy and Literature, After Derrida, The Uncanny* (forthcoming) and (with Andrew Bennett) *An Introduction to Literature, Criticism and Theory*. He is co-editor of the *Oxford Literary Review*.

MARQUARD SMITH is Commissioning Editor for Cultural History at Reaktion Books. He is a founder of *parallax*, the cultural theory journal, and is currently working on a book entitled *Disfigures: Prosthetic Technologies in the Visual Arts*.

ALLAN STOEKL is Professor of French and Comparative Literature at Pennsylvania State University. He is the author of *Agonies of the Intellectual: Commitment, Subjectivity, and the Performative in the Twentieth Century French Tradition*, and his latest work is a translation, Maurice Blanchot's *The Most High*.

STEVE SWEENEY-TURNER is Lecturer in the Department of Music at the University of Leeds. His interests include popular music, the Scottish Enlightenment and Gilles Deleuze and Félix Guattari.

SCOTT WILSON is Director of the Institute for Cultural Research, University of Lancaster, and a managing editor of the journal *Cultural Values*. His publications include *Cultural Materialism* and, as co-editor, *Diana: The Making of a Media Saint*. He has co-edited, with Fred Botting, *Georges Bataille: A Reader* and *Georges Bataille: A Critical Reader*. They have two books forthcoming: *Holy Shit: the Tarantinian Ethics* and *Bataille*.

Editors' foreword

death is that to which, or
in which, there is birth:
once again, exposure to
the limit.

Jean-Luc Nancy, *The Experience of Freedom*

How to begin the impossible task of talking about death?

As one might expect, an immediate stumbling block confronts our efforts to respond to the challenge of this question, the question to which the articles in *The limits of death* attend: death itself. Is it possible to talk about 'death itself'? What is it? What, and how, does it mean? What is at stake in our attempts to give meaning to an experience – through figures, narratives, representations – that can never be present as such, and which, because of this, marks the edges of the possible? How to begin to explore the figurations of the *im*possible and, simultaneously, the very impossibility of figuration? In effect, does the empirical fact of death and its impossible metaphysical self-identity preclude figuration? How might one grasp the singularity of a finitude that refuses the chance of dialogue and exchange, that is also, at one and the same time, indiscriminate, motivated, criminal? How might we establish the terms of a conversation on or with this stark nothing, this differend, this mark of radical incommensurability that knows no justice? Must death necessarily elude the possibility of knowing and meaning? And how, then, to find the right words with which to begin such a struggle?

At this point one might imagine hesitation or anxiety. But the contributions gathered in this volume do not shy away from confronting the difficulties of such dilemmas. In fact, they offer striking ways of thinking and writing about these predicaments by weaving together disparate philosophical and material threads from contemporary cultural theory, Continental thought, literature, art, photography, film and music. This is not to say that their authors adhere to disciplinary boundaries, but to suggest that they move *beyond* these precise spaces would also be a mistake. They do not know the limits that restrict the possibility of thinking impossibility. They have learnt the lessons of Hegel, Nietzsche, Freud, Heidegger, Bataille, Levinas, Lacan, Derrida, Barthes and Clément, but they are not restricted to or by these teachings. Sometimes in harmonious concord, at other times desperately jarring, the pieces collected here often do not sit well with one another. This is their success: they refuse the consolations of comfort. Each of them acts as an intimation of a distinct confrontation with the limits of death, each one is a splintered piece of the incomplete that strains to map the intricate condition that is the twilight of modernity.

The work of death is never done. It provokes, it interrupts, it frays. And yet it also demands a certain intimacy.

The authors of the studies that make up *The limits of death* know that it is impossible *not* to begin to talk about the matter of death. They know that the spectral and imminent presence of death is unavoidable. They *feel* it. It touches and is touched by them. They know that death is some*thing* that must be opened out to discussion, for many reasons – not least in an effort to do justice to the dead. For there is an experience given to us by death, by the death of the other. It is perhaps the one experience that is unavoidable, that must intervene in any relationship, whether between family members, friends or lovers. How can this experience be understood? Is it available to understanding? There is an inevitable opening to the personal here, where we are touched in this intimacy: where we love, where we speak, listen, laugh, make contact. Here, we are touched by the law, by the demands of reciprocity, by ethics, by the political. This touching calls us towards responsibility: towards the impossibility of knowing, towards our knowledge of the mortality of the other, and towards the invention of an other justice.

Each of these essays marks a thought at the limit of thought, a knowledge of the borders of knowledge. Each attends to a certain rigour, in the name of a certain rigour. Each opens thought to an exemplary singularity – a text, a voice, a life, a death – that strips bare and disarticulates the practice of thinking itself. Each addresses the consequences of the death of the other for the life of the living, testifying to life. As such, death must not be condemned out of hand; it will not be shut out, for its contagion, too, endangers those left behind.

Knowing this, we ask again, how to begin to talk about death?

Through the disparate voices of love, remembrance, mourning, disappointment, bemusement, frustration, unease, inarticulacy, compulsion, anger, joy and ecstasy, the studies in this book write of the materiality of death at its limits. From the bedside of a dying body whispering its last secrets, they begin to speak with the haunting, haunted tone of a death which is never far away. For in knowing that the final destination is, without a doubt, a foregone conclusion, they seek to communicate the inadequacies of coming at death head on. In confronting this task of writing of death obliquely, we might say, the intensity and originality of these essays – heavy with the melancholic timbre of human finitude – lies in their approach to what it means to live in despair, in the radical ungraspability of death. And not only in this, for in refusing any thorough quest – a futile enterprise – to reclaim death itself for the domain of intelligible knowledge and experience, and in neither taming nor fearing mortality, they also offer ways to begin living again. Not content to announce the inexorable waning of the human and the rise of the post-human, to proclaim the efficacious overcoming of the limitations of the body and being, these essays act as weighty reminders that such triumphalism may be premature, that the corporeal and the ontological cannot wholly be dispensed with. That, at best, perhaps at worst, we are witnessing the *gradual* obsolescence of the integrity of a body (of thought), and that, as such, we are being led away from a mourning of somatic death and towards a refusal to grieve for that which is incompatible with the persistence of life: what we might call molecular death. For these studies are not concerned with the finitude of life so much as with death's infinite life, with the possibilities of life at death's end. And they also wish to establish the infinitude of death as it lives on in the historical, social and more philosophical, as well as private, circumstances of those bound to life. From the physicality of death itself, their speculations strive to mark personal contingencies, inscribing the cultural and collective memory of death as an arrangement of familiar, uncommon, but always singular encounters.

With the singularity of these encounters in mind, *The limits of death* is torn into three separate but interanimating parts. 'Death and philosophy' addresses the thought of some of the most influential thinkers in twentieth-century Continental thinking, focusing on complex questions relating to the possibility of a knowledge and experience of death. 'The body of death' brings together contributions that explore the ways in which a consideration of the material body, the human and the post-human affects attempts to conceptualize death. 'Death and testimony' offers a series of narratives which attempt to speak with the dead through emotive council with the very borders of death itself.

In the end these studies, joined in these singular differences from one another, show themselves to teeter on the very edge of experience itself. They walk along the limit of experience, marking out the event horizon of the limit experience while staggering across the limit of that experience. They cannot *not* attempt to bridge the caesura between death and life. They must try to come together uncomfortably. And, ultimately, then, the works gathered in *The limits of death* are here to talk about life.

We would like to thank the School of English, the Centre for Cultural Studies and the Department of Fine Art at the University of Leeds for supporting the conference 'Death and its Concepts' (24–26 March 1997) from which this book springs. In addition to institutional support, we extend our warmest thanks to the speakers and audience at the conference, who contributed to the enthusiasm and excitement which was this event. Similarly, our gratitude is extended to friends who were on hand in so many ways, especially Omayra Cruz, Ray Guins and Steve Sweeney-Turner. Thanks also to the other contributors to this volume who were not present at the conference and who responded with great passion and thoughtfulness to this project. Finally, we would like to thank Matthew Frost, Lauren McAllister and all at Manchester University Press.

Joanne Morra, Mark Robson and Marq Smith
London and Manchester

Death. A preface

ELISABETH BRONFEN

Death is a solitary, highly individual and incommunicable event, perhaps the most private and most intimate moment in the life cycle of the human subject. Whether it marks, in religious terms, an exchange whereby the dissolution of the body is coterminous with an entry into a new spiritual existence and, thus, the return to divinity, or whether, in the more secular encoding of what Sigmund Freud calls the death drive, it merely initiates the return to that tensionless, undifferentiated state of the inanimate that is beyond, grounding and prefiguring biological and social human existence, the finitude of death is generally acknowledged as the one certainty in any given life. At the same time it is impossible to know in advance what the experience of dying will be like, as it is also impossible to transmit any precise and definitive knowledge of this event to those surviving it.

Yet dying, burial and commemoration are always also public matters. As cultural anthropology has shown, death, in that it removes a social being from society, is conceived as a wound to the community at large and a threatening signal of its own impermanence. The dying person and then the corpse of the deceased occupy a liminal place, no longer fully present in the world of the living and about to pass into a state inaccessible to them. Rituals of mourning, falling into two phases, serve to redress the disempowering cut that the loss of a group member entails, creating a new identity for the deceased and reintegrating her or him back into the community of the survivors. On the one hand, a phase of disaggregation marks the dangerous period of temporal disposal of the corpse and the mourners' separation from everyday life, celebrating loss, vulnerability and fallibility. On the other hand, a phase of reinstallation or second burial reasserts society because it emerges triumphant over death. Thus, rituals of mourning, acknowledging the wound to the living that death entails, always also work with the assumption that death is a regeneration of life. Especially once death can conceptually be translated into sacrifice, it serves as a cultural ruse that works against death. The sacrificial victim, representing the community at large but placed in the position of liminality between the living and the dead, draws all the evil or pollution of death on to its body. Its expulsion is then in turn coterminous with purifying the community of the living from death. While the loss of a cherished family or community member evokes grief and the pain of loss for the survivors, viewing and commemorating the death of another is also a moment of power and triumph. Horror and distress at the sight of death turn into satisfaction since the survivors are not themselves dead. Visual or narrative representations of death, meant to comfort and reassure the bereaved survivors as is the case in tragic drama and elegiac poetry, ultimately serve to negotiate a given culture's attitudes to survival. Signalling such a gesture of recuperation after the disempowering impact of loss, a given society will perpetrate stories about sacrifice, execution, martyrdom and commemoration so as to affirm its belief in retribution, resurrection or salvation, much as an individual family will generate stories about its deceased ancestry to express its coherence after the loss of one of its members.

In discussing the more personal psychic aspects of grieving the loss of a beloved person, Freud has suggested that the normal affect of mourning bears resemblances to melancholia. In both cases the response to the loss of a loved one is a turning away from all worldly activity such that the mourner instead clings almost exclusively to the deceased love object. However, whereas melancholia describes a pathological condition that arises because the afflicted person is unwilling to give up his or her libidinal investment in the lost love object, in the case of mourning the lost love object is ultimately decathected, but only after an extended period during which the survivor works through the memories, expectations and affects attached to the dead. With worldly reality once more gaining the upper hand, the process of mourning comes to an end and the afflicted subject is again liberated from the painful unpleasure it had been cultivating during the mourning process. Cultural rituals such as attending wakes and seances were designed to assist such a working-through process, for they allow the mourner to enter into a dialogue with the deceased, but under the condition that this exchange will ultimately find closure, in the first case when the body is buried or in the latter when the spirit is once again released. Visits to cemeteries, or in the case of those who died as a result of wars and other political catastrophes, to memorial sites of collective commemoration, furthermore, work with the presupposition that the living no longer harbour a libidinal investment in the lost objects, even while they are meant to assist the survivors in preserving their memory of the dead.

Any discussion of the aesthetic rendition of death is thus fraught with contradictions. On the one hand, it must account for the fact that dying is always a solitary act, a highly ambivalent event of fissure both for the person dying and for the survivors. It can elicit both psychic distress and serenity, induce a sense of burden and relief and fulfil both a desire for and an anxiety about finitude, so that any images or narrative of mortality inevitably touch emotional registers in relation to an event of loss that enmesh the terrifying with the uplifting as well as with the inevitable. What emerges is a highly complex interplay of grief, anger, despair, acceptance and commemoration of the deceased, an interplay so highly personal, individual and specific that it is seemingly performed outside historical and social codes. Indeed, because the transitory nature of human existence and the possibility of an afterlife have always preoccupied the living, because all earthly life is directed toward death and one's conduct is fashioned in view of death and the possibility of salvation, representations of death seem to be an anthropological constant that defies periodization.

On the other hand, precisely because burial rites are used to reinforce social and political ideas, with tombs and funerary sculptures endorsing concepts of continuity, legitimacy and status, historians have also been eager to demonstrate that different periods are characterized by different cultural images of death and attitudes to it. The most prominent, Philippe Ariès, offers a linear development that begins with an early European acceptance of death as an inevitable fact of life, as an organic and integral part of a harmonious reciprocity between living and death. With the emergence of individualism, however, the destiny of each individual or family takes precedence over that of the community and a new emphasis is placed on the funeral as a sign of social status and material wealth. At the same time the focus on the self provokes a passionate attachment to an existence in the material world and hence a resentment of death. By the mid-eighteenth century an attitude of denial, conjoining the fear of with a fascination for death, becomes the norm. While cemeteries are symbolically removed to the outskirts of the city, the dying person and the corpse become objects of erotic, mystic and aesthetic interest. Ariès calls this the 'period of beautiful death', and, in a sense that has permeated well into the late twentieth century, aestheticization hides the physical signs of mortality and decay so as to mitigate the wound that death inflicts on the survivors.

Whether through spiritualism, which offers an androcentric domestication of heaven as a continuation or repetition of earthly existence, or through a cultivation of burial and mourning insignia – consolatory literature, elaborate tombstones and pompous cemetery monuments – aesthetic beautification renders the terror and ugliness of death's reality palatable by placing it within the realm of the familiar as well as the imaginary. By the mid-nineteenth century visits to morgues, houses of mourning and wax museums had become comparable to visiting a picture gallery. This death so lavishly represented was, however, no longer death but rather an illusion of art. Yet a seminal contradiction came to be inscribed in this allegedly modern attitude toward death, persisting today in our visual, narrative, cinematic and cyber-representations of violence, war and destruction as well as in the sentimental stories about victims our cultural discourses engender so as to idealize and make into heroes those smitten by death. The more Western culture refuses death the more it imagines and speaks of it. Aestheticization, meant to hide death, always also articulates mortality, affirming the ineluctability of death in the very act of its denial. With death's presence relegated to the margins of the social world, representations of death also turn away from any reference to social reality, only to implant themselves firmly in the register of the imaginary. Self-reflexivity comes to be inscribed in images of death in that, because their objects of reference are indeterminate, they signify 'as well', 'besides', 'other.'

Locating at the end of the eighteenth century the epistemic shift that reinstalls a discourse of mortality, which insists that all knowledge is possible only on the basis of death, Michel Foucault has highlighted the contradiction at issue. Death, which is the absolute measure of life and opens on to the truth of human existence, is also that event which life, in daily practice, must resist. The metaphor Foucault uses to illustrate how death is the limit and centre toward and against which all strategies of self-representation are directed is that of a mirror to infinity erected vertically against death: 'Headed toward death, language turns back upon itself. To stop this death which would stop it, it possesses but a signal power: that of giving birth to its own image in a play of mirrors that has no limit'(1977, p. 54). As death becomes the privileged cipher for heroic, sentimental, erotic and horrific stories about the survival and continuity of culture, about the possibility and limits of its knowledge, it self-consciously implements the affinity between mortality and the endless reduplication of language. What is called forth is a literature where aesthetic language is self-consciously made into a trope that refers to itself, seeking to transgress the limit posed by death even as it is nourished by the radical impossibility of fully encompassing this alterity. In a similar manner Martin Heidegger has argued that all life is a 'being toward death', with all existence forcing the human subject into a recognition of this abyss, into a realization that one is never at home in the world. Such an encounter with the nothingness of the veiledness (*Verhülltheit*) of death, although it initially calls forth anxiety, ultimately leads to the recognition of the truth of being, namely, an experience of the ontological difference between being (*Sein*) and beingness (*Seiendes*), with the former overcoming the latter. Representation for Heidegger is authentic when it bows into the silence evoked by the measurelessness of death, while any language that avoids death is for him mere idle chatter. Similarly Georges Bataille describes the trajectory of human existence as a move from a discontinuous state of earthly fracture and difference to a state of unlimited continuity through death.

Speaking of the aesthetic rendition of death thus ultimately brings into play the issue of misrepresentation, for the paradox inherent in representations of death is that this 'death' is always culturally constructed and performed within a given historically specific philosophical and anthropological discourse on mortality, resurrection and immortality. Since death lies outside any living subject's personal or collective realm of experience, this 'death' can only be rendered as an idea, not something known as a bodily sensation. This idea, furthermore, involves imagery not directly belonging to it, so that it is always figural, the privileged trope for other values. Placed beyond the register of what the living subject can know, 'death' can only be read as a signifier with an incessantly receding, ungraspable signified, invariably always pointing back self-reflexively to other signifiers. Death remains outside clear categories. It is nowhere because it is only a gap, a cut, a transition between the living body and the corpse, a before (the painful fear, the serene joy of the dying person) and an after (the mourning of the survivor), an ungraspable point, lacking any empirical object. At the same time it is everywhere, because death begins with birth and remains present on all levels of daily existence, each moment of mortal existence insisting that its measure is the finitude toward which it is directed.

Put apodictically, death is the one privileged moment of the absolutely real, of true, non-semiotic materiality and facticity as these appear in the shape of the mutability and vulnerability of the material body. On the one hand, then, it demarcates figural language by forcing us to recognize that even though language, when faced with death, is never referentially reliable, it also cannot avoid referentiality. Non-negotiable and non-alterable, death is the limit of language, disrupting our system of language as well as our image repertoire, even as it is its ineluctable ground and vanishing point. On the other hand, signifying nothing, it silently points to the indetermination of meaning so that one can speak of death only by speaking other. The aporia at issue can be formulated in the following manner: as the point where all language fails, it is also the source of all allegorical speaking. But precisely because death is excessively tropic, it also points to a reality beyond, evoking the referent that representational texts may point to but not touch. Death, then, is both most referential and most self-referential, a reality for the experiencing subject but non-verifiable for the speculating and spectating survivor.

Yet the numerous literary depictions of deathbed scenes also illustrate that representations of death not only attest to the fallibility of aesthetic language and the impermanence of human existence but that they also confirm social stability in the face of mortality precisely by virtue of a language of death. The force of these narratives resides in the fact that in their last moments the dying have a vision of afterlife, while at the same time the aesthetic rendition of the deathbed ritual includes the farewell greetings from kin and friends and the redistribution of social roles and property that serve to negotiate kinship succession. Thus a sense of human continuity, so fundamentally questioned in the face of death, is also assured in relation to both ancestors and survivors. Indeed, as Walter Benjamin argues, death is the sanction for any advice a storyteller might seek to transmit. Speaking in the shadow of one's own demise, as well as against this finitude, is precisely what endows these stories with supreme authority.

Representations of death, therefore, ground the way a culture stabilizes and fashions itself as an invincible and omnipotent, eternal, intact symbolic order, but they can do so only by incessantly addressing the opposition between death and life. As the sociologist Jean Baudrillard argues, the phenomenon of survival must be seen in contingency with a prohibition of death and the establishment of social surveillance of this prohibition. Power is first and foremost grounded in legislating death, by manipulating and controlling the exchange between life and death, by severing the one from the other and by imposing a taboo on the dead. Power is thus installed precisely by drawing this first boundary, and all supplementary aspects of division – between soul and body, masculinity and femininity, good and bad – feed off this initial and initiating separation that partitions life from death. Any aesthetic rendition of death can be seen in light of such ambivalent boundary drawing.

Referring to the basic fact of mortal existence, these representations fascinate because they allow us indirectly to confront our
own death, even though on the manifest level they appear to
revolve around the death of the other. Death is on the other side
of the boundary. We experience death by proxy, for it occurs in
someone else's body and at another site, as a narrative or visual
image. The ambivalent reassurance these representations seem
to offer is that, although they insist on the need to acknowledge
the ubiquitous presence of death in life, our belief in our own
immortality is nevertheless also confirmed. We are the survivors
of the tale, entertained and educated by virtue of the death
inflicted on others. Yet, although representations of death may
allow us to feel assured because the disturbance played through
in the narrative ultimately finds closure, the reader or spectator is
nevertheless also drawn into the liminal realm between life and
death so that partaking of the fantasy scenario often means hesi-
tating between an assurance of a recuperated mastery over and
submission before the irrevocable law of death.

Any representation of death, therefore, also involves the disturbing return of the repressed knowledge of death, the excess
beyond the text, which the latter aims to stabilize by having
signs and images represent it. As these representations oscillate
between the excessively tropic and a non-semiotic materiality,
their real referent always eludes the effort at recuperation that
representations seek to afford. It disrupts the system at its
very centre. Thus, many narratives involving death work with a
tripartite structure. Death causes a disorder to the stability of a
given fictional world and engenders moments of ambivalence,
disruption or vulnerability. This phase of liminality is followed
by narrative closure, where the threat that the event of death
poses is again recuperated by a renewed return to stability.
Yet the regained order encompasses a shift because it will never
again be entirely devoid of traces of difference. Ultimately these
narratives broadcast the message that recuperation from death
is imperfect, the regained stability is not safe and the urge for
order is inhabited by a fascination with disruption and split.
The certainty of survival emerges over and out of the certainty
of dissolution.

Ultimately, the seminal ambivalence that subtends all representations of death resides in the fact that, while they are morally educating and emotionally elevating, they also touch on the knowledge of our mortality, which for most is so disconcerting that we would prefer to disavow it. They fascinate with dangerous knowledge. In the aesthetic enactment, however, we have a situation that is impossible in life, namely, that we share death vicariously and return to the living. Even as we are forced to acknowledge the ubiquitous presence of death in life, our belief in our own immortality is confirmed. The aesthetic representation of death lets us repress our knowledge of the reality of death precisely because here death occurs in someone else's body and as an image or a narrative. Representations of death, one could say, articulate an anxiety about and a desire for death, functioning like a symptom, which psychoanalysis defines as a repression that, because it fails, gives to the subject, in the guise of a ciphered message, the truth about his or her desire that he or she could not otherwise confront. In a gesture of compromise, concealing what they also disclose, these fundamentally duplicitous representations try to maintain a balance of sorts. They point obliquely to that which threatens to disturb the order but articulate this disturbing knowledge of mortality in a displaced, recoded and translated manner, and by virtue of the substitution render the dangerous knowledge as something beautiful, fascinating and ultimately reassuring. Visualizing even as they conceal what is too dangerous to articulate openly but too fascinating to repress successfully, they place death away from the self at the same time that they ineluctably return the desire for and the knowledge of finitude and dissolution, upon and against which all individual and cultural systems of coherence and continuation rest.

Literature used

Ariès, P., *The Hour of Our Death*, trans. H. Weaver (Oxford: Oxford University Press, 1981).

Barthes, R., *Camera Lucida*, trans. R. Howard (New York: Hill and Wang, 1981).

Bataille, G., *L'Erotisme* (Paris: Editions de Minuit, 1957).

Baudrillard, J., *L'Echange symbolique et la mort* (Paris: Gallimard, 1976).

Bauman, Z., *Mortality, Immortality, and Other Life strategies* (Stanford: Stanford University Press, 1992).

Benjamin, W., 'Der Erzähler', in *Gesammelte Schriften 2.2*, ed. R. Tiedemann and H. Schweppenhäuser (Frankfurt am Main: Suhrkamp, 1977), pp. 438–65.

Blanchot, M., *The Gaze of Orpheus and Other Literary Essays*, ed. P. Adams Sitney, trans. L. Davis (Barrytown, N.Y.: Station Hill, 1981).

Bloch, M., and J. Parry, eds, *Death and the Regeneration of Life*, (Cambridge and New York: Cambridge University Press, 1982).

Choron, J., *Modern Man and Mortality* (New York: Macmillan, 1964).

Derrida, J., *The Gift of Death*, trans. D. Wills (Chicago: Chicago University Press, 1995).

Foucault, M., *Language, Counter-Memory, Practice: Selected Essays and Interviews*, trans. and ed. D. F. Boucard and S. Simon (Ithaca, N.Y.: Cornell University Press, 1977).

Freud, S., 'Mourning and Melancholia', in *Standard Edition of the Complete Psychological Works of Sigmund Freud 18*, ed. J. Strachey (London: Hogarth Press, 1955 [1917]).

Freud, S., 'Beyond the Pleasure Principle', in *Standard Edition of the Complete Psychological Works of Sigmund Freud 18*, ed. J. Strachey (London: Hogarth Press, 1955 [1920]).

Heidegger, M., *Sein und Zeit*, 15th edn (Tübingen: Max Niemeyer, 1979).

Kofman, S., *Mélancholie de l'art* (Paris: Galilée, 1985).

Kristeva, J., *Powers of Horror: An Essay on Abjection*, trans. L. S. Roudiez (New York: Columbia University Press, 1982).

Vernant, J.-P., *Mortals and Immortals: Collected Essays*, ed. F. I. Zeitlin (Princeton: Princeton University Press, 1991).

Part 1
Death and philosophy

1

To die laughing

SIMON CRITCHLEY

'Wie heisst du denn?' fragt man ihn. 'Odradek', sagt er. 'Und wo
wohnst du?' 'Unbestimmter Wohnsitz', sagt er und lacht; aber es
ist nur ein Lachen, wie man es ohne Lungen hervorbringen kann.
Es klingt etwa so, wie das Rascheln in gefallenen Blätter. Damit ist
die Unterhaltung meist zu Ende.

Kafka, 'Die Sorge des Hausvaters'

Although in these indifferentist times one normally only finds it
written on toilet walls, let us begin by considering the meaning of
the following proposition: God is dead.[1] It means, I think, that any
philosophical thinking through of the meaning of human finitude –
and thus the question of death – has to begin with acceptance of
religious disappointment. Such disappointment is the realization that
religion is no longer capable of providing a meaning for human
finitude or a framework for thinking through the question of death.
The religious disappointment that follows the awareness of the death
of God provokes and opens the question of meaning: namely, what
might count as a meaning for life in the absence of religious belief?

The great metaphysical comfort of religion, its existential balm,
surely resides in the claim that the meaning of life lies outside of
life and outside of humanity; and even if, as Kant insisted, this
outside is beyond our limited cognitive powers, we can still turn
our faith in this direction. For me, any philosophical thinking
through of the meaning of human finitude, and of the event that
we call death, has to begin from the literal in-credibility of this
claim. Namely that the possibility of belief in God or in some God-
equivalent, whether vindicable through reason or faith alone, has
decisively broken down.

Of course, the proper name for this breakdown is *modernity*, and the task of philosophical modernity, at least in its peak experiences – Hegel, Nietzsche, Heidegger – is a thinking through of the death of God in terms of human finitude. Importantly, such a thinking through does not only entail the death of the God of the Judaeo-Christian tradition, but also the death of all those ideals, norms, principles, rules, ends and values that are set above humanity in order to provide human beings with a meaning to life, or at least serve to justify a certain social–political–economic arrangement. Such is the twilight of the idols. As Heidegger notes in a striking remark from 1925, thinking of Nietzsche, 'Philosophical research is and remains atheism, which is why philosophy can allow itself "the arrogance of thinking"'. As some of you will be painfully aware, philosophy is nothing if not arrogant, and furthermore it *should* be arrogant, a continual arrogation of the human voice. But the source of philosophical arrogance, its unquestionable hubris, is a disappointment that flows from the dissolution of meaning, the frailty that accompanies the recognition of the all too human character of the human. So, under the conditions of modernity, philosophy is atheism.

Now – and here's the rub – if atheism produced contentment, then I think philosophy would be at an end. Contented atheists, like happy cattle, have no reason to bother themselves with philosophy other than as a rather mediocre cultural distraction or as a technical means of sharpening their common sense and becoming a bright chap. However, on my view, atheism does not provide contentment, but rather *unease*. And it is from this mood of unease that philosophy begins its anxious, melancholy dialectics, its tail-biting paradoxes, as Nietzsche writes in the *Will to Power*, 'Not to esteem what we know, not to be *allowed* to esteem the lies we should like to tell ourselves'. Those familiar with the lunar landscape of philosophical modernity will recognize this uneasy situation as a description of the problem of nihilism, a problem provoked by the realization of the death of God. It is through an engagement with the problem of nihilism, I believe, that the problem of human finitude and death is best approached.

I cannot in this context give the necessary genealogy of nihilism that would enable us to see how finitude has been approached in the *Atheismusstreit* of philosophical modernity. Such a genealogy would involve us in a veritable Cook's tour of German idealism and romanticism (Jacobi's critique of Fichte, Jean Paul's critique of poetic nihilism) and would have us looking at Feuerbach, Stirner and Russian literature of the 1860s and 1870s, in particular Turgenev and Dostoevsky.

But nihilism obviously receives its definitive philosophical articulation in Nietzsche, where it is defined necessarily paradoxically: 'That the highest values devalue themselves' (emphasis here should be placed on the reflexive character of this formulation, '*dass die obersten Werte* sich *entwerten*'). Nihilism is the breakdown of the order of meaning, where all that was posited as a transcendent source of value becomes null and void – the true world becomes a fable – and there are no skyhooks on which to hang a meaning for life. Through a self-reflexive process of historical degeneration (in other words, the Reformation), all transcendent claims for a meaning to life have been reduced to mere values, and those values have become incredible, standing in need of what Nietzsche calls 'transvaluation' or 'revaluation'. For Nietzsche, nihilism as a psychological state is only attained when we realize that the categories by means of which we have tried to give meaning to life and the universe are themselves meaningless. Further – reflexively once again – for Nietzsche, nihilism is not simply the negation of the Christian-moral world-view, as it is for Jacobi and Dostoevsky, it is rather the *consequence* of that world-view. That is to say, nihilism is the consequence of moral valuation, it is the consequence of the Christian-moral interpretation of the world, or more precisely it is the consequence of the disappointment with that interpretation.

Because we can no longer believe in God, existence is suddenly declared meaningless – *incipit* Schopenhauer. Nietzsche puts it sharply: 'Faith in the categories of reason is the cause of nihilism.' We therefore require new post-rationalist categories and new post-Christian values that will permit us to endure the world of pure becoming without either inventing a new God or declaring that sheer becoming is meaningless. Such is obviously the motivation for Nietzsche's teaching of eternal return, namely the affirmation of 'existence as it is, without meaning or aim, yet recurring inevitably without any finale in nothingness'. Although the teaching of eternal return is highly enigmatic and open to conflicting interpretations, the doctrine can perhaps simply be understood as that which enables one to endure the world of becoming without resenting it or seeking to construct some new hinter-world, some new God.

To put this argument in a slightly different register, the historical pathology of modernity of which nihilism is the diagnosis consists in the recognition of a double, reflexively tail-biting, failure:

1 That the values of modernity or Enlightenment do not connect with the fabric of moral and social relations, with the stuff of everyday life, failing to produce a fusion of pure and practical reason in a new rational or aesthetic totality. The moral values of the Enlightenment – and this is the core of Hegel's critique which is inherited by the Left Hegelians and the young Marx (where Enlightenment values become bourgeois values) – lack any effectivity, any *Wirklichkeit*, and connection to praxis.
2 However, the worse news is that not only do the moral values of Enlightenment fail to connect with the fabric of moral and social reflections, but they lead instead to the progressive degradation of those relations through processes that we might call with Weber, rationalization, with Marx, capitalization, with Adorno and Horkheimer, instrumental rationality, and with Heidegger, the oblivion of Being. Such is Enlightenment's fateful and paradoxical dialectic.

Thus a (arguably, the) governing problem of philosophical modernity, on this admittedly crude sketch, is how to confront the problem of nihilism after one has seen how the values of Enlightenment not only fail to get a grip on everyday life but lead instead to its progressive disintegration. In Lacanian terms (and, incidentally, I think that Freudian psychoanalysis only makes sense as a consequence of and response to the problem of nihilism, where Freud pulls up the floor in the house of being to find out where the smell is coming from and where the bodies are buried) the Sadean universe of anti-morality is only conceivable on the basis of the Kantian elimination of the pathological object, passion and sentiment from the realm of morality. Kantianism is the necessary precondition for its perverse inversion into Sadism.

As will have already become clear, to accept the diagnosis of modernity in terms of the problem of nihilism is to accept the ubiquity of the finite, the irreducibility of the question of human finitude. That is to say, the question of the meaning of life must be approached from within the awareness of the death of God. That is to say, if God is dead, and if all Enlightenment God-equivalents have become devalued and degraded in nihilism's tail-biting dialectic, then the response to the question of the meaning of life must be sought *within life*, conceived of as a finite temporal stretch between birth and death. So, under the nihilistic conditions of modernity, the question of the meaning of life becomes a matter of finding a meaning to human finitude. In this way we rejoin Cicero's question, restated by Montaigne as: 'That to philosophise is to learn how to die'. The difference between this conception of modernity and Ciceronian antiquity is that there is little sense of philosophy as a calmative influence, as a consolation as it was for Boethius, that prepares the individual stoically for the passage on to either oblivion or eternal bliss. Beckett's Murphy strapped to his chair, or Kafka's Jäger Gracchus, in 'The Hunter Gracchus', drifting in his barge unable either to live or die, have replaced the Garden of Epicurus as images of the philosopher in late modernity. To philosophize in the epoch of nihilism is to learn how to die *this* death, *my* death, knowing that there is nothing else after this death. One can still mime the sophistical procedures of Pascal's wager, but the bank has long been broken in God's heavenly casino.

Death can obviously, and sometimes painfully, simply be a brute fact from which it is difficult to extract a meaning. Death can strike meaninglessly and, contrary to Biblical wisdom, it can sting with the sudden meaninglessness of a bereavement. However, if death is not just going to have the character of a brute fact, mortality is something in which one has to find a meaning. In the vocabulary of Heidegger's *Being and Time,* death is something that one has to project freely in a resolute decision (*Entschlossenheit*). Thus, the acceptance of the ubiquity of the finite is not simply expressed in the fact that human beings are mortal – this is merely banal – but rather that the human being must *become* mortal. '*Werde was du bist!*' as Nietzsche said and as Heidegger was fond of quoting in *Being and Time*. For the early Heidegger death is something to be achieved; it is the fundamental *possibility* that permits us to get the totality of existence, and hence authenticity (according to Heidegger's logic of *Ganzheit*), into our grasp. The human being is death in the process of becoming. Death is the possibility of impossibility – a proposition upon which Levinas and Blanchot will wreak havoc, inverting it into 'the impossibility of possibility'. But I will come to that presently.

A pervasive, active and highly romantic response to nihilism, which continues to bewitch people who should really know better and which haunts Heidegger up to the period of his commitment to National Socialism, is to see the collapse of theological certainty that follows on the death of God as the occasion for an explosion of creative energy in which death becomes one's work and nihilism is heroically overcome in a blazing affirmation of finitude. A key text for this question in relation to Heidegger is his utterly distasteful eulogy to Albert Leo Schlageter, supposed early martyr of the Third Reich, delivered on 26 May 1933, in which Heidegger praises Schlageter's 'hardness of will', which allowed him to endure the 'most difficult' and 'greatest' death of all:

> As he stood defenceless facing the rifles, the hero's inner gaze soared above the muzzles to the daylight and mountains of his home that he might die for the German people and its Reich with the Alemannic countryside before his eyes.

In the face of a god-less world, individual authenticity produces itself through acts of self-invention and self-creation, acts in which the self is invented or created through a relation with death, in which death becomes the work of the subject and suicide becomes the ultimate existential possibility. This is, of course, a description of what Dostoevsky calls 'logical suicide'; it is logical because Dostoevsky argues that once the belief in the immortality of the soul, the 'loftiest idea' of which humans are capable, has broken down, suicide is the only logical conclusion. Such is the position that he puts into the mouth of Kirilov in *The Devils*:

> Everyone who desires supreme freedom must dare to kill him-
> self. ... He who dares to kill himself is a god. Now everyone can
> make it so that there shall be no God and there shall be nothing.
> But no one has done so yet.

Cruelly and crudely, there is an almost logical contradiction at the heart of this romantic-heroic conception of suicide, namely that if death is my ownmost possibility, it is also precisely the moment when the 'I' and its possibilities disappear. In suicide, *the 'I' wants to give itself power to control the disappearance of its power.* If the resolute decision of the suicide is to say, 'I withdraw from the world, I will act no longer', he or she wants to make death an act, a final and absolute assertion of the power of the 'I'. *Can death be an object of the will?* That is the question. Blanchot, whose arguments I am following closely here, writes:

> The weakness of suicide lies in the fact that whoever commits it
> is still too strong. He is demonstrating a strength suitable only
> for a citizen of the world. Whoever kills himself, could, then,
> go on living: whoever kills himself is linked to hope, the hope of
> finishing it all.

The desire of the suicide is too strong and too hopeful because it conceives of death as the action of an 'I' in the realm where the 'I' and its action no longer pertain. The contradiction of the suicide is analogous to that of the insomniac, who cannot will him- or herself to sleep because sleep is not an exercise of the will – sleep does not come the person who wills it.

Paradoxically, the suicide, in desiring to rid him- or herself of the world, acts with an affirmativeness that would equal the most resolute, heroic and Creon-like of worldly citizens. Blanchot continues:

> He who kills himself is the great affirmer of the *present.* I want to
> kill myself in an 'absolute' instant, the only one which will not
> pass and will not be surpassed. Death, if it arrived at the time
> we choose, would be an apotheosis of the instant; the instant in
> it would be that very flash of brilliance which mystics speak of,
> and surely because of this, suicide retains the power of an
> exceptional affirmation.

Suicide is the fantasy of total affirmation, an ecstatic assertion of the absolute freedom of the subject in its union with nature or the divine at the moment of death, a mystical sense of death as the *scintilla dei*, the spark of god. One can find analogies with this conception of death in Hölderlin's fascination with the death of Empedocles (a figure who – happily enough – he was never able to kill as the various drafts of the play show) or more widely in the Jena romantics, where Friedrich Schlegel writes of 'the enthusiasm of annihilation', in which 'the meaning of divine creation is revealed for the first time. Only in the midst of death does the lightning bolt of eternal life explode.' The moment of annihilation is the becoming-enthused, the possession by and the identification with the god – rapture, fervour, intensity. The moment of the controlled extinction of the subject is also, paradoxically, the moment when the subject swells to fill the entire cosmos, becoming, like Walt Whitman, a cosmos and the uncreated creator of the cosmos. The death of the self confirms its deathlessness. As Baudelaire defines pantheism in his 'Fusées': 'Panthéisme. Moi, c'est tous; tous c'est moi.' Such is also the death ecstasy of eternal return in Nietzsche, expressed in a stunning fragment from the *Nachlass*:

> Five, six seconds and no more: then you suddenly feel the presence of eternal harmony. Man, in his mortal frame, cannot bear it; he must either physically transform himself or die ... In these five seconds I would live the whole of human existence, I would give my whole life for it, the price would not be too high. In order to endure this any longer one would have to transform oneself physically. I believe man would cease to beget. *Why have children when the goal is reached?*

The romantic and post-romantic affirmation of annihilation – which justifies both the right-wing radicalism of the young Heidegger or Ernst Jünger and the leftist terroristic radicalism of someone like Ulrike Meinhoff, and which continues to this day in the shabby intellectual provincialism of cyber-antihumanism – is an attempt at the appropriation of *time*, to gather time into the living present of eternity at the moment of death. The affirmation of finitude takes place through the transformation of the temporal into the eternal through the suicidal leap into the void: 'only in the midst of death does the lightning bolt of eternal life explode'.

By contrast, and this is the counterposition I will try to develop, the person who *actually* lives in despair, those lives of quiet desperation that make up so much of the untheorized content of everyday life, dwells in the interminable temporality of dying, in what Blanchot calls *le temps mort*, where time is experienced as passing, as slipping away – the wrinkling of the skin, the murmuring of senescence, crispation. Such a person has all the time in the world and, paradoxically, has no time and, as Blanchot remarks in a wonderful image, 'no present upon which to brace himself in order to die'. If the suicidal affirmation of finitude ultimately denies the temporal by transforming it into the eternal, then the more difficult task is living in the temporal, being moved within the endless procrastination of a time that exceeds the will. Such an experience of time can be described as *temporization* – time as delay, as waiting, as deferral, as procrastination.

This temporality of dying is wonderfully evoked in Beckett's *Malone Dies*. The 'I' that speaks in Beckett's books has no time and yet has all the time in the world: 'I could die today, if I wished, merely by making a little effort. But it is as well to let myself die, quietly, without rushing things.' Or again, the final lines of 'Dante and the Lobster':

'Well, thought Belacqua, it's a quick death, God help us all.
"It is not".'

The point I want to make here can also be made with reference to the theme of *laughter*, to which I shall return below. On the one hand, there is the laughter of eternal return, laughter *as* eternal return, the golden Nietzschean laughter of affirmation, which laughs in the face of the firing squad; a laughter that I always suspect emanates from the mountain tops – a neurotic laughter, solitary, hysterical, verging on sobbing. On the other hand, there is Beckett's laughter, but equally the comic genius of a Frankie Howerd or a Tommy Cooper, which is more sardonic and sarcastic, and which arises out of a palpable sense of inability, impotence, impossibility. For me at least it is this second laughter that is more joyful (not to mention a lot funnier): 'If I had the use of my body I would throw it out of the window. But perhaps it is the knowledge of my impotence that emboldens me to that thought.'

As Stephen Dedalus remarks with what Joyce calls 'saturnine spleen', 'Death is the highest form of life. Ba!'

To want to commit suicide is to want to die *now*, in the living/dying present of the *Jetztpunkt*, and, as Wittgenstein says in one of those unvisited corners of the *Tractatus*, the eternal life is given to those who live in the present. As such, within suicide *there is an attempt to abolish both the mystery of the future and the mystery of death*. Suicide – or euthanasia for that matter – wishes to eliminate death as the prospect of a contingent future that I will not be able to control, to avoid the utter and undeniable misery of dying alone or in pain. 'But', as Blanchot points out, 'this tactic is vain'. The ultimate (but perhaps necessary) bad faith of suicide is the belief that death can be achieved, and eliminated – as in Chaucer's words from *The Pardoner's Tale* 'deeth shal be deed' or from Donne's 'Divine Poems', 'One short sleepe past, we wake eternally,/And death shall be no more; death, thou shalt die' – through a controlled leap into the void. However, once this heroic leap is taken, all the suicide feels is the tightening of the rope that binds him more closely than ever to the existence he would like to leave, the horror of what Levinas calls the *il y a*, the irremissibility of Being or being-riveted to oneself which I have discussed at length elsewhere. Blanchot writes chillingly in *Thomas l'obscur*':

> Just as the man who is hanging himself, after kicking away the stool on which he stood, the final shore, rather than feeling the leap which he is making into the void feels only the rope which holds him, held to the end, held more than ever, bound as he had never been before to the existence he would like to leave.

Death is not an object of the will, the *noema* of a *noesis*, and one cannot, truly speaking, *want* to die. To die means losing the will to die and losing the will itself as the narcissistic motor that drives the deception of suicide. This means no longer conceiving of death as possibility and attempting to accept the harder lesson of the impossibility of death – to learn to live with time, to temporize, to have time on one's hands.

You might have noticed that we now have two concepts of death at play: *death as possibility,* to which we have attached the name of Heidegger; and *death as impossibility*, which can be associated with the names of Levinas and Blanchot. A double death, then. In *L'espace littéraire* Blanchot writes:

> There is one death which circulates in the language of possibil-
> ity, of liberty, which has for its furthest horizon the freedom to
> die and the power to take mortal risks – and there is its double,
> which is ungraspable, it is what I cannot grasp, what is not linked
> to me by any relation of any sort, that never comes toward me
> and to which I do not direct myself.

The experience of death is double, and the most extreme exposure to the first conception of death as possibility in suicide opens on to the second conception of the impossibility of death. In believing that death is something that can be grasped – in plac-ing the noose around my neck or the gun in my mouth – I expose myself to the radical ungraspability of death; in believing myself able to die, I lose my ability to be able.

To these two concepts of death we might add two paradigms for thinking through the question of human finitude and responding to the problem of nihilism. We might say that the conception of death as possibility constitutes a *tragic-heroic paradigm*, which can be traced back through Heidegger and Nietzsche to elements within German Idealism and romanticism. I would even go so far as to join Lacoue-Labarthe and call this an *archi-fascistic* concep-tion: death as martyrdom, as meaningful sacrifice.

To this tragic-heroic paradigm I would like to oppose a *comic-antiheroic* paradigm based on the conception of death as impossi-bility, where finitude is radically ungraspable and where laughter – a certain sort of laughter – opens up a weak and ever weakening relation to finitude. This will hopefully provide us with another take on the framing problem of nihilism and will allow us to digress briefly into Beckett, and beyond that into Tommy Cooper, who of course literally died laughing.

I shall try to formalize this second conception of death as impossibility to make good some of the claims I have been making and will then explore this comic-antiheroic conception of death.

In phenomenological terms, death is not the *noema* of a *noesis*; that is, it is not the meaningful fulfilment of an intentional act. Death is not an object of the will. It is ungraspable and exceeds both intentionality and the correlative structures of Husserlian or Heideggerian phenomenology. Thus, there can be no phenomenology of death because it is a state of affairs about which I can find neither an adequate intention nor intuitive fulfilment.

In other words, death is radically resistant to the order of representation. Representations of death are misrepresentations, or, rather, representations of an absence. The paradox at the heart of the representation of death is best conveyed by the rhetorical figure of *prosopopeia*, the trope by which an absent or imaginary person is presented as speaking or acting, a form which indicates the failure of presence, a face that withdraws behind the form which presents it. The representation of death is always a mask – a *memento mori*, a death mask – behind which nothing stands, rather like the way in which the face of Tadzio appears to von Aschenbach as he dies on the beach at the end of Mann's *Death in Venice*.

Thus, if there can be no phenomenology of death because it is a state of affairs about which I can find neither an adequate intention nor intuitive fulfilment, this entails that *the ultimate meaning of human finitude is that we cannot find meaningful fulfilment for the finite*. In this specific sense, death is meaningless and the work of mourning is infinite. Of course, this is also to say that mourning is not a work (*Trauer-Arbeit*), for my relation to the death of the other does not permit any adequation with the dead other such that I might eventually detach myself from the other and work through their memory, eventually becoming 'free and uninhibited' as Freud says. Of course, if the impossibility of death entails the impossibility of mourning, this leaves us with the choice between melancholia and mania, which of course are two ends of the same piece of pathological string; between melancholia as the ethos or philosophy in Aristotle's words themselves taken up and transformed by Freud and later by Kristeva, and mania as the anti-philosophical Falstaffian rage of the belly turned mind, bodily materialism as absolute idealism.

Let me return to the framing problem of nihilism. The difficulty here is that if one accepts that one cannot find meaningful fulfilment for the finite, if death (and consequently life) is strictly meaningless, how does one avoid moving from this claim into the cynical conformism and sheer resignation of what Nietzsche calls 'passive nihilism'?

The response to the crisis of meaning within nihilism does not consist in the restoration of a new totality of meaning derived from the datum of finitude: a new thesis on being, the achievement of philosophy as revolutionary praxis, or whatever. Such would be what Adorno calls 'the more and more faded positivities' of the true nihilists, like Ernst Jünger, with their active desire for an over-coming of nihilism. So, rather than restoring meaning, a response to nihilism might lie, I believe, in *meaninglessness as an achievement*, as a task or a quest – what I have described elsewhere as the achievement of the ordinary or the everyday without the rose-tinted glasses of any narrative of redemption.

Incipit Beckett. Contrary to the usual sloppy prejudice, Beckett is not a nihilist; that is, in no way is he flatly stating or even celebrating the meaninglessness of existence. Rather, Beckett indicates obliquely, I think, how meaninglessness can be seen as an achievement. That is, Beckett's work in its steadfast refusal to mean something exhibits an aesthetic autonomy that, far from conspiring with apolitical decadence or existential hopelessness, gives the faintest indication of the transformative praxis from which it resolutely abstains, namely, in Adorno's words, '*die Herstellung richtigen Lebens*'. Such is the necessarily weak messianic power of Beckett's work, a power conditioned by the refusal of any strong messianism, any false positivity. This is why, as Adorno writes, artworks must 'efface any memory-trace of reconciliation – in the interest of reconciliation'.

The problem here is that, in responding to nihilism, the world is all too easily stuffed full of meaning and we risk suffocating under the combined weight of the many competing narratives of redemption – whether religious, socioeconomic, scientific, tech-nological, political, aesthetic, psychoanalytical or astrological. The problem of nihilism is missed in the manic desire to over-come meaninglessness in the erection of some new positivity. What Beckett's work offers, I think, is a radical decreation of these salvific narratives (Clov to Hamm in *Endgame*: 'Do you believe in the life to come'. Hamm to Clov: 'Mine was always that'), an approach to meaningless as the achievement of the ordinary, *a redemption from redemption.* My wild little hypothesis is that this redemption from redemption, this achievement of the ordinary, this weak messianic power, is profiled in the phenomenon of laughter, a certain laughter.

The recognition of meaninglessness as an achievement leads to a deeper recognition of the profound and happy limitedness of the human condition, of our frailty, our vulnerability and our separateness from one another. I think this has something to do with Beckett's use of language, his syntax of weakness, the endlessly proliferating series of non-sequiturs, planned inconsistencies and contradictory sayings and unsayings that make up his texts. For example:

> I shall have to speak of things, of which I cannot speak, but also, which is even more interesting, but also that I, which is if possible even more interesting, that I shall have to, I forget, no matter.

Or again (and it is this very repetition that interests me, and what is always interesting about jokes, the uneasy silence that follows the laughter at a good joke is the silent demand for another):

> I resume, so long as, so long as, let me see, so long as one, so long as he, ah fuck all that, so long as this, then that, agreed, that's good enough, I nearly got stuck.

Beckett's sentences are a series of weak intensities, sequences of antithetical inabilities, unable to go on, unable not to go on. It is this double inability which describes, I think, the weakness of our relation to finitude, the ungraspability of death, a dwindling, a stiffening, enfeebling corporeality – which is *not* a recipe for despair but for a kind of *rapture*: 'There is rapture, or there should be, in the motion crutches give'. In other words, what seems at best like stoicism in Beckett, 'I can't go on, I'll go on', entails as Adorno rightly remarks 'a legacy of action' that 'silently screams that things should be otherwise' – a negative utopianism under the sanction of the *Bilderverbot*. The impossibility that, on my view, seems to pervade the relation to death, nihilism and finitude is articulated, as Adorno writes in the final words of *Minima Moralia*, 'for the sake of the possible'. The very impossibility of death and redemption leaves open the horizon of the possible understood as the realm of future action, namely '*die Herstellung richtigen Lebens*'.

Now, coming to my final point, my hypothesis, such as it is, and it is not much – very little in fact – is that this conception of the impossibility of death, which is articulated for the sake of the possible, is articulated as comedy. The syntax of weakness is a comic syntax, the very ubiquity and ungraspability of the finite is evoked comically, in laughter: 'Nothing is funnier than unhappiness, I grant you that'.

There is a joke in Frankfurt concerning the little *Denkmal* that was erected by Gretel Adorno outside the apartment in which she and Theodor lived from 1949 until Adorno's death and which I used to pass every morning. Adorno's smooth, moonlike face stares out at you, like a fat potato-head crowned by a little pair of NHS spectacles, and the motto reads '*Kein richtiges Leben im Falschen*'. One reading of this would be perfectly consistent with Adorno's somewhat austere social analysis of the post-war world; another reading would suggest that the motto is Gretel's final ironic, bitter comment on Teddy's legendary womanizing, the fact that he was indeed living unjustly *im Falschen.*

Now, Adorno's writing, although in itself perhaps witty in its hyperbolic black gusto, in not really known for being a laugh a minute. This lack of comic effect is particularly evident in his reading of Beckett, where, despite the fact that Adorno offers, to my knowledge, the philosophically most powerful and hermeneutically most nuanced piece of writing on Beckett, he comes nowhere close to understanding the comic effect and humour of Beckett's writing. Let me explain.

Adorno inserts Beckett into his own contestable account of contemporary society as one characterized by total reification and the domination of identity thinking: 'Beckett's trashcans are emblems of a culture rebuilt after Auschwitz', his language is a 'jargon of universal disrespect', his characters inhabit 'the pre-established harmony of despair' and are like 'flies twitching after the fly swatter has half squashed them'. For all its many merits, one cannot help but feel that Adorno's hectoring – even bullying – hyperbole comes nowhere near close to evoking the recoiling evasiveness and uncanny ordinariness of Beckett's language, and that the latter's syntax of weakness is drowned out by the former's declamatory and slightly triumphalistic antithesis.

Beckett's humour does not, as Adorno suggests, evaporate 'along with the meaning of the punchline'; rather, humour is this very experience of evaporation, which is the disappearance of a certain philosophical seriousness, interpretative earnestness or ideological posturing. Humour does not evaporate in Beckett; rather, laughter is the sound of language trying to commit suicide but being unable to do so, which is what is so tragically comic. It would be a question here of linking humour to idiom, because it is surely humour that is powerfully and irreducibly idiomatic in any natural language, which is perhaps why jokes are so tricky to translate. It is humour that resists direct translation and can only be thematized humourlessly – *ergo* the mortal tedium of philosophical discussions of laughter, including this one, in fact especially this one.

Adorno insists, in a formulation of which he was fond, and whose Beckettian source might well be in Dante, that 'A dried up, tearless weeping takes the place of laughter. Lamentation has become the mourning of hollow, empty eyes.' And again, 'the only face left is the one whose tears have dried up'. I can find no textual authority for tearless weeping in Beckett; on the contrary, both the protagonist in *The Unnamable* and Worm are described as crying without ceasing. However, textual authority is not really what interests me here; it is more that I find Adorno's remarks on this point intuitively unconvincing and I would claim that Beckett's humour does not exhaust itself in the manner suggested. If we laugh until we cry, it is because we are laughing so hard, not because we are unable to laugh. Admittedly, Beckett's humour is dark, very dark – 'Nothing is funnier than unhappiness' – and his lightning traces of wit illuminate a moonless, starless night, but those traces also allow us to see the night as such. Let me offer some examples, some of which you may have heard before:

1 Mahood to himself: 'The tumefaction of the penis! The penis, well now, that's a nice surprise, I'd forgotten I had one. What a pity I have no arms.'
2 Molloy on Lousse's parrot: 'Fuck the son of a bitch, fuck the son of a bitch. He must have belonged to an American sailor, before he belonged to Lousse. Pets often change masters. He didn't

say much else. No, I'm wrong, he also said Putain de merde!
He must have belonged to a French sailor before he belonged
to the American sailor. Putain de merde! Unless he had hit on it
alone, it wouldn't surprise me. Lousse tried to make him say,
Pretty Polly! I think it was too late. He listened, his head on one
side, pondered, then said, Fuck the son of a bitch. It was clear
he was doing his best.'

3 Moran hallucinating Youdi's words to Gaber: 'Gaber, Gaber, he
said, life is a thing of beauty, Gaber, and a joy for ever. He brought
his face nearer mine. A joy for ever, he said, a thing of beauty,
Moran, and a joy for ever. He smiled. I closed my eyes. Smiles
are all very nice in their own way, very heartening, but at a rea-
sonable distance. I said, Do you think he meant human life?'

4 Molloy on the impermeability of the *Times Literary Supplement*:
'Even farts made no impression on it. I can't help it, gas escapes
from my fundament on the least pretext, it's hard not to mention
it now and then, however great my distaste. One day I counted
them. Three hundred and fifteen farts in nineteen hours, or an
average of over sixteen farts an hour. After all, it's not excessive. Four farts every fifteen minutes. It's nothing. Not even one
fart every five minutes. It's unbelievable. Damn it, I hardly fart
at all, I should never have mentioned it. Extraordinary how
mathematics help you to know yourself.'

Beckett's humour at its most powerful – and perhaps verbal
humour as such, one thinks of the genius of Groucho Marx – is a
paradoxical form of speech that defeats our expectations, produc-
ing laughter with its unexpected verbal inversions, contortions
and explosions, a refusal of everyday speech that lights up the
everyday: estranged, indigent and distorted 'as it will appear one
day in the messianic light'. Laughter is an acknowledgement of
finitude, precisely not a manic affirmation of finitude in the solitary, neurotic laughter of the mountain tops, but as an affirmation
that finitude cannot be affirmed because it cannot be grasped.
As Beckett quips in his *Proust*, '"Live dangerously", that victorious
hiccough *in vacuo*, as the national anthem of the true ego exiled in
habit'. Laughter returns us to the limited condition of our finitude,
the shabby and degenerating state of our upper and lower bodily

strata, and it is here that the comic allows the windows to fly open on to our tragic condition. The very comic exaggeration of the body, which runs back through the tradition of clowning to ancient Greek satyr plays with their absurdly large phalluses, is what recalls us to the weakness and vulnerability of the body.

Pushing this a little further – maybe too far – I would even go so far as to claim that the sardonic laughter that resounds within the ribs of the reader or spectator of Beckett's work is a site of uncolonizable resistance to the alleged total administration of society, a node of non-identity in the idealizing rage of commodi-fication that returns us not to a fully integrated and harmonious *Lebenswelt* but lights up the comic feebleness of our embodiment. Laughter might here be approached as a form of resistance, of critique, of the sudden feeling of solidarity that follows the eruption of laughter in a bus queue or watching a party political broadcast in a pub. Laughter is a convulsive movement, like sob-bing or like an orgasm, involuntary and contagious, the solidarity of giggling.

Now, to pull the rug from under my feet, as I think I should in a paper like this, I confess that I have not even begun to get close to what really interests me, which is the way in which the comic antiheroic relation to finitude, this experience of death as impos-sibility, is articulated in the peculiar idiom of *actual examples* of comedy. This would be a question of empirical research, which is something of a novelty for me. In particular, I am thinking of the comic syntax of weakness that refuses or is apparently unable to tell a joke, a refusal and an inability which somehow result in laughter, whether this is in Tommy Cooper's perfectly timed incompetences, Frankie Howerd's mannered ineptitude and hesitancy or Eddie Izzard's wildly plausible implausibilities, his endless parentheses and deviations. But in the face of such phenomena the always false humility of the philosopher should draw breath and shut up, not out of any sense of false piety, but simply because I don't know what I would say, or rather I don't know how what I would say would be in any way adequate to the phenomenon of comedy. Perhaps it's a good thing that the second half of Aristotle's *Poetics* was lost, despite Umberto Eco's fictions. As Spike Milligan said of Tommy Cooper, 'There's only one moment when a joke becomes funny and Tommy felt it instinctively'. At such a moment you can literally die laughing. A philosopher might simply die or corpse in the theatrical sense in trying to explain laughter.

In one of those fascinating byways of the *Critique of Judgement* Kant writes, rightly: 'Voltaire said that heaven has given us two things to compensate for the many miseries of life, *hope* and *sleep*. He might have added *laughter* to the list'. Indeed, Kant might have added orgasm to the list, but the point is well made. However, if laughter compensates for the miseries of life, it is not simply because it allows us to escape them, to compensate or *economize* on the expenditure of affect as Freud claimed in his *Jokes and their Relation to the Unconscious*. Laughter does not *just* economize on expenditure of affect, it also indicates obliquely the source of that affect, as Freud was also well aware. What is opened in that endless play of nonsense we call comedy is the life of the drives, a life itself governed by the death drive. If psychoanalysis shows us one thing, it is that the It, the Es, the Id speaks where there is pain. And maybe it only hurts when you laugh.

Notes

1 This is the text of a lecture presented at the University of Leeds in March 1997 (at the conference *Death and its Concepts*). I have not sought to erase its impromptu oral character with a scholarly apparatus. Those seeking the latter can find similar arguments with complete references in my *Very Little … Almost Nothing: Death, Philosophy, Literature* (London: Routledge, 1997) and *Ethics – Politics – Subjectivity* (London: Verso, 1999).

2

The impossibility of Levinas's death

JOHN LLEWELYN

> For I have but the power to kill,
> Without – the power to die –
>
> Emily Dickinson

Emmanuel Levinas died in Paris on the morning of Monday, 25 December 1995. It is a fact that he died there and then. It is a consequential fact that he is now dead. The event has taken place. And, since it is valid to argue from being to possibility, it was possible that that event should take place. From at least as early as the date of his birth, his death was a possibility. As was the death of Heidegger. But this empirical possibility of Heidegger's death is not to be confused with the phenomenological possibility of *Dasein*'s death, which in *Being and Time* Heidegger called a *Seinkönnen* and *Seinsmöglichkeit*.[1] Both empirical possibility and logical possibility, he maintains there, are derived from the possibility which is *Dasein*'s way of transitively existing its world. The verbality of the verb–noun *sein* means that the power or possibility of the way in which *Dasein* exists its being in the world, *Dasein*'s worlding, is not to be construed in the manner of Aristotle and Scholasticism, where possibility or potentiality is conceived on analogy with a reservoir from which activity might spring. The possibility of being here referred to is being's possibility, where the possibility is constitutive of being's verbality and where what Heidegger wishes to convey is a notion in which the classical contrast between activity and passivity is exceeded. It could be said that that notion is a 'condition of possibility' of that contrast, provided that this condition is not construed in the manner of Kantian transcendentalism as an analytic or synthetic *a priori* principle of judgement. The existentials into which *Being and Time* analyses the possibility of being in the world are not *Grund-sätze* understood as principles, judgements or contents of assertions. Contents of assertions have the status of what can be presented to a mind, whereas it is one of the aims of *Being and Time* to show that such presentedness to mind, like the present-edness to hand of material objects – their being on display – is secondary to an engagement or an involvement which is the point of pointing to, referring to and intending any kind of object. It is therefore viciously circular to construe this involvement as ultimately a correlation of *noesis* and *noema* or *doxa* in the style of Husserl, who describes even axiological and practical mindsets as such correlations.

This objection to Husserl is underlined in Levinas's book on that philosopher.[2] In making this objection Levinas is in agreement with Heidegger. It is an objection concerning the scope of intentionality considered in abstraction from temporality. But neither for Husserl nor for Heidegger nor for Levinas can intentionality be separated from the temporality of consciousness. Heidegger writes in his foreword to *The Phenomenology of Internal Time Consciousness* that the book is 'an exposition of the intentional character of time consciousness and the developing fundamental elucidation of intentionality in general'.[3] And Levinas takes intentionality to imply protentionality and retentionality. He refers to protentionality and retentionality in a clause placed in apposition to a reference to intentionality in a sentence which proposes a reason for thinking that 'the structure of time is not intentional, is not made up of protentions and retentions'.[4] The reason he suggests is that maybe my relation with death exceeds the possibility of experience and the experience of possibility. Maybe it exceeds even the possibility of impossibility of my being toward my death that according to Heidegger is architectonic of all other possibilities of mine and of my very own mineness – of the *Eigentlichkeit* of which each individual I is capable. Maybe there is evidence of this, Levinas further suggests, in the excessive weeping of Apollodorus and Xanthippe and the other women at the scene of the death of Socrates described in the *Phaedo*. This may well be an indication that there is more than measure to the humanity of a life that appears to be limited and measured by death. And maybe this indicates not only something about what the death of another means for me as opposed to what my own death means for me. After endorsing Heidegger's warning against confusing the latter with the former, Levinas goes on to warn his readers against endorsing what he takes to be Heidegger's view that the death of the other is ontologically secondary compared with my concern for being, in that the latter embraces both concern for the other's death and concern for my own.

Heidegger observes that for *Dasein* its death is certain. He says that it is *gewiss*, and in saying this he prepares the ground for his statement that *Dasein*'s being toward its death underlies the ordinary concept of conscience, *Gewissen*. Heidegger does not take over without revision Husserl's conception of intentionality. Indeed, he seizes the opportunity of the above-mentioned foreword to *The Phenomenology of Internal Time Consciousness* to remark that 'Even today, this term "intentionality" is no all-explanatory word but one which designates a central problem'. A year or so before writing this he had been attempting to cast light on that problem by substituting for Husserl's triad of retention, presence and protention a triad of temporal ecstases not based, as Husserl's is, on representation: being already there in the world, being alongside things in the world and being ahead of oneself. Now this non-representational structure, considered by Heidegger to be fundamental to *Dasein*'s everyday way of being in the world, is considered by Levinas to be an exercise of *conatus*. It is worth noting, therefore, that although involvement with things in their readiness or unreadiness to hand is plausibly described as one in which *Dasein* is trying to do something, and that the term *conatus* is derived from the Latin verb *conari*, to try, the philosophical and psychological notion of conation traditionally contrasted with cognition and emotion is associated with the notion of willing. But Heidegger sees willing as the fundamental concept of German Idealism and sees his own thinking as an endeavour (so in that sense a *conatus*) to bring to attention a way of being that is more fundamental than willing and is a kind of freedom which is prior to freedom of will. One of his words for this is *Seinlassen*, and it is arguable that this letting-be belongs to a modality or voice which it is also Levinas's aim to bring to his reader's attention as prior to *conatus* as will, as power and as will to power. For Levinas in turn sees his own thinking as an attempt to show that room must be found for a freedom which is older than freedom of will. Aided by Heidegger's explication of *Seinlassen* as a kind of listening and obedience, notions to which Levinas too appeals, the latter sometimes goes as far as to adapt Heidegger's expression *Seinlassen* to his own purpose.

Nevertheless, their purposes do differ. It is being that calls to be let be according to Heidegger, and this is a calling from and to the being of *Dasein* in its being towards its own death. According to Levinas it is from the other human being in his or her mortality that the call comes. It is a call to not leave the other to die alone, a call to non-indifference to the other's suffering and isolation, a summons summed up in the commandment 'Thou shalt not kill'. The difference that this non-indifference introduces is other than the ontological difference between being and beings. It is therefore different from the meontological difference, the difference between being and non-being. Intervening into the realm of light and darkness, of concealing and unconcealing, to which *Dasein*'s being toward its own nothingness is confined, responsibility for the other human being is a response which defines mortality as the impossibility of possibility rather than, as in Heidegger's definition, the possibility of impossibility. That is to say, prior to power is impower or unpower; prior according to a temporality which is not that of recollection, but of *accueil au-delà du recueil*, of welcome beyond recall: of acollection or adcollection, one might say, in recollection of the tie between *cueillir* and *colligere*, to tie together, where the sense of ligature is that which stirs, as Heidegger is fond of reminding his readers, in the word *legein*, to read, and in *logos*, a saying or a word. This word of welcome would be the first always already spoken word of allegiance which makes the stranger a neighbour – and *accolere* is to dwell near or be a neighbour to.

This confirms what was hinted at earlier, that a false dichotomy is made when it is asked whether it is my death or the death of the other that Levinas calls the impossibility of possibility. My being toward my death is my being toward the death of the other in me and under my skin, as Levinas writes, the other who is a source of irritation. I am ab-aboriginally, from a time always already beyond the beginning of memory – like the silent first letter in the aleph-bet which precedes the first letter of the first word of the first book of the Hebrew Bible, *Bereshit* – infected and affected by the other whose coming (*venir*) is not within memory (*souvenir*). The mortal other intervenes and advenes, but this event (*événement*) is not the *Ereignis* of being or of the non-being which heralds being as such in the temporality described in *Being and Time*. *Ereignis* is another Heideggerian word that Levinas recruits, by no means put off by the sense of appropriation and possession that the German word bears. Translating this word as *événement* and with caution as 'event', we can say that Levinas writes of an event of this event where sameness is broken into and broken up by otherness, an event even other than the nominalized abstractness of the -ness of otherness.[5] The event in question, in the question of the question that Levinas raises, is not the taking possession of myself when I become possessed by the question of the meaning and the truth of being. It is that dateless always already happened happening of my having become possessed of myself through being possessed by the other: psychosis. My being possessed by the other is my being self-possessed by a self (*soi*) which is more than only my ego (*moi*) interested in its own survival. That self-hood is a singularity and uniqueness more complicated than the each-for-itselfness of what Heidegger calls *Jemeinigkeit*. In the *conatus essendi* of each for-itself, for whom the question of its own being and death is what is of primary interest, the disinter-estedness, *dés-intér-esse-ment*, of the for-the-other is implicated. As the *posse* is superseded by the *imposse*, the *esse* is put in service to the otherwise than *esse* and beyond essence. Alterity is diachronically anteriorly ulterior to egological sameness – which does not mean that the latter cannot be naturally altruistic or benevolent.

These are not simple reversals. If intentionality is *conatus*, what subverts intentionality is not a simple counter-*conatus*. To suppose that it is would be to overlook Levinas's frequently repeated denials that the relation of all relations of responsibility for the other is a relation of power or force. It is not a relation of *energeia*. Primary sociality is not allergy, as it is said to be by philosophers as diverse as Hobbes and Hegel and Sartre. If it were, systematicity would be paramount, an interrelationship of terms affecting each other like Hegel's master and slave. Yet, as the above-mentioned notion of being irritated by the other under my skin leads us to expect, Levinas's conception of my primary dyadic rapport to *autrui* is no more comfortable than is the relation of the slave or bondsman to the master.

In the *Philosophy of Right* Hegel says: 'Just as life as such is immediate, so death is its immediate negation and hence must come from without, either by natural causes or else, in the service of the Idea, by the hand of a foreigner [*von fremder Hand*].'[6] Some key differences between Hegel and Levinas can be brought out by reflection on this statement. Death, which Hegel elsewhere calls the absolute master, is not according to Levinas a simple negation of life. And when it is threatened by the hand of someone who comes from without, it is not just a condition necessary to mutual recognition. Before being the foreigner who seeks to master me and the one with whom I would want to see eye to eye and be on equal terms, the other is the one by whom I am already seen, *déjà vu*, *eräugnet*, before he becomes *visé* or *vu* by me. Before I comprehend him in my gaze, *il me regarde*: his eyes are the source of my ethical concern, my *souci*. *Souci* is the word which Levinas also uses to translate *Sorge*, the word used by Heidegger that is usually translated as 'care' or 'concern'. But Levinas agrees with Hegel and Heidegger in emphasizing that whether death approaches by the hand of another or as accident or disease and ageing, it comes as a threat. It comes, according to Levinas, as an accusation. The other's look is an accusing look. This does not only mean that I am *accusé* by the other in the sense of made by the other's look to stand out like a figure on a ground. In Levinas's destructuring ethical revision of this figure-ground structure of Gestalt or Form Psychology, my physiognomical and phenomenological appearance as *apparaître* is dis-figured by my appearance as *comparaître* before the face of another who pursues and prosecutes me as though in a court of law.

The face of the other expresses the command 'Thou shalt not kill'. It also commands me to command others likewise. This command is expressed also in the words of Leviticus 19:18: 'Love thy neighbour as thyself'. But it should not be overlooked that at the very moment of the utterance of those words (*en ce moment même*), after and before and again and again in the pages in which Leviticus records the words addressed to Moses, come the words 'I am the Lord'. The other human being is the Lord. Not, however, the Lord of the relation of lordship and bondage or master and slave analysed in the *Phenomenology of Spirit*. The other human being is the master as *magister*, teacher. And although he teaches the laws and the statutes – 'You shall keep my statutes' says the Lord to Moses – the other human being teaches that the statutes are not kept if they are applied to every human being in the way that laws of nature apply. The moment of their application must be a moment of response to the singularity of the other just as, in being addressed and having the law addressed to him and through him to the people gathered at the foot of the mountain, Moses is one and unique because he is chosen.

But surely justice demands not only that Moses, and those waiting at the foot of the mountain, be chosen but that every human being be chosen? And if he is to avoid the injustice of elitism, must not Levinas say this of every human being? He does say this, and he cannot avoid saying this in expounding his doctrine philosophically in the 'Greek' concept of philosophy as love of wisdom. But he says that philosophy thus understood must be understood at the same time as the wisdom of love or Desire. What that means can be partly explained by reference to Kant's statement that the person of good will is one who lives not only according to the law but out of respect for the law. What Levinas underlines is that systematic respect for the law in the realm of ends in themselves is not enough. The good unwill calls too for respect for the singular other human being with whom I am face to face, notwithstanding that a second other and a third and a fourth speak through that first other's eyes. It is of this that the philosopher must repeatedly remind her or his readers and listeners. Philosophy must speak with an equivocal voice – Critically and hypoCritically.[7] It must by an abuse of language indicate the immediate responsibility I am under as a philosopher and a human being not to be content with the indifference implied by treating universalizability as what is primordially ethical. Universalizability may be the foundation of the ethical, but prior to the foundation and the bedrock of law is unfoundational, pre-principial, an-archic responsibility which for me is a responsibility entailing the sacrifice of my egological, though not therefore necessarily egoistic, persistence in being, and which substitutes for substance substitution for the other.

Dasein is such persistence in being toward its own death, whether or not the everydayness which it mostly is is also in ownmost possession of itself. *Dasein* has to be the possibility of its impossibility. That is what Levinas's philosophy would relegate to a second place. Levinas's philosophy is first of all phenomenological in its method, even if it employs that method in order to show that it deconstrues itself. In its first steps it is also ontological. Its point of departure is phenomeno-ontological, Husserlian and Heideggerian up to a certain point, to the point where certainty is sacrificed, and to the point where Levinas deems it necessary to increase notch by notch the shockingness of his descriptions, moving from saying that the self is subjectivity to saying that it is sub-jection, from saying that it is host to saying that it is hostage, from saying that it is for the other to saying that it is persecuted by the other. This acceleration in the torrential haemorrhage of Levinas's tropes can be compared to the unceasing refusal of Heidegger and Derrida to work with a settled lexicon. Their lexicon of paleonyms, neonyms and anonyms must be worked *through* open-endedly and unendingly if through it are to be performed what Heidegger, Derrida and Levinas philosophically constate.

This rhetoric of increasingly exasperating hyperbole suggests another comparison between Levinas and Heidegger. This rhetoric seeks to work against the rhetoric invoked by the irresistible inclination to construe the secret ethical moment as a public display, if not of intention, at least of intentionality, that is to say of meaning and giving of sense. But it is Levinas's claim that such giving of noetico-noematic sense ultimately depends for its sense on the non-sense of traumatizing affectivity in which signification is reduced ultimately to my being a signifier that says 'Hear me, call me, send me' (*hineni*). And that saying speaks for itself prior to and more pluperfectly than any conative activity and more passively than the passivity to which activity is traditionally opposed. Does this mean that Levinas may be charged with quietism, as Heidegger often is? Or, rather than charging him with this, should we congratulate him on it? Has he not opened up a way to a language which speaks peace, a language which says, from its heart, *shalom*? Is not his incessant insistence on the absolute past-participiality of sacrifice to be welcomed? Whether it is or is not, the feeling that Levinas's account of non-indifference makes no difference may derive from misplaced expectations. In reading him, misled by his practice of supplementing what he calls formal or dialectical description with what he calls concrete application (a new ethical schematism beyond the schematism of the theory of application outlined in the *Critique of Pure Reason*) we can easily forget – and a similar forgetting threatens in reading Heidegger – that, like Heidegger and like Husserl, Levinas is regressing beyond transcendentally rational conceptual analyses or 'expositions' such as are conducted by Kant to an exposition which he sees as their phenomenological and more than phenomenological ethical quasi-condition. The universe of discourse of his philosophical texts is quasi-transcendental. 'Metaphysical' is the word he himself uses, pouring new wine into the old bottle of metaphysics as this has been classically understood. This means that no claims are made for the validity or invalidity of specific moral maxims, any more than claims are made for the truth of any particular empirical laws in the *Critique of Pure Reason* (whatever we may think of Kant's attitude to some of the maxims cited in the second *Critique*, the *Groundwork*, 'On a supposed right to tell lies from benevolent motives' and elsewhere). Hence, whether the disquietude into which the other throws me is to express itself as quietism in my moral relations with members of my family and in the marketplace is not a question for which we should expect Levinas's philosophy to provide an answer.

Levinas underscores his denial that his philosophy of death aims to make death inoffensive, to justify it or to preach eternal life. Its aim is to show how death confers meaning on 'the human adventure, that is to say, on the ess*a*nce of being or on the beyond of ess*a*nce', where, as Levinas elsewhere explains, the spelling of this word with an *a* marks the verbal sense of being via a 'suffix *ance* derived from *antia* or *entia* which gave birth (*naissance!*) to abstract nouns of action'.[8] Despite this denial, does he not take the sting out of death by saying that what dies is not this man or this woman or this child but, let us say, using his word, the 'virility' of the man (and of the woman and of the child?)? It may seem that this reading blunts the acuity of death, sublimes its sharpness away. For it seems to require only that the ego's will to survive must succumb, allowing the responsible self to outlive that partial demise. This partialness of death is only an appearance, however, arising from the partialness of our account. The account can be taken a step further by putting into context Levinas's statement 'Suicide is a contradictory concept'.[9] In *Time and the Other* Levinas isolates the moment when Macbeth learns from Macduff that the latter was not born of woman. Macbeth learns thereby that he cannot count on the protection he believed was assured by the witches' prediction that no man born of woman could hurt him. Referring to the announcement Macbeth thereupon makes to Macduff, 'I'll not fight with thee', Levinas comments: 'Here is that passivity when there is an end to hope. Here is what I have called the end of virility. But straight away hope is reborn, and here are his last words: "Though Burnam wood be come to Dunsinane, And though oppos'd, being of no woman born, Yet I will try the last."' That is to say, trying, *conatus*, and the hope which the 'I can' of the will to activity implies, implies in its turn the absolute passivity of death. That passivity is, so to speak, the principle of hope, *das Prinzip Hoffnung*, hope's *Urprinzip* or, more precisely, its *Unprinzip*.[10] How so? 'To be or not to be', Levinas says, is an expression of Hamlet's realization of the impossibility of annihilating oneself. Hamlet grasps that he cannot grasp death. Because Levinas – notwithstanding what Heidegger calls the other thinking, *das andere Denken* – takes all thinking to be noetic-noematic, that is to say directedness at an object or objective, he maintains that death cannot be thought. But if death cannot be thought, neither can the nothingness to the thought of which Heidegger maintains the thought of death gives access; nor can being be thought if the way to the thought of being is the way to the thought of nothingness, as is maintained in *Being and Time*. Hence, Levinas concludes, that book's aim to be a fundamental ontology is not achieved. By pursuing it Heidegger cannot reach a description of the meaning of being. If the meaning of being is claimed to be temporality, if that meaning can be reached only through the thinking of nothingness, if the thinking of nothingness can be reached only through the thinking of death, and if the thinking of death is not a possibility, then perhaps instead of attempting to make sense of temporality via the nothingness indicated by mortality, we should attempt to make sense of mortality by first making sense of temporality. And that is Levinas's project.

Death is not nothingness. Ever to come, *à venir*, *avenir*, future, death is imminence which menaces the immanence of *Dasein*'s being toward its death. *Minari*, meaning to menace and be imminent, is a deponent verb, and what the deferment intrinsic to death deposes is the persistent imperialist ego positing itself in its place in the sun, *Da*, there, ready to usurp the world. It is as though this Pascalian *pensée* leads to that other Pascalian *pensée* on the terror inspired by the silence of the infinite outer spaces occupied by the sun and the starry skies above, and as though the starry skies above were symbolic of the sublimity of the moral law and of the still higher height of the face of the other human being. But the face, although glorious, is not entirely benign. As observed earlier, it prosecutes me. It even persecutes me. Again like the sublimity of the moral law, it is inimical to my monadic endeavour to survive. It haunts the phenomenological threat of death. That threat is phenomenologically social. This is the meaning Levinas takes from the statement 'The Eternal brings death and brings life'.[11] The Eternal is he over whom I can have no power, Levinas goes on to explain, and his explanation seems to entitle his reader to infer that what the Eternal stands for here is what also Satan stands for, for Levinas brackets the enemy and the accuser with God. What he is talking about is evil, as his essay 'Transcendence and Evil' confirms.[12] The evil or badness to which that essay points is not the evil which is opposed to the good. It is the primordial malevolence beyond the errance which according to Heidegger is the primordial partner of primordial truth. It is the menace beyond the opposition of evil and good and in virtue of which we may say that the good beyond being is also the ultra-ontological bad. We have already said that according to Levinas goodness pursues and persecutes me from the face of the other. We may say too, recalling that the French *mal* is either evil or illness, bad health, malady, that the evil of my death's imminence is an occasion for vigilance. Even in the approach my death makes to me in my growing old, vigilance is prescribed as indelibly as in the word *vieillissement* is inscribed the word *veille*. For the approach of death is not my approach towards it, not *Sein zum Tod*, but its approach towards me, and its approach to me is passive synthesis.

The phrase 'passive synthesis' is Husserl's. Having cast Husserl as one of the sources of the misleading proposition that all consciousness is noetico-noematically intentional, Levinas acknowledges that Husserl's doctrine of temporality as operatively intentional non-representational passive synthesis is a source of his own correction of that error. 'The room made in Husserlian phenomenology for non-representative phenomenology promised a significance (*significance*) not proceeding from knowledge, but the promise was not kept.'[13] The promise is kept only where room is kept open for what Levinas here refers to as non-representative intentional consciousness and elsewhere refers to as non-intentional consciousness and inverse intentionality or intentionality *à rebours*. This last phrase has the sense of being against the grain or upstream, as when Levinas writes that the time of death flows upstream.[14] Its literal meaning is against the lie of the hair. Against the lie, against the direction, against the *sens*, against *Sinn*, against straightforward sense. Remembering, as Heidegger does, that being healthy is a being *sanus*, and remembering, as Nietzsche does, that *sanus* is cognate with *salvus*, *salve*, *salut*, salvation, Levinas maintains that it is thanks to the countersensicality, nonsensicality and insanity announced in bad health and the death it announces that sense is saved for the life of the egological self. The bad health or insanitariness which announces death also announces the good health of sanctity, the *Heiligkeit* which falls short of wholeness because it is the height of madness, of *folie*, of *Unheiligkeit*. Other than the *Angst* of being toward the indeterminacy of non-being which according to Heidegger is incorporated in the certainty of death, other than intension and intentionality, *meinen* and *jemeinen*, the affectively alterological fear of death is the apology for life egological.

It may seem that another step, a *pas encore*, has to be taken before we can understand why the meaning of egological *jemein-iges meinen*, meaning which is mine (Hegel), is rescued by the danger – the *Gefahr* (Heidegger, Hölderlin), the *beau risque* (Levinas, Plato) – of what we might call the *deinen*, the 'thining', the being for the other whom the for-itself is to serve. It may seem that Levinas has still not told us how he gets from the fear *of* the other of which he writes in one paragraph of *Totality and Infinity* to the fear *for* the other of which he writes two paragraphs later.[15] But how this step is to be taken is implicit in what has already been said. This *pas encore* has already been taken there. If my death approaches as though inflicted on me by a hostile other, and if the one thus menaced is the ego persisting in its being, it is already a murderous being. The other's hostility is already accusation. I am the culpable survivor of the murderer I have always been from before my birth, before any commitment of myself to a contract that I could break and before the commitment of any other particular offence. So Levinas is able to write: 'My death is my part in the death of the other and in my death I die this death which is my fault. The death of the other is not simply a moment of the mineness of my ontological status.'[16]

My part in the death of the other is my participation in the death of the other. We can glimpse how Levinas gets from the fear *of* the other to the fear *for* the other only if the menace of my mortality is not construed as the menace of an encounterable force. If my death is conceived as a force approaching me like a vehicle with which I am about to have a head-on collision, it will continue to be a puzzle to us how my involvement with such a physical *Anstoss* resisting my progress along the highway of life can carry any accusatory charge. Why should I not simply resent it? Levinas's lecture course on time and death gives the last word to Abraham: 'The relation with the Infinite is the responsibility of one mortal for another. As in the passage in the Bible (Genesis 18:23 f.) where Abraham intercedes for Sodom, Abraham fears for the death of others and takes upon himself the responsibility of interceding. That is the moment when he says "I am myself but dust and ashes."' It would be quite wrong to suppose that Levinas takes Abraham's words as tantamount to the statement that he knows what it is to be mortal and can therefore experience sympathy with the Sodomites. Prior to feeling-with that can be symmetrically returned – an unconditional condition of the sympathy that is primary according to moral theories such as Hume's – is my being immediately and asymmetrically affected by the other in me and in the ever-present menace of my ever-future death. But it is not this latter feeling either which Levinas takes Abraham's words to express. Abraham's feeling is expressed rather in his taking upon himself the responsibility to intercede. What is expressed in his exclamation 'I am myself but dust and ashes' is the absurdity of his death and the consequent gratuity of his taking upon himself that responsibility to intercede. He does it for nothing. That is how the nothingness of my death afflicts me: not as that which turns me back to the question of my own being, but as that which turns me, the culpable survivor, forward toward those who survive me in a time that is not an extension of my time but is a time for the other without me, a time which would not be without me if it were imagined as some sort of afterlife; for the imagination of an afterlife would lend itself all too readily to becoming a consolatory way of once more being toward my death, another possibility of impossibility instead of the impossibility of possibility which alone secures the absolute gratuity without which responsibility toward the other might be recompensed if only by the self-congratulatory thought of my self-sacrifice.[17]

Abraham and the narrative of Genesis supply Levinas with the clues for the familial categories whose crossing with those drawn from Greek thinking and mythology *Totality and Infinity* describes. Abraham is the one who, in contrast with Ulysses, does not return to his home. The primacy of separateness and the irreducibility of alterity to sameness are already implicit in Levinas's analysis of femininity. Femininity according to this analysis is more than biological and sexual femaleness. Femininity, paternity, maternity, fecundity, filiation and fraternity are 'categories', 'conditions of the possibility' of the empirical biological concepts that they commonly denote. They are not genetic concepts, so they can apply where there is no woman in the house and where there is no biological son or daughter; they can apply, for example, to the relation of teacher and student.[18] They are not generic concepts in the sense of the classificatory 'catholic' universals of Plato and Aristotle. They are not abstract modes of representation, nor concrete universals in the manner of Hegel. They are concrete ways in which human being is accomplished, realized and produced. Not being essences, genera or species, they are not strictly conditions of possibility in the sense of formal or Kantian transcendental logic. Nor are they possibilities in the sense of Heidegger. Already beyond description in terms of 'I can' is the innocent youthful enjoyment of oneself, not yet disturbed by bad conscience and not yet amounting to straightforward intentional consciousness of noematic objects, but rather living from them. This 'from' anticipates the inversely intentional affect of the erotic enjoyment of another human being, of feminine alterity. Erotic love is beyond concupiscent need; it does not seek satisfaction through possession. Yet, being a relation with an intimate thou, neither is it fully ethical desire of a You. Rather is it transcendence beyond the face of the other toward an ever more remote future of generations more future than my possibilities, incomprehensible in terms of the opposition of being and nothingness. For filiation is also disaffiliation. The temporality of filiation is a temporality of ethical filiation which severs ontological filiation, severs the head of Father Parmenides. Timeless being is killed by the commandment 'Thou shalt not kill'. All time is the time of death, but instead of being a time of which the length is defined as the persistence in being of a being running up toward its own death, it is a time of which the length is that of an infinite patience in the face of and beyond the face of another.

The deponence of the verb *patior* marks a time in which imminence puts off, defers, deposes the ontological persistence of a finite being's perdurance in favour of a persistence which is infinite ethical endurance:

Endurance, because a burden is carried.

Ethical, because the burden is not the burden of biological ageing but the burden of responsibility arising from no contract or act performed in the time of biography or memoir, but going back to an absolutely and immemorably lapsed past of an ageing which gives sense and direction to biological senescence by commanding vigilance on behalf of the other human being.

Infinite, because the responsibility (like the God of Descartes' *Meditations*) exceeds definition and comprehension within the frame of an idea and breaks up the flow of time finishing in death, whether this time be conceived as time measured by the position of the sun or the hands of a clock (Newton, Kant), as accumulative lived duration (Bergson), as ecstasis toward death (Heidegger) or as history totalizing itself in the end of history (Hegel). Into and cutting across temporal continuity there intervenes an interval which Levinas refers to as dead time. This is the between-time of the separation between me and the other human being, whether the other human being is the one who is excluded from and threatens my egological enjoyment, the one who faces me and is welcomed into my home, or the son beyond the face.[19]

Biological ageing is produced, accomplished and emphasized in an ageing where the always already elapsedness of a past that was never present is my always already having lapsed in being overdue in taking up my responsibility. As ageing is accomplished in the ethical absolute past, so filiation is emphasized as the ethical absolute future, the absolute youth of the son and his ability to give absolute forgiveness. As absolute culpability is not defined by empirical fault, neither is it for an empirical fault committed earlier in time that it receives absolute pardon. Pardon, understood absolutely, as the quasi-condition of the experience of the happiness of reconciliation (*felix culpa*) is constitutive of time.[20] Across the space of dead time in which I do not go up to death but death comes to me, I am resurrected in the son, the uniquely chosen son who is nevertheless also the brother face to face with a brother, one among a plurality of brothers each of whom is unique. Pardon as the judgement of human beings of future generations is ab-solution, that is to say, disaffiliation in filiation, the undoing of the judgement passed by history. Judgement is thereby delivered from anonymity, truth is kept in touch with the truthfulness of a person, freedom is invested in responsibility for the other. When the other's death becomes the key to the concept of death, when death is described as the impossibility of possibility and is emptied of the pathos that comes to it from the fact of its being mine, the concept of death is modified, Levinas says.[21] So too is the concept of concept. For when the concept is conceived across conception, femininity, paternity and the dead time of transubstantiative filiation – where these expressions stand for the metaphysical and ethical meaning of what is meant by their biological and theological homonyms – Desire is Desire for a being that Desires, so that the concept of concept transcends the egological finitude of *sein zum Tod* and the impersonal infinitude of *sein zur Totalität*. Levinas's modification of the concept of death is at the same time a modification of the concept of concept because, in locating the centre of gravity of life in the death of the other human being, it dislocates the limit of limit. Limit gets de-fined as *limen*, the threshold across which strangers are invited to enter, and across which they and the child and the widow may call me to exit for good.

Notes

1 See J. Llewelyn, 'The "Possibility" of Heidegger's Death', *Journal of the British Society for Phenomenology*, 14:2 (1983), 127–38.
2 E. Levinas, *La Théorie de l'intuition dans la phénoménologie de Husserl* (Paris: Alcan, 1930); *The Theory of Intuition in Husserl's Phenomenology*, trans. A. Orianne (Evanston: Northwestern University Press, 1973).
3 E. Husserl, *The Phenomenology of Internal Time Consciousness*, trans. J. S. Churchill (The Hague: Nijhoff, 1964), p. 15.
4 E. Levinas, *Dieu, la mort et le temps* (Paris: Grasset, 1993), p. 19.
5 Levinas, *Dieu, la mort et le temps*, pp. 131, 134.
6 G. W. F. Hegel, *Philosophy of Right*, trans. T. M. Knox (Oxford: Oxford University Press, 1967), p. 57 (§70).
7 See J. Llewelyn, *The HypoCritical Imagination: Between Kant and Levinas* (London: Routledge, 2000).
8 Levinas, *Dieu, la mort et le temps*, p. 130; compare p. 16n., and E. Levinas, *Autrement qu'être ou au-delà de l'essence* (The Hague: Nijhoff, 1973), p. ix, *Otherwise than Being or Beyond Essence*, trans. A. Lingis (The Hague: Nijhoff, 1981), p. xli, and E. Levinas, *De Dieu qui vient à l'idée* (Paris: Vrin, 1982), p. 78n.

9 E. Levinas, *Le Temps et l'autre* (Paris: Presses Universitaires de France, 1983), p. 60; *Time and the Other*, trans. R. A. Cohen (Pittsburgh: Dusquesne University Press, 1987), p. 72.

10 In *Dieu, la mort et le temps* at least one thesis of Ernst Bloch's work of this title is endorsed by Levinas. See also 'Sur la mort dans la pensée d'Ernst Bloch', in *De Dieu qui vient à l'idée*.

11 E. Levinas, *Totalité et infini: essai sur l'extériorité* (The Hague: Nijhoff, 1971), p. 210; *Totality and Infinity: An Essay on Exteriority*, trans. A. Lingis (The Hague: Nijhoff, 1969), p. 234.

12 In E. Levinas, *Collected Philosophical Papers*, trans. A. Lingis (The Hague: Nijhoff, 1987), pp. 176–86.

13 Levinas, *Dieu, la mort et le temps*, p. 82.

14 Levinas, *Totalité et Infini*, p. 213, *Totality and Infinity*, p. 235.

15 Levinas, *Totalité et Infini*, p. 213, *Totality and Infinity*, p. 235.

16 Levinas, *Dieu, la mort et le temps*, p. 50.

17 E. Levinas, 'La signification et le sens', in *Humanisme de l'autre homme* (Montpellier: Fata Morgana, 1972), pp. 19–63 (see pp. 42–5); 'Meaning and Sense', in *Emmanuel Levinas: Basic Philosophical Writings*, ed. A. T. Peperzak, S. Critchley and R. Bernasconi (Bloomington: Indiana University Press, 1996), pp. 33–64 (see pp. 49–51).

18 E. Levinas, *Ethique et infini* (Paris: Fayard, 1982), pp. 73–5, *Ethics and Infinity*, trans. R. A. Cohen (Pittsburgh: Duquesne University Press, 1985), pp. 70–2.

19 Levinas, *Totalité et infini*, pp. 29, 260, *Totality and Infinity*, pp. 58, 284.

20 Levinas, *Totalité et infini*, p. 259, *Totality and Infinity*, p. 283.

21 Levinas, *Totalité et infini*, p. 217, *Totality and Infinity*, p. 239.

3

Rigor mortis: the thirteen stations of philosophy's passion
(following Bataille's *Conferences on Un-Knowing*)

BORIS BELAY

Death and its concepts – concepts trying to seize, circumscribe, understand death – concepts to grasp the disappearance, the vanishing, the ungraspable – concept*s*: several of them is not too many – thirteen concepts: like the twelve stations of that oft-celebrated death – thirteen steps along the path of passion, the way towards death – each of them impossible, each thus leading to the impossibility of conceiving death – thirteen tormented concepts towards an impossible knowledge of the unknowable, self-sacrifice of philosophy – the concept and its death.

Death.

Death teaches nothing, since in dying we lose the benefits of its teachings. True, we can think about the death of another. We can apply to ourselves the feeling elicited by the death of others. We often imagine ourselves in the situation of those we see dying, but precisely, we can only do so on the condition of living. The reflection on death is all the more vain that to live is always to scatter one's attention, and we can struggle all we want, when death is at stake, it is the greatest sham to speak about it. (p. 560)[1]

So begins 'The teachings of death': death teaches nothing. But that a reflection on death is vain, that it is fraudulent to speak about death as a living to the living, does not prevent Bataille's endeavour to do so. Necessary contradiction which only mirrors the limits of thought, where thought confronts its ignorance of that limit: separation as such.

1 Ignorance

> Position of someone who does not know what is within a locked
> trunk which he cannot open. This is the point where we revert
> to literary language, in which there is more than what is neces-
> sary to say. Only silence can express what we need to say, thus
> in a confused language, in a state of perfect despair, which can-
> not be compared, in one sense at least, to that of who is looking
> for something and does not have it; it is a much deeper despair,
> which we have always known, which comes from the fact that
> we have a project in mind which cannot be completed, that we
> are about to fail at it, while we essentially care for its object.
> This despair is equivalent to that which death can amount to.
> As foreign to death as ignorant of the content of the trunk I
> mentioned earlier. (pp. 192–3)

Death is this foreign realm: closed to us and yet it haunts us. The
despair we feel in front of death is deeper than any other, it is
depth itself: the despair of what cannot be achieved – not now,
not ever. Still death is. And we have always known this despair:
it confronts us like the impossible itself, like our own ignorance.
Death is our ignorance because we want to know it, because it is
here, there. But the frontier between here and there is such that
what we have in mind cannot be completed. Our despair is perfect because death is incomplete. The project of death, the movement of the mortal is incompletion, it is the project of despair
itself. It is thus the ever-present project of knowledge – that which
must yet be known because it cannot be. Ignorance insists not
only in the project of knowledge but as that project. Impossible
project, perfect despair. Perfect despair, perfect project.

2 Knowledge

It is only if I knew everything that I could claim to know nothing, if this discursive knowledge were in my possession that I could claim in an unfaltering way to have reached un-knowing. ... In the end, I do not think this can be formulated in a perfect way. Nevertheless, it seems to me that the fundamental question is posed only when no formulation is possible, only when the absurdity of the world is heard in silence. I have done all I can to know what can be known and what I have sought is what cannot be formulated in my innermost. I am myself in a world which I recognize to be altogether inaccessible to me, since in all the ties I have sought to establish with it, there remains something unknown that I cannot overcome, leaving me in a sort of despair. (p. 192)

The end of knowledge is the end of knowledge. The circularity of knowledge knowing that it knows everything allows it to reach its end – having reached its end, it still has to proceed to what it cannot know, and accede to ignorance. Nothing is the end of knowledge: thus it has to know everything to know its end. The end of knowledge is nothing: thus it has to know everything to know that its end is beyond knowledge. Even if circularity denotes completion, it still only circumscribes what remains foreign to the circle, what contradicts completion. Knowledge has nothing to do with the absurd until it is complete; then the absurd appears: an unknown which cannot be overcome. Thus the perfect end of knowledge lies in the inaccessible. But even this is confusing, ambiguous, the circle from one end of knowledge to another closing far too quickly on itself to prevent absurdity. But even that shows that it is precisely insofar as the problem of the end of knowledge cannot find a perfect formulation that it remains as the end-problem of knowledge. Unformulated, the inaccessible becomes the fundamental question of knowledge, the despairing condition of its impossible completion.

3 Sovereignty

> It is subordinated things – at least subordinated in time to what will result from them – that science considers. It is also things, in a sense, that will be considered in the study the principles of which I now attend to, but the subordinated character of these things will not be the object of my research. Indeed, I will not consider an object of thought insofar as it is identical to the one I could turn it into, insofar as it contains this or that possibility of transformation or of reduction. On the contrary, the moments of this thing (represented as a thing by default) I will consider as sovereign moments, that is, as moments having their ends in themselves and not as middle terms. This is how from the death of thought ensues not exactly a science, but what I could call a study of sovereign moments. (p. 206)

What haunts, insists, resists, what we have always known but finds no formulation – disrupts the temporality of knowledge. Science: progressive knowledge requires objects that can be accumulated through time, that can be amassed until the completion of its project. But death is both too punctual and too evanescent to allow itself to be transformed or reduced into an object. Persistent in the menace of its unexpected event, it proceeds according to its own rules: it gives itself its own temporality and thereby subjects that which attempts to seize it. Death is sovereign, it comes at its own time, and the moments of its appearance disturb the coherence of the self-identical thing. In fact its time is the disruption of what lasts: altogether unpredictable, we know it has come, gone, when we discern a fault in self-subsistence. We have no other words besides those of objectivity for it, only the default in language which imposes itself as the mark of its sovereignty. Its seal is that of the end: the self-referential end which, by the lack of middle terms, marks the end of both self and reference.

4 Language

Here we meet the continuation of the persistent difficulty, encountered since the beginning, which distances thought from its object when it is a sovereign moment. The sovereign is in the domain of silence, and if we speak of it, we jeopardize the silence which is constitutive of it. It is always a comedy, a fraud. We can certainly proceed with the study, but only in the most unfavourable conditions, the most difficult ones. With respect to the sovereign moment, language obscures everything it comes to touch, it alters it, corrupts it, debases it through an operation only fit for vulgar activities, such as planing wood or ploughing a field. And it is not even enough to say: of the sovereign moment one cannot speak without altering it, without altering it as really sovereign. In fact, as much as to speak about them, it is contradictory to *seek* these movements. (p. 207)

As sovereignty demands its own time only to disrupt time, it would need a language known only to itself if only to prevent its ever being circumscribed. The force of its commands lies entirely in the impossibility of knowing what they mean, of finding a translation from here to there, a way to compromise with it. To deal with sovereignty is thus always a fraudulent matter, it always involves a medium which, in its very role of intercessor, debases the end it seeks to bring up. Language, inasmuch as it attempts to bring sovereignty within the realm of discursive knowledge, only manages to lose it as an object of thought. Sovereignty is negated in its essence when it is equated with known objects through a common language; it is then lost as loss when it is transposed in a simulacrum of knowledge which thinks the sovereign may be mastered, understood. In front of sovereignty language becomes a comic double of itself, able only to portray the limits of its power to represent: comedy of language as language, a medium ever impotent in reaching its end when its end is the end.

5 Love

> In front of a woman, as long as one knows her, one knows her unsatisfactorily, that is, this 'acquaintance' ['*connaissance*'] has to do with knowledge [*savoir*]. To the extent that one seeks to know a woman psychologically without being carried away by passion, one withdraws from her. It is only when trying to know her with respect to death that one gets closer. Inescapable series of contradictions: it is when a being is sinking that one gets close to it, but one must deny the feeling of the 'perishable'. In love, the will to project the beloved into the imperishable is a contrary one. It is to the extent that a being is not a thing that it can be loved, to the extent that it resembles this sacred. ... Love cannot be a success. In this effort to aggrandise a human being, its grandeur is reduced to the world of practical knowledge. (p. 195)

If language has any value, the loved being has all value: commanding incommensurability. I love this being for itself, beyond any comparison with all else. And it has this value for me for this very reason: in its separation. If I were to know it in a coherent way, related to known objects, it would withdraw incongruently – passion giving way to, slipping away from, objectivity. But death opens the breach, and passion follows, removing with it loved and lover. For if the dissolution of death were not threatening, knowledge could get a permanent hold of the loved one, but it would thereby vanish – lost for both. Yet loss insists in love too, as the love of a mortal being is itself perishable: unmasterable effect of disappearance. Love cannot preserve itself if it is to remain sovereignly itself: for itself, and not for its object. The needed identification of the loved one can only be frustrated – thus maintained as the need, the demand, of love – in the loss of that identity. Mortality removes it from this world of practicality, and by losing itself as loved, the loved one prevents its being preserved as object of love. Adulated, it is lost; lost, it demands to be adored.

6 Sacred

> What motivates the feeling of the sacred is horror. This feeling
> is dying from the weakness of the people of this day: who do not
> know any more, do not want to know, that nothing is more fas-
> cinating than horror. What causes us the most horror is death,
> and in the feeling of the sacred, existence lies close to death:
> as if, in a dream, the contents of a coffin drew us to it. Yet, it is
> not as if death only has the meaning given to it by people who
> try not to think about it. Indeed, life has its greatest intensity in
> the chilling contact with its contrary. The image of corruption
> and annihilation fascinates us, it decomposes us and freezes us.
> (p. 188)

Death gives us to love, and to love life. The greatest intensity of
life is reached at its limit, beyond which it opens on to the other.
But this limit motivates it, fascinates it, arouses the most extreme
feeling – feeling of the ultimate, and its tremor. The sacred is this
feeling: it is nothing, nothing but what is aimed at by this terrifying arousal. It is thus everything, it is its end above and beyond all
objects, discernible in the annihilation of objectivity. The sacred
is that nothing: what lies beyond our reach, forever removed,
untouchable, unspeakable, unfathomable. That horror stupefies
knowledge – only those who refuse to think about it can think
they know it. The others have stopped before – the sacred: frozen,
unable to move beyond the awe that announces it; drawn to death,
they are engulfed and decomposed along the only way that leads
to it.

7 Sacrifice

> The slaughtered cow has nothing to do with all of these practical conceptions. ... Once we have taken part in the ritual destruction of the cow, we have destroyed all notions to which simple life had accustomed us. Man needs to grant himself a perspective of un-knowing under the guise of death. These are not legitimate intellectual operations. Cheating is always involved. We all have the feeling of death, and we can surmise that this feeling played a large part in sacrifice. ... At bottom, sacrifice quite frequently involves seeking horror. In this respect, it seems to me that the mind takes in as much destruction as it can stand. Atmosphere of death, of the disappearance of knowledge, birth of this world we call sacred. (p. 194)

Sacrifice is the way, the passage from this world to its beyond. Sacrifice is the sacrifice of this world for another: impractical path away from practicalities, from what we know, to another end – unknown. Chilling slaughter, fascinating destruction opening on to an end that withdraws of necessity. Irregular passage, there can be no calculations from here to there, no planned path, no justification for the destruction. Because sacrifice seeks the end, an ultimate end, because it is a medium towards what defeats all mediation and withdraws behind horror, sacrifice can only attain its end if it becomes its own end. Sacrifice thus loses its end as it finds itself: as a virulent, parodic representation of its operation. Sacrifice is only the sovereign simulacrum of the sacred, and only as such does it become sacred – fraudulent. Knowledge can follow this path towards the unknown on a single condition: the disappearance of knowledge. In an atmosphere of death, the sacred is only born of consciousness seeking destruction.

8 Communication

> In the several presentations I have done here, I have attempted
> to communicate my experience of un-knowing, which, to a cer-
> tain extent, is personal, but which I believe to be communicable
> insofar as it seems *a priori* to differ from that of others only in a
> sort of defect of my own: the consciousness that this experience
> is one of un-knowing. Of course, I can never speak of un-knowing
> without facing the same difficulty. Thus I have to recall it every
> time. But I move beyond this, and I admit it without hesitation:
> what I will develop in front of you will once more be this para-
> dox – the knowledge of un-knowing, a knowledge of the absence
> of knowledge. (p. 210)

Self-sacrifice of knowledge, communication is impossible: possible
by default, when all else fails. Communication happens in and as
that failure – the breach of and to the other. The end of communication is the unknown: the passage across the limit from here
to there. I communicate from my personal experience to an other
beyond me, another beyond. So, communication is the passage
of the unknown: what communicates and how persists as a difficulty, an ultimate problem. But communication moves beyond
this: precisely by moving to un-knowing – it is the project, the
event of the unknown, so it happens, and it does. Then we know:
something has happened. Without hesitation, the paradox that
disturbs regular knowledge opens the space of knowledge, marks
its possibility in the impossible sign of the advent of un-knowing.
And so it is that it can never speak without bearing the mark of
this difficulty. Exactly as it moves beyond.

9 Play

[The way I see things] consists in saying that everything is play, that being is play, that the universe is play, that the idea of God is unfortunate, and what's more, unbearable, insofar as God, who initially, outside of time, can only be play, is tied by human thought to the creation, and to all of the implications of the creation, which are contrary to play. Thus it in fact weighs down the most ancient human thought, which hardly moves beyond play when it comes to what is considered in its totality. ... Christianity is no doubt not the first religion to cease having the strength to situate human action in the universal play. All the same, Christianity, Christian thought, still is the screen that separates us from what I would readily call the beatific vision of play. (p. 211)

If sacrifice, language, median terms become comic parodies of themselves as they seek communication, it is because sovereignty, in the end, incites play. The sovereign, God above all, sets the rules – they may as well be the rules of play, indisputable mark of that sovereignty. In play, the sovereign marks its ultimate irreducibility: it is none of its effects, elsewhere. The objects of knowledge cannot but veil the injustifiability of a creation which asserts its utmost end at the level of play. But knowledge loses itself there, it loses its reason, which is to be for a reason – serious. Serious knowledge, practical reason misses totality, remaining too effective in front of what can have no completion because it has no reason. Still, the sovereignty of play affects the totality, and God, before the Verb, before finding His reason in the Creation, has none that is serious enough for words. Beatitude, ecstasy is nothing but this absence: of seriousness – unmasterable play that disempowers thought, dispossesses words of a referentiality, leaving them inoperative, besides themselves, defeated by un-knowing.

10 Failure

> The death of thought always fails. Indeed, it is only a *powerless movement*. Similarly, ecstasy is powerless. In ecstasy, there remains a sort of constant consciousness of ecstasy, placing ecstasy on the same inappropriate plane as a head of cattle for the farmer, on the plane of things offered for property. In fact, it is inevitable in the end to take it as a thing fit to be turned into an object of teaching, as I mean to do. I will not insist on this difficulty. It is the one that I have encountered since the beginning, and I can even say that the failures which will result from it will be mixed up with the achievements, in terms of knowledge, which I am approaching because of my very powerlessness. (p. 205)

Aberrant seriousness, parodic play of the inappropriate: thought can only be a simulacrum of death even as it enacts the death of thought. Ecstasy, rapturous knowledge, remains knowledge, just as the sacrificial animal remains a dead cow for practical reasons. The project of knowledge persists all the way to the point of death, and then vanishes – altogether. The thought of death ends in failure, even as the death of thought. Even then it cannot escape the end of knowledge: objectification, conceptual commodification. Nor should it – as it would thereby lose its sense: knowledge means to do so, it has a sense on the condition of doing so. There is no need to insist on this difficulty: it insists on its own, inevitability as the very own, the very property of knowledge. Proper failure, then: simulacrum at the end of knowledge parodying the death of knowledge. It may thereby reach the limit of the knowledge of death: confusing success, confusing success with failure.

11 Un-knowing

> Since, by un-knowing, I mainly mean an experience, I remain, despite the break with any possible knowledge, in the richness of the experience I had previously known. Un-knowing, as I understand it, does not prevent the possibility of an experience which I consider as rich as the religious experience given in this maximum of knowledge that revelation constitutes. In the end, it is in posing being as problematic, being as unknown in its entirety, and in throwing myself in this non-knowledge, that I find an experience not only as rich, but, it seems to me, richer yet, deeper if that is possible, because in this experience, I remove myself even more from common experience (p. 223).

If it is to be a failure, un-knowing must be an experience. It bears knowledge only to the limit of experience, and then throws itself beyond the limit-experience, casting knowledge into un-knowing. There – nowhere within thought's bearings – revelation takes place: it takes the place of knowledge where knowledge has no place. Revelation is thus beyond knowing: it is the experience of the too-much of consciousness. Richer than it can properly handle, it saturates the accumulating economy of knowledge in one instant – that instant which transgresses the temporality of the maximum. Besides itself, in space and time, the excess is also that of ignorance: being unknown in its entirety, being thrown in the impossibly deep abyss of negative revelation – richer than any positive knowledge. As the sacred appears in its separation from common experience, the experience of un-knowing exceeds religious revelation as the communication of ignorance itself. This should not even be said.

12 Silence

> I believe I can introduce here a fundamental proposition. Considering tragedy and the emotion it causes, not only does it appear as sovereign in relation to this world ... but what it introduces is precisely the inadequation of any word. Yet this inadequation must nevertheless be said. ... At this point, I must object to myself the fact that there was no need for me, and that tragedy itself can express itself. When, at the end of the tragedy, the hero, mired in crime, in violence, succumbs to violence, he himself can say: all the rest is silence. A tale told by an idiot, which means nothing. All the rest is silence. ... In other words, what tragedy teaches is silence, and *silence is nothing if it does not, at least for a time, put an end to thought.* Of course, there is nothing to say about death. (pp. 200–1)

Fundamental proposition: the inadequation of anything said. Inadequation to what is sovereign, to the end of saying, then – inadequation ultimately to silence, death. But silence is no more adequate: its violence reverts to idiocy, it means nothing. The self-sacrifice of saying cannot escape this suffering: silenced, it remains inadequate to its own tragedy – and this must yet be said. Speaking for itself, it only points to my own inadequacy: in front of it, I remain necessarily self-contradictory, needlessly, noisily, insisting, teaching myself silence. Experience of incompletion: fundamental knowledge, philosophy restlessly put to rest, the rigorous torment of philosophy – approaching death.

13 Philosophy: *rigor mortis*

In the end, I will begin from the statement of a general philosophy,
which I could give as my philosophy. I must say so to begin:
it consists in a very crude philosophy, a philosophy which must
lead one to think that it is all too simple, that a philosopher able
to put forth such vulgar affirmations has nothing in common
with the subtle character that deserves today the name of
philosopher, for in the end, anybody could have an idea of this
kind. I know it well, this thought I find vulgar is my thought.
(p. 211)

Yet philosophy reclaims its rights insofar as it alone can lay
out the problems. Philosophy, to my mind, intervenes as a
demand for rigour. ... The point is to push things to the end,
without stopping with the first way out, and to see clearly that,
on the contrary, if anything deserves to be carried to the end,
this is it. *It is not even a philosophy any more.* (pp. 201–2)

Only philosophy can accomplish the rigorous movement
that leaves one speechless in a consistent manner, that refuses
diversions. Yet, if we attempt this, we quickly come to see that
philosophy cannot accomplish this movement while remaining
on its own ground. It intervenes only negatively, not to accomplish itself, but accessorily tied to the effort of the mind suffering from its inability to experience death. It can only refuse
the presuppositions and denounce, in the answers of science,
what conceals, etc. But having drawn nearer to this experience,
it nevertheless refuses it. Insofar as it is reflection and work, it
steers away from it. (pp. 202–3)

At bottom, the philosophy of play appears as truth itself,
indisputable, vulgar, but it remains unsettled insofar as we suffer
and we die. The other solution: we can think and be the play,
make of the world and of ourselves a play, on the condition of
confronting suffering and death. Major play – more difficult than
we believe.

In this way it seems we are leaving the philosophy of play, we
are at the point where knowledge gives way, and what appears
is that the major play is un-knowing – the play is the indefinable,
what thought cannot conceive. Such thought exists in me only
in a timid way, a thought I do not feel apt to bear. I do think it
indeed, it is true, but I must say, as a coward, as somebody who

covers his eyes, who hides, and who, in the end, is delirious with fear. (pp. 212–13)

Here begins, based on the abandonment of knowledge, an ordered reflection which it is possible to pursue about the experience of un-knowing. (p. 203)

Notes

1 All the citations in this essay are taken from Georges Bataille's *Conférences du non-savoir*, a series of lectures given at the Collège Philosophique in 1951–53 (except that about the sacred, taken from 'Le sacré au XXème siècle', a related talk from the same period). For a while Bataille had considered gathering these lectures into a book (tentatively entitled *Dying of laughter and laughing to die* or *The unfinished system of un-knowing*); later, he offered *Tel Quel* the opportunity to publish them but died before being able to give them a definitive form. What remains, in the form of either Bataille's manuscripts or transcriptions by the Collège, has been gathered in volume VIII of the *Œuvres complètes* (Paris: Gallimard, 1976). The numbers following each of the citations refer to this edition; all the translations are my own.

Part 2
The body of death

4

Dead time (a ghost story)

FRED BOTTING AND SCOTT WILSON

Death does not authenticate human existence. It is an outmoded evolutionary strategy. The body no longer need be *repaired* but simply have parts *replaced*. Extending life no longer means 'existing' but rather of being 'operational'.

Stelarc[1]

Crash!
HELEN We can look at it again on the monitors. They're showing it in slow motion.

An audience of thirty or so gathers at the trestle tables to watch a slow-motion replay on a huge television monitor. As the hypnotic, grotesque ballet unfolds, the crowd's own ghostly images stand silently in the background, hands and faces unmoving while the collision is re-enacted. The dream-like reversal of roles makes them seem less real than the mannequins in the car.

James looks down at the silk-suited wife of a Ministry official standing beside him. Her eyes watch the film with a rapt gaze, as if she were seeing herself and her daughters dismembered in the crash.[2]

As a cinema audience watches James Ballard watch a Ministry official watch herself being dismembered in slow motion in a scene from David Cronenberg's screenplay of *Crash* depicting a test at a road research laboratory, that audience also sees itself reflected in the ghostly image of the spectators reflected on the screen. A host of bodies in physical space, in different times and spaces, are transformed into faint shadows of corporeal presence.

Reflected in the video replay of the crash test they have just watched, the ghostly images of the spectators signal their absorption into the screen collision that they see as if for the first time. Since the actual crash occurred so quickly, perception can only occur with the technological capacity to vary speed. The crash is a brutally comic literalization of the death drive determining the relationship between technology and human bodies; the dismemberment of the impacting bodies ironically provides a satisfying *tableau vivant* for the spectral mutilation, by the motorized lens, of the silent and motionless group of spectators. In an age of omnipresent prostheses of vision, movement and labour, bodies become no more than the shadows of ghosts, receding figures supplanted by the tele-cinematic machine. Writing of the 'last vehicle' – the 'vector-velocity' of motorized vision and communication – Paul Virilio comments: 'It is thus our destiny *to become film*'.[3] And when we become film, captured and captivated by our own ghostly images, an older, more corporeal spectre is left behind.

Ghosts have no doubt always haunted technology, perhaps from the moment the first primitive tool became a murder weapon, but contemporary ghostliness accelerates towards an ever more evanescent and virtual world. In a letter concerned with letter-writing, Franz Kafka discussed the ghosts that haunt the temporal and spatial gaps of epistolary communications technology. Letter-writing, which introduces 'a terrible disintegration of souls', is 'an intercourse with ghosts, and not only with the ghost of the recipient but also with one's own ghost which develops between the lines of the letter one is writing'. Epistolary communication is failed communication, deferring and dislocating presence and self-presence in a world of ghosts: 'Writing letters ... means to denude oneself before the ghosts, something for which they greedily wait. Written kisses don't reach their destination, rather they are drunk on the way by the ghosts. It is on this ample nourishment that they multiply so enormously.' At the same time as communications technology absents oneself from oneself as much as others, the Other of writing extending its spectral realm, technology is invented to compensate for temporal and spatial distance, railways, cars and aeroplanes being constructed 'in order to eliminate as far as possible the ghostly element between people and to create a natural communication'. 'But', Kafka exclaims, 'it's no longer any good, these are evidently inventions being made at the moment of crashing. The opposing side is so much calmer and stronger; after the postal service it has invented the telegraph, the telephone, the radiograph. The ghosts won't starve, but we will perish.'[4] For Virilio, facing up to another revolution in technical innovation, the computer-aided development of telecommunications only accentuates this 'ghostly dimension'.[5]

> Thanks to so-called 'force-feedback' technologies, to feedback from the *teleact* DataGlove recently put on the market and, in the near future, to the full teletactile bodysuit in which touch and impact will involve the whole body, we will see industrial production of a personality split, an instantaneous cloning of living man, the technological recreation of one of our most ancient myths: the myth of the *double*, of an electromagnetic double whose presence is spectral – another way of saying a ghost or the living dead.[6]

The ghosts living their death in the glowing array of networked machines, feeding vampirically on the circuits of undead digitally generated imaging systems, leave something, less than living and less than dead, blinking in front of spectral screens.

Death match

Maybe sometime soon, then, death will have met its match. Cyberstrategists, genetic engineers and science and science fiction writers are anticipating the death of death. For the Australian performance artist Stelios Arcadiou, AKA Stelarc, technology will continue to transform the nature of human existence, redesigning the body in a modular fashion so that malfunctioning parts can be infinitely replaced, or extended, to the point where life will become totally unrecognizable. Geneticists have apparently discovered the molecular structure, the telomeres, that renders some cells immortal while letting others age and die; they have the knowledge that, potentially, will enable scientists to 'stop the biological clock' and allow some to live forever.[7] In the near future described in William Gibson's novel *Neuromancer* (1984) computers and artificial intelligences are able to access, replicate and 'realise' or concretize, virtually, the thoughts, mental images, memories, dreams and fantasies of human subjects;[8] human consciousness, subjectivity and will can be recorded on ROM disks and played indefinitely; and life persists in the cybernetic matrix, biological death no longer providing a limit point for human experience. Naturally this situation has decidedly dystopian possibilities: the absolute freedom promised by the release from death simultaneously threatens to become an eternal life sentence of exploitation or manipulation by the technological powers that can access and employ the data. The novel describes the potentialities of a neuromantic, cybernetic, in-corporate life-in-death. Such a description of the future may seem far-fetched, or too pessimistic, or even, in its pathos concerning the fate of humanity, sentimental. But for Virilio the dystopian vision evoked by Gibson should be taken very seriously indeed, since he believes that in many respects it has already been realized. Much of the technology that Gibson imagines is theoretically feasible, as Jean-Pierre Changeaux contends in *L'Homme neuronal*: 'The materiality of mental images can no longer be doubted', and that materiality will surely enable the translation or preservation of 'mental phenomena' on to disk.[9] The erasure of the limit of death has thus become the threshold for human scientific imagination and its attendant anxieties concerning the future present. The death of death promises to dissolve the temporality, the sense of finitude, that has defined humanity for modernity, inaugurating a completely new order of existence.

This essay is about dead time, about the death of time as it has been understood in the modern epoch, and the new time of the undead. Modernity changed time, so the story goes, from an 'organic' or 'natural' time of cycles and seasons to the mechanical time characterized by the organized urban mass. The *flâneur* of Baudelaire and Benjamin, idling along without purpose or direction, is the witness and surplus to this modern temporality. But time is no longer credibly organized by the progressive ascent of the grand narratives of modernity; the symbolic and subjective structure of temporality is no longer anchored by a general equivalent that allows time to be exchanged for money. Instead temporality accedes to aleatory movements beyond the end of history, to an a-temporality whose mirror is the drifts, speed and hyperconductivity of electronic pulsation. The virtual reality of rapid binary exchange

leads to an order of mechanical and abstracted digital symbolization, a machinic temporality on to which corporate structure is
grafted: cybertime, computer time, real time, global time. And the
death of time as modern humanity has lived it. Unrecognizable,
incomprehensible, time's pulse beats to alien rhythms, death-
driven by the exponential incursions of speed. And no pulse at all,
but a residual, ghostly non-machinic temporality. Dead time.

To establish the time of death of the death of time it would be
necessary to take a photograph, no doubt with a 1930s flash bulb.
For it is perhaps only photographs, as shades or phantoms of the
past, that can speak authoritatively of death, and of time, of the
passing of the symbolic boundary between life and death, past
and present, even as they mark that boundary in a state of limbo
that is neither one nor the other. Photographs, scars of time frozen,
prostheses of sight and memory, signal a connection and disconnection from the Other. The invention of the photograph marked
a significant shift in modern conceptions of death and time. For
Barthes, in *Camera Lucida*, the spectral force of the photographic
image manifests the distinctive temporality and reality of modernity. Bound up with what Edgar Morin called 'the crisis of death'
in the second part of the nineteenth century, the photograph
grounds the passing of real time in death. In a society confronted
by the scientific secularization of its symbolic order, the photograph becomes the primary means by which society can register
death through commemorating life. The photograph marks the
intrusion of 'an asymbolic Death', dying placed outside religion as
'a kind of abrupt dive into literal Death. *Life/Death*: the paradigm
is reduced to a simple click, the one separating the initial pose
from the final point'.[10] The punctum of the photograph which arrests
the eye and challenges the gaze discloses another punctum:
'this *new punctum*, which is no longer of form but its intensity,
is Time, lacerating emphasis of the *noeme* ("that has been"),
its pure representation'.[11]

> By making the (mortal) Photograph into the general and some-
> how natural witness of 'what has been', modern society renounced
> the Monument. A paradox: the same century invented History
> and Photography. But History is a memory fabricated according
> to positive formulas, a pure intellectual discourse which abol-

ishes mythic Time; and the Photograph is a certain fugitive
testimony; so that everything, today, prepares our race for this
impotence: to be no longer able to conceive of *duration*, affectively or symbolically: the age of the Photograph is also the age
of revolutions, contestations, assassinations, explosions – in
short of impatiences, of everything which denies ripening.
And, no doubt, the astonishment of *'that has been'* will also
disappear. It has already disappeared.[12]

Even as the photograph testifies to a past, it exists at the point
where its possibility, in respect of future time, vanishes. That has
been, the statement of past presence and the duration traced
upon the surface of the photograph as a pause in time, becomes
absorbed in a fugitive flight from a time, death and reality governed by the monumental symbolic world. The 'that has been',
marking the cathexis of a subject before a past, is virtually gone:
it will disappear, says Barthes, 'it has already disappeared'. Looking backwards in the mode of the anterior future in which death
does its work, the photograph, tracing something that will be no
longer, is pitched forward despite itself, caught up in a movement
alien to History. For the photograph also partakes of the events,
the speeds and drives of revolution which invent History only to
supersede it, wanting an immediacy in which presence jettisons
the past and speed overtakes time, an instantaneity which simulates a past in the vision machines of the future in the form of new,
prospective ghosts that never have been.

For Barthes, the photographic punctum arrests the gaze, draws
it back in time, pinned to the void of death, of all too human
mortality, a point of connection and disconnection. For Vaughan
in *Crash*, the photograph captures the moment of impact, the click of
the shutter no longer separating life and death but freezing their
moment of fusion as a body part is violently imprinted by the
machine. Death and presence are conjoined in this moment, the
condition of the union celebrated, ritualized and monumentalized
in the photographic testimony. Human mortality is itself eclipsed,
death has been but will be no longer in the eternal instant of erotic
fusion with the machine. The photographs become visionary,
prophetic, prospective, anticipating a future in which they will
remain as the only prehistory, a moment, a pause of instantaneous

fatal impact before all moments, and all time, cease in machinic apocalypse. Duration disappears in this explosive, momentous impact; human impatiences and challenges disappear in the time-lessness of this assassination. Only the crash itself has been. The rest is history to be simulated in the future of the machine.

If history has any future in the machine, it will no doubt unfold beyond the threshold of the human subject according to the arti-ficial death drive of an entirely machinic process. Photography, which once preserved the perception of past presence and a lost reality, now finds itself determined by the rule of speed: 'Today professional and amateur photographers alike, are mostly happy to *fire off shot after shot*, trusting to the power of speed and the larger number of shots taken. They rely slavishly on the contact sheet, preferring to observe their own photographs to observing some kind of reality.'[13] The trace of duration and past reality, necessary to human history, that is glimpsed in Barthes' gaze upon the photographic image vanishes as the development of vision machines gathers momentum. Cameras become motorized, image and vision production becomes automated, operating without regard to human perception but according to the possibilities of technological perception: 'After the ascendance of *distance/time* in the nineteenth century to the detriment of space, it is now the ascendance of *distance/speed* of the electronic picture factories'.[14] Spatial distance cedes to temporal distance and the determining factor becomes speed of acceleration, transmission and light. Speeding, notes Virilio, involves the 'elimination of expectation and duration'; everything collapses 'in the instantaneous apoca-lypse of messages and images'.[15] In cinema, alterity is optically replaced by lens and projector, presenting absence and erasing the 'stereoscopic couple' which 'previously composed and gave life to the social depth of the real'.[16] As duration gives way to instantaneity, life, for Virilio, occurs within 'a system of techno-logical temporality, in which duration and material support have been supplanted as criteria by visual and auditory instants'.[17] We inhabit, according to Virilio, 'a depressive culture where tech-nological acceleration means that departure and arrival – birth and death – blur to such an extent they look the same'.[18] The com-puter technology that dominates daily and banal existence offers

only a 'momentariness without history'.[19] Video cameras connected to and controlled by computers produce a 'sightless
vision', an 'automation of perception' in which humans have no
place, no ability and no relevance.[20] Virtual reality enmeshes
future humans in control systems to the point that man will be
'dispossessed of his shadow'.[21] For the residually human figures
populating the world of automated lenses and monitors and TV
screens, the hyperrationality of speed-perception is something
of a shock, a violent experience of trauma as the perceptual and
cognitive faculties of organic beings 'crash'.

Half time

In *The Art of the Motor* Virilio warns of the 'enslavement' of humans
by intelligent machines.[22] Technology, its speed and hyperrationality, drives towards a fundamental reversal of the status of the
imaginary human Other: machines no longer, if they ever did,
serve a human order of production but transform that relation
to enslave humans, their reality, their bodies, their temporality,
their life and death, within a new order of machinic instantaneity.
There are two consequences of this reversal in the relation of
human and machines in respect of a machinic Other: acquiesence
before the machine and inertia, passivity before the stupefying
array of informational screens, or utter obedience to the injunctions of machinic speed, an enhancement of performance according to machinic requirements. Whether a particular relationship
is one of passivity or enhancement does not depend on whether it
takes the form of work or leisure, even if it were possible to maintain that sociological distinction. Passively looking at television
monitors, making the minimal hand movements necessary to
work a computer game, or enhancing one's sporting or corporate
performance are equivalent pursuits in a world where sport is big
business and corporations rank, regulate and staff themselves
like football teams. As J. G. Ballard writes, reviewing Robert
Heilbroner's *Visions of the Future* (1995), 'The future, he suggests,
may belong to neither work nor leisure but to a violent and ultra-
competitive form of play – linked to American football and the
Olympic games – where virtual reality will make its marriage with
psychopathology, and the Marquis de Sade will find his ultimate

home in the domestic video sensorium'.[23] For Ballard, then, the psychopathological core of mortal being discovers its path to death, to organic extinction, in the images in which it is consumed and remains as the ghost in the life–death of internalized electronic pulsation. In this ghost story, narrative has ceded to play, just as the ideological function of national culture (English literature, for example) was taken over by the corporatization of sporting excellence (Team Nike).[24]

It is precisely this Sadean alternation between a Justine-like docile passivity and a Juliette-like superhuman capacity for violent excitement, in relation to a future consumed with Sadean Nature's deadly categorical imperative, that sustains the current novelty of the ghostly human shape in the machine. While passivity relates to television viewing and the playing of computer games, sporting and corporate practices instrumentalize the acquiescence to machinic imperatives. The two modes of contemporary humanity's being are determined by the dominance of the machinic Other:

> Rendered passive, if not inert, by the employment of various prostheses of transport and instantaneous transmission, man will no longer feel the need to economize physical effort. Hence the emergence of a new law entailing the opposite; this time it will be a matter of treating the living being like a motor, *a machine that needs to be constantly revved up*.[25]

Sport is one evident means for the transformation of the human body to the demands of the machine: technology enables the 'territorial body' to be 'rigorously reconfigured in the manner of the "animal body" of the runner or the athlete', to be 'wholly reconstituted by speed'.[26] The Nietzschean notion of the 'super-species' is thus also transformed through sport, the body bionically reconfigured in accordance with the vector-velocity of machinic atemporality: 'Aren't sports practices a sure index of this "postmodern" attempt to speed up the living, the animate, the way that the inanimate, the machine, has always been made to go faster'.[27]

Speed dictates processes of human temporality, transforming the relation between life and death: 'Rapidity is always a sign of precocious death for the fast species'.[28] Of course there is nothing particularly new in a sense of human enslavement by machines, nor even in a sense of passivity and plasticity towards the different speeds of a machinic process of production where life expectancy is foreshortened by the pressures of physical exertion and mechanical overload. At the start of the industrial age workers died young, exhausted by the 'frenzied pace of daily slave labor'. The aging slows, however, with the mechanization of production and, with a longer span of life, a new sense of time emerges: 'the perception of *too much time, time to spare*'.[29] The deadly imperative therefore takes time as its primary object. The point is now to find newer and more intense ways of *killing time*. Activities are developed to occupy the extended periods of leisure and vacation, activities that 'serve no purpose – except to kill lengthening time'.[30]

Sports and visual leisure activities, once surplus to or byproducts of organized, industrial temporality, come to occupy a more central and dominant place in the age of automated instantaneity. Killing time, deleting it, produces both an excess and a deficiency: automation, for those in the machine, means there is not enough time to do everything: it is a question of the speed at which one works or enjoys one's leisure time by playing energetic games or rewards oneself, and one's nearest and dearest, with episodes of quality. Time is to be used up, exhausted in instants of intensity:

> Postmodern man's inertia, his passivity, demands a surplus of excitement not only through patently unnatural sports practices, but also in habitual activities in which the body's emancipation due to real-time remote-control technology eliminates the traditional need for physical strength or muscular exertion.[31]

Sports, unnatural until the excess of industrial time removed the requirement for a standing or reserve army, overstimulate and accelerate the body in unnecessary physical exertion. Correlatively, television, video and multimedia offer excessive stimulation without physical effort. It is the overstimulation of the organism that is the crucial issue, not excuses of health or fitness. Activity, generated by games or images, has as its primary purpose the expenditure and exhaustion of useless time.

That snooker may become an Olympic event indicates the extent to which ideals of corporeal and post-martial excellence – 'faster, further, higher' – no longer apply. The address of the Olympic ideal now reaches out to the television audiences that consume and make popular televised pastimes: they are enjoined to excel by watching more channels 'longer, later, harder'. Sport and vision machines are thus defined in the same machinic relation of stimulating the void of boredom left by excess time. The overstimulation, of the instant by instant real-time global coverage conveyed by satellite, blurs the relation between time and space, life and death, to the point that excitement is now what solely defines 'life'. In quasi-sporting activities the thrill of the immediate and instantaneous serves to obliterate or homogenize time. Virilio describes the pleasures of bungee-jumping as 'repeated simulations of the ultimate getting off, anticipating *near death experience*'.[32] Simulating an approach to death, the acceleration of sensation through the work of gravity alone, the jumper does nothing. As Nick Cave remarks of his experience of bungee-jumping: 'That's good because it's the sport where you don't have to take your clothes off or anything. You just strap something on your leg and jump, and you can be a hero for the day. Hur hur'.[33] Instant heroism, a quick thrill and the absence of any need for exertion make bungee-jumping a fine example of the contemporary sport that is not a sport. In jumping, or falling, one accedes only to the force of gravity, gives oneself up to its pull, accelerating as fast as a falling body can before the instant when life snaps back from death. The thrill simulates life as it ought to be lived, according to the instantaneity dominating global exchange: for the moment, in intensity, on the thrilling point of simulated death. That is, according to an atemporality, a speed, that is no longer human.

Full time
Sports and leisure activities relate to the production of simulations in that they are determined by the same process, the same law of speed and instantaneity, the same injunction to expend energy, to consume life, at the point of life–death's thrilling instant. The narcissism of these pleasurable expenditures is nonetheless determined by the image, but not as the glass of vain reflection:

the image is the object one loves as and in place of oneself. Narcissus, Baudrillard observes, is no longer in love with the image that is other: he is absorbed into the seductive surface, beyond reflection to the extent that reflection and the beyond no longer exist: *'death itself shines by its absence'*, death 'can be turned into a brilliant and superficial appearance, that is a seductive surface'.[34] The 'digital Narcissus' is consumed by a 'strange bioelectronic mirror' and slides 'along the trajectory of a death drive' to 'sink in his or her own image'.[35] The utter absorption in the image, the erasure of any temporal or spatial distance and difference, the foreclosure of the possibility of reflection, consumes not only the body in the image but obliterates subjectivity in its Cartesian sense.

It is not the limit of death, nor its thrilling proximity, which forms the central thrust of a culture of speed and stimulation. The excitements of dangerous sports, like the visual shocks of video and multimedia, are secondary, though attractive, benefits for the participants. Amy Anderson, a paraglider and mountain biker, comments on the increasingly common pleasures of adrenalin sports like skydiving, bungee-jumping and climbing in an increasingly familiar manner: 'I get a buzz from the sense of danger.' Risk, speed and physical peril, the imminence of death affirming life, underlie the activity. On the topic of mountain biking Anderson states: 'I want to go really fast downhill through steep woods. That's the most incredible buzz.'[36] The buzz of danger, while it defines the contemporary thrill-seeker, becomes banal for the hardened extreme sportsperson. Mike Frost, who, with his cameraman Andy Ford, is a world class skysurfer, argues that 'It's not about the exhilaration or fear any more, it's about performing the move that no one else can do and doing it as well as you possibly can'. In the interests of the perfect execution of a carefully choreographed fifty-second set of filmed manoeuvres the danger is minimized through technical means: Frost wears a watch that tells his height and beeps a warning; his parachute rig contains a computer that monitors his altitude a thousand times a second and releases a reserve if he falls below 750 feet. 'So, it's a safe sport.'[37] An array of technical devices thus expels the very danger of life reaching towards the point of death that makes the sport thrilling in the first place. Beyond life and death the desire is to achieve the optimum performance of sporting excellence.

The object of sport, too, is not the enhancement of feeling or speed of thought but the obliteration of any autonomous and reflective subjectivity: the process, performance and primacy of physical training and technique are all that count:

> It is now a matter of severely limiting *time for conscious interven-tion* on the part of the subject, to the point where the body seems to act of its own accord, without the aid of reflection, oblivious to the present world and freed from doubt and hesitation.
>
> Top sportspeople are not supposed to lose time listening to themselves think. They no longer take their own counsel; they listen instead to their video monitor.[38]

Subjectivity, the space and time for reflective self-consciousness, is now a waste of time, an inefficient pause that is detrimental to the most efficient performance of the finely tuned sporting body-machine. Reflection, automated, replayed in slow motion, happens after the fact, detached from the process and the immanence of the game, itself an almost automated, non-conscious technique. Its retroactive value, moreover, is no longer an attribute of the performer but a function of the vision machine, a supplement that supplants subjectivity in the interests of excellent performativity.

But even at the point of absolute passivity, it is by no means certain that the human body, in its current shape and form, is robust enough to support or sustain the 'expectations of its images'. For Stelarc,

> It is time to question whether a bipedal, breathing body with binocular vision and a 1400cc brain is an adequate biological form. It cannot cope with the quantity, complexity and quality of information it has accumulated; it is intimidated by the pre-cision, speed and power of technology and it is biologically ill-equipped to cope with its new extraterrestrial environment.[39]

Stelarc's project is not only to question the efficiency and practi-cality of the human body but to declare it obsolete in its present form. Further, his project is to redesign the body in order to enhance its performance: 'As an object, the body can be amplified and accelerated, attaining planetary escape velocity. It becomes a post-evolutionary projectile, departing and diversifying in form and function'. 'The body is neither a very efficient nor a very durable structure. It malfunctions often and fatigues quickly; its performance is determined by its age.' In his goal of redesigning the body to increase its efficiency and maximize its performance and operativity, Stelarc reveals himself to be the corporate artist par excellence: life 'no longer means "existing" but rather of being "operational"' as part of 'an extended system'.[40] Divested of emotions, subjectivity and self-reflection, the 'cyberbody' is thereby able to 'extend performance possibilities' and 'cope with the complexity of controlling information'.[41]

For Virilio the non-reflective trajectory offered by vision machines takes ocularcentrism on a hyper-optic course towards cyberspace: '*It is the eyeball that now englobes man's entire body*'.[42] Indeed, in fictional accounts of cyberspace the determination of everything by the coordinates of sightless, directly injected vision depends on the erasure of reflection and the subsumption of the body within the eye:

> He came in steep, fueled by self-loathing. When the Kuang program met the first of the defenders, scattering the leaves of light, he felt the shark thing lose a degree of substantiality, the fabric of information loosening.
>
> And then – old alchemy of the brain and its vast pharmacy – his hate flowed into his hands.
>
> In the instant before he drove Kuang's sting through the base of the first tower, he attained a level of proficiency exceeding anything he'd known or imagined. Beyond ego, beyond personality, beyond awareness, he moved, Kuang moving with him, evading his attackers with an ancient dance, Hideo's dance, grace of the mind–body interface granted him, in that second, by the clarity and singleness of his wish to die.[43]

In *Neuromancer*, William Gibson's 'console cowboy', 'jacked in' to cyberspace, lives in vast space and at virtual speed, accelerating his life to the point of braindeath and flatline. He lives–dies, despite the thrills and *jouissance* of acceleration in virtual space, in the service of the machine that unfolds within his cerebral and optical neurones. His movement, balletic and martial in technical art, leaves no room for reflection, an absolute fusion of 'him' and the artificial speed-images englobed by his optical nerve. The beyond, of ego, personality, consciousness, is an inner, image-generated englobement, the 'intrastructure' of the interface.

Stelarc's work is of course an attempt to embody or realize, in different ways, the elements that characterize Gibson's fictional world. The work exists at the 'interface and interplay of virtual and machine systems, of simulating and physical action, of actuation and automation'. One of his plans is to 'hollow out' the body of its organs so that they may be replaced by new technological components. His 'Stomach Sculpture' of 1993 was a stop on that road. In this work Stelarc attempted to distend his stomach so that it could host a machine, a closed capsule complete with bleeping sound and flashing light. The machine was swallowed and guided down into the stomach on a flexidrive cable. Once inserted, an endoscope was used to suck out excess stomach fluid and the stomach was inflated with air. Then the capsule was opened and extended. Documentation was done using video endoscopy equipment. Although imaging was possible, there were nevertheless difficulties: 'Even with a stomach pump, excess saliva was still a problem, necessitating hasty removal of all the probes on several occasions.' Ultimately, 'for medical reasons' it proved impossible to image the opened and extended sculpture inside the stomach.[44]

A third term, then, intervened in this interplay between machine and physical systems: Stelarc's saliva. A substance that, from a functional point of view, is designed to lubricate the smooth passage of objects down the gullet to the stomach, is also employed as spit and associated with loathing, disgust, disease and death. Stelarc's salivary glands expended in such excessive quantities that they disrupted the smooth imaging of the 'interface' between man and machine to the point that the artist nearly drowned in his own spit.

Appropriately enough, this third element also has a place in Gibson's universe. This 'something else' precipitates the utter immersal in the internalized machinic image, and, like saliva, it is some Thing that is human (in the sense of being non-machinic), but non-human in the sense of being heterogeneous to the unity and dignity that defines the human figure. Like saliva, this Thing enables the becoming of a fusion of body and machine. This something, which is neither body nor machine but interior and alien to them both, pertains to the 'meat' in Gibson's world insofar as the 'meat' – that useless corporeal remainder discarded by the machine – retains an excess that cannot be reduced to the lumpen mass of fleshy existence. It is not purely inert; it is, or can be, as in the case of Stelarc's saliva, animate and excessive.

Injury time

The Thing's space and movement is that of the drive. The death drive which propels the mind–body to a peak of technical prowess in harmonious dance with the software machine takes its bearings precisely from the meat. Locus of rage and hate, the meat opens on to something in an intimate exteriority to the core of being that situates desire in relation to death. For the human who is incorporeally unravelling in the cybernetic matrix, the 'talking' of the meat is linked to the death drive and a *jouissance* that takes desire and subjectivity beyond itself. Indeed, without the meat the machines cannot be joined as a transcendent artificial intelligence. While it injects the energy for 'synthanatos' to occur, propelling the fusion of meat and machine, the drive remains in excess of the *jouissance* it inaugurates. Jettisoned body parts, no use to the machine, are left over from the crash, but libidinal energy remains in excess of the fatal expenditure.

The death of time at the pixellated points of technological instantaneity is not dead time. Dead time only emerges as the excess of corporate time. Dead time is to corporate time as meat is to machine, the time of the meat. Derogating human corporeality to the extent that it connotes all that is useless, the excremental remainder of abject physicality, lumpen, inefficient and obscene, the meat is visible in Stelarc's saliva and in the obese bodies, slumped in their designer sport and leisure wear, consuming buckets of Haagen Daas and their own image on Jerry Springer or Rikki Lake. These obscene, meaty objects, for all their meatiness, remain crucial to the system of corporate time and consumption as its inverse and antithesis. Their destiny, too, is that of the image-screen, their meat and non-performance is determined by the instant injunctions of the machine.

Corporate time, structured by the imperatives of technological speed, succeeds the temporality of production and consumption by means of the empty performative models associated with excellence: time must be used as efficiently as possible, every instant must be accounted for, every action determined by mechanical utility. Virilio cites a worker in the French textile industry, commenting on record-breaking contemporary work practices: 'I make the same movement six hundred times an hour. With the old machines, you could have a bit of a break. Now it's the computer that controls the assembly time and sets the pace.' For Virilio,

> With this level of hyperproductivity, in which a person can no longer keep up with the racing of his digital command tools, we are seeing a new epidemic, following the outbreak of stress. Repetitive Strain Injury, or RSI – acute inflammation of the bones and joints – is a new professional disease.[45]

From the shopfloor to the higher echelons of corporate management hierarchies a machinic hyperrationality sets the pace. For blue-collar workers the physical stress of repetitive and enforced exertion displays the inability of the body to live up to the speeds of performance demanded by the corporate computer. For those in white collars, whose passivity at work is rewarded by the injuries of fitness programmes and sporting play, stress is a failure of cognition, a mental inability to cope with the pressures of informational and performative speed represented by the desktop personal computers dominating the office and the laptops that dog their every move. Meat must race to keep up with the machine; it must pay the price exacted by speed in burn-out, early retirement or sudden death, to be replaced as malfunctioning parts of the corporate system.

Speed dominates corporate, performative time, dictating use of time according to models of efficiency, commodity and hyperrationality: one must maximize the use of time by minimizing delay and deferral, thereby optimizing performativity. Time is thus restructured according to the imperatives of a corporate capitalist order, an order organized according to the models of computerized networks. Unanchored by anything other than the

injunction to excel in one's use of time, the atemporal flows and
pulsations of machinic corporatism disclose a different, corporate
superego beyond reason, morality or humanity, beyond anything,
indeed, other than performativity. Recently businesses have introduced digital timesheets into the personal computers of their
employees: the packages – 'Carpe Diem', 'Tempo', 'Viz Topia' –
are designed to improve output and efficiency by restructuring
the working day into commodifiable and accountable units.
For example, the accountancy firm Coopers and Lybrand divides
the day into twenty-eight units of fifteen minutes and workers are
given codes so that all the day's activities can be monitored,
costed and credited by designating which units were devoted to
which projects and which clients are to be charged for the time.
Offering greater precision in the process of invoicing customers,
the timesheets also measure performance: the ratio of chargeable
to non-chargeable work provides the gauge of an employee's
efficient and profitable use of time.

In the face of this hyperhomogeneous order of things a void and
attendant horror consumes the residually human world: 'Let one
consider the abyss that is facing humanity. Could minds ready to
draw back from the horror possibly measure up to the problems
put in front of them by the present time, *the accursed time par
excellence?*'[46] Georges Bataille's notion of 'accursed time' situates
dead time in non-productive relation to corporate time. In its inert
sense, dead time remains utterly opposed to the hyperrationality
that organizes the Western corporate world. Dead time calls up
the spectre of a temporality that cannot be used, put to work or
rendered efficient: it is unproductive, an expenditure or waste of
time which cannot return a profit, a consumption of a precious
commodity in excess of corporate comprehension or use, and
thus thoroughly alien to the incorporation of time. Dead time has
no reference to exchange, productivity or performativity; it consumes time without purpose and thus defies corporate superegoic
injunctions to be excellent. Like dead air in broadcasting, it haunts
corporate time with a void that cannot be incorporated, assimi-
lated or explained, introducing a heterogeneity that has no place
in the machinic order of things. In this respect, dead time is akin
to what Bill Readings, writing on Lyotard, calls '*unaccountable*

time', a '*temporal alterity*' that resists 'the hegemony of the economic genre in the linking of phrases, a resistance to capitalism'.[47] Indeed, dead time appears only as appalling blanks in the ledgers of corporate accountants.

The elements abjected by corporate time take various forms. Hyperrationality consumes workers, incorporated as operatives, at hitherto unimaginable speeds, stressing them out, retiring them, killing them off. At the opposite pole are the ghostly others, reflections in the screens that consume them as they sit passively, obscenely, in porcine quiescence. Beyond them, however, automated production spits out a reservoir of excess and desolation that cannot be used, delivering more disturbing forms of waste and superfluity, an enforced idleness situating bodies outside corporate time:

> In modern democracies, the transmission revolution reenacted last century's revolution in industrial transport. The dysfunctional society of the ghetto soon reflected that of the waterside towns and obsolete enclaves that rail travel had created. Modern *tourists of desolation* have replaced the tourists of spleen, of tuberculosis or neurasthenia who haunted the seaside resorts of the nineteenth century, in the grip of hatred of the present world. Unemployment, anomie, and the most dire poverty have led to an idleness comparable to that produced by wealth or disease, to flight as far away as possible from a familiar world that really has become unhealthy and unlivable.[48]

For Virilio, the scale of this waste of time and bodies is an effect of the machine's supercession of corporeal effort in production and their consumption of all temporal rhythms other than their own: 'The passivity of individuals made useless, hence supernumerary, becomes a social menace because of the strong component of boredom and discontent'.[49] The passivity evinced in this wasteland and wastetime is of a different order to the stupefied and contented bodies captivated by the stimulation of simulations, inert consumers of the images of contemporary culture. 'Supernumerary', the detritus of corporate time remains unaccountable, in excess of, and beneath, the bottom line of corporate speed, beyond budgetary requirements and provision. Disconnected from the machines of vision and stimulation, the machine's excess grows bored and rumbles with discontent. Here, perhaps, the meat begins to talk, the growling voice of the no one, without (corporate) identity and career structure, speaks from the position of the death drive. For Lacan, the drive has the form of a 'headless subjectification, a subjectification without a subject':[50] it is 'a will for an Other-thing' that 'challenges everything that exists. But it is also the will to create from zero, a will to begin again'.[51] In contrast to the corporate will to produce in nothing and nowhere, in the virtual space of technological atemporality, the headless dejecta, themselves nothing and nowhere in terms of corporate accounting, slowly evince the discorporated, unproductive energies that twitch in boredom and discontent. Their accursed time retains an accursed share of the death drive, an acephalic and unemployed negativity.

Dead time, like the lumpen mass and thieving rabble who, according to Bataille, spit sovereignly on morality and the Good, remains the time of the meat. And meat, in its second sense, remains the impossible object around which the drive circulates; dead time is the time of pure drive situated within but in excess of, unaccountable to, corporate time. Where the latter is tied to a temporality of pleasure and desire, dead time is implicated in an eroticism beyond the consumption of objects. Virtuality seizes and transforms objects of reality: erasing the distance and deferral of desiring in line with a consumptive gratification which obliterates any object of value or desire, it discloses only the void beyond the virtual. Eroticism is not an immediate seizure of objects of desire but a precipitation beyond objects and images. The erotics of time circulate around the formless, base materialism of an object that cannot be delivered or presented. In contrast, corporate time incorporates infinity as the matrix, the totality of data but, in the process, cannot fail to incorporate the unthinkable void of dead time. Even as it attempts to abolish death and unaccountability, as it drives to overwrite the Real, corporate time rapidly re-inscribes the unbearable void of fatal *jouissance* within itself. Crash! Goal!

Notes

1 Stelarc, 'From Psycho to Cyber Strategies: Prosthetics, Robotics and Remote Existence', *Cultural Values*, 1:2 (1997), 241–9, 246.

2 D. Cronenberg, *Crash* (London: Faber, 1998), p. 40.

3 P. Virilio, 'The Last Vehicle', in *Looking Back on the End of the World*, ed. D. Kamper and C. Wulf, trans. D. Antal (New York: Semiotext(e), 1989), p. 115.

4 F. Kafka, *Letters to Milena*, ed. W. Haas, trans. T. and J. Stern (New York: Schocken Books, 1953), p. 229.

5 P. Virilio, *Open Sky*, trans. J. Rose (London: Verso, 1997), p. 66.

6 Virilio, *Open Sky*, p. 39.

7 See, for example, the *Guardian*, 27 November1997, p. 14.

8 W. Gibson, *Neuromancer* (London: HarperCollins, 1993).

9 Cited in P. Virilio, *The Lost Dimension* (New York: Semiotext(e), 1991), p. 112.

10 Roland Barthes, *Camera Lucida* (London: Flamingo, 1984), p. 92.

11 Barthes, *Camera Lucida*, pp. 94–5.

12 Barthes, *Camera Lucida*, pp. 93–4.

13 P. Virilio, *The Vision Machine* (London: British Film Institute, 1994), p. 13.

14 Virilio, 'The Last Vehicle', p. 112.

15 Virilio, *The Art of the Motor*, trans. J. Rose (Minneapolis: University of Minnesota Press, 1995), p. 92.

16 Virilio, *The Art of the Motor*, p. 8.

17 Virilio, *The Lost Dimension*, p. 84.

18 Virilio, *The Art of the Motor*, p. 93.

19 Virilio, 'The Last Vehicle', p. 118.

20 Virilio, *The Vision Machine*, p. 59.

21 Virilio, *The Art of the Motor*, p. 146.

22 Virilio, *The Art of the Motor*, p. 135.

23 J. G. Ballard, 'Anything Could Happen', *Guardian*, 6 October 1995.

24 See F. Botting, 'Culture and Excellence', *Cultural Values* 1:2 (1997), 139–58.

25 Virilio, *The Art of the Motor*, p. 123.

26 Virilio, *The Art of the Motor*, p. 104.

27 Virilio, *The Art of the Motor*, p. 122.

28 Virilio, *The Art of the Motor*, p. 81.

29 Virilio, *The Art of the Motor*, pp. 81–2.

30 Virilio, *The Art of the Motor*, p. 90.

31 Virilio, *The Art of the Motor*, p. 103.

32 Virilio, *The Art of the Motor*, p. 93.

33 N. Cave, *New Musical Express*, 8 March, 1997, p. 23.

34 J. Baudrillard, *Seduction*, trans. B. Singer (London: Macmillan, 1990), p. 97.

35 Baudrillard, *Seduction*, p. 160.

36 Amy Anderson, *Observer*, 13 July 1997, p. 18.

37 See the *Guardian*, 26 September 1998, p. 11.

38 Virilio, *The Art of the Motor*, p. 94.

39 Stelarc, 'From Psycho to Cyber Strategies', p. 242.

40 Stelarc, 'From Psycho to Cyber Strategies', pp. 246, 248.

41 Stelarc, 'From Psycho to Cyber Strategies', p. 248.

42 Virilio, *The Art of the Motor*, p. 148.

43 Gibson, *Neuromancer*, p. 309.

44 Stelarc, 'Hollow Body/Host Space: Stomach Sculpture', *Cultural Values* 1:2 (1997), 250–2.

45 Virilio, *The Art of the Motor*, p. 134.

46 G. Bataille, *The Bataille Reader*, ed. F. Botting and S. Wilson (Oxford: Blackwell, 1998), p. 240.

47 B. Readings, *Introducing Lyotard* (London: Routledge, 1991), p. 132.

48 Virilio, *The Art of the Motor*, pp. 96–7.

49 Virilio, *The Art of the Motor*, p. 129.

50 Jacques Lacan, *Four Fundamental Concepts of Psychoanalysis*, trans. A. Sheridan (London: Harmondsworth, 1976), p. 184.

51 Jacques Lacan, *The Ethics of Psychoanalysis*, trans. D. Porter (London: Routledge, 1992), p. 212.

5

Death's incessant motion[1]

JONATHAN DOLLIMORE

Human consciousness is inseparable from the perceptions of time and space and, therefore, of death: it is in time and space that things die. To know death is perhaps to fear dying; more woundingly, it is to experience the trauma of loss as it is everywhere experienced as time, or its effects: change, flux, mutability, transience. For poets and philosophers, to know death is to see *eventual* oblivion in the here and now. Death in life. This is one of the great artistic and philosophical preoccupations, indeed obsessions, of Western culture. If we no longer want to learn from that obsession, we call it a commonplace or catalogue it as a tradition. Either way, we look the other way.

In 1614 Sir Walter Ralegh, imprisoned in the Tower of London, and himself expecting to die, meditates on death. It is, he tells us, more omnipotent even than God; despite God's best efforts, it is actually only death that can make man know himself. It reveals to us the futility of every endeavour and every vanity; it 'holds a [looking] glass before the eye of the most beautiful, and makes them see therein their deformity and rottenness and they acknowledge it'.[2]

Shakespeare tells the young man of the *Sonnets*: 'thou among the wastes of time must go'. But no one, especially not the narcissist, has to wait to know the eventual effects of time; we can see it now, in the sundial – and the mirror:

> The wrinkles which thy glass will truly show
> Of mouthèd graves, will give thee memory;
> Thou by thy dial's shady stealth mayst know
> Time's thievish progress to eternity.[3]

The mirror glass only reflects the moment of looking. So why do both Ralegh and Shakespeare insist on 'seeing' in that immediate moment the later reality of decay and death? Perhaps because it shares its name with the 'hour-glass' which measures time – and loss.[4] But it is also that they are engaged in the melancholy search for the reality concealed within the appearance.

Always historicize. Yes. But not now. That injunction – always historicize – in its dedication to the specific, has its own kind of consolations and evasions, just like the complacent universalism it rightly challenged and is superior to.

Living death

The human ability to comprehend time brings with it the curse of seeing oblivion in the here and now. The 'most beautiful' search the mirror for the flattering reflection of their appearance only to 'see' within beauty the ruin which is its ineluctable fate. A temporal process is telescoped back into the present moment in a way which says death is latent within life itself.[5]

Ralegh and Shakespeare tell us to confront this truth of time, and remember it all the time. When we need to know the time we are of course least aware of Time. Social life requires a timetable whose very precondition is that we repress the truth of Time: if we really knew and remembered that truth in our everyday lives we would never get anxious about not being on time. Thus the skull clock (a skull with a clock recessed into it), the ultimate aid to living wisely and possibly the only time-piece to actually encourage a disregard of punctuality.

For Ralegh and Shakespeare death is experienced as mutability; yes, there is the future event of dying, but more wounding even than that is the permanently present experience of death as mutability, transience and decay. Our loss accumulates with every minute that passes. It has been said that death is not an event in life, that I cannot 'experience' my own death. These are the phrases of the chop-logician: I do know death, and I experience it most acutely as the passing of time and of the death of others in time. Death is co-extensive with the span of the life it terminates – not as the permanent fear of dying, but as the trauma of ceaseless change and loss. To be mortal is to be subject to time.

In early December 1623, five years after Ralegh was finally executed, the poet John Donne fell dangerously ill. He survived, but at the time believed, with good reason, that he was going to die. So he wrote about the experience, feverishly – literally – and obsessively. Illness becomes the occasion to feel on the (failing) pulse the effects of death as change and loss: 'Variable, and *therefore* miserable condition of Man'.[6] Donne, like Ralegh, thinks of mutability or change as the living agency of death.

Unusually among the early moderns, Francis Bacon tells us *not* to be overwhelmed by death.[7] But even he, in another mood, writes: 'Who then but to frail mortality shall trust/But limns [paints] the water or but writes in dust'.[8] Decline, ruin, decay and oblivion are the fate of all. Felt on the pulses, that is what mutability means: it is the living experience of mortality.

Mutability also suggests that to experience change and decline *in time* is worse than the idea of not being at all. To experience the loss and betrayals of this life is, for Bacon, eventually to despair: 'What then remains, but that we still should cry/Not to be born, or, being born, to die?' ('The World's a Bubble'). And it is desire which suffers the trauma of loss most acutely; as W. B. Yeats put it three centuries later: 'Man is in love and loves what vanishes,/What more is there to say?'.[9] There is, of course, endlessly more to say. Arguably, art, philosophy and religion would not exist without the traumatic experience of change, loss and death. For certain, that experience exerts an incalculable influence on the intellectual and spiritual development of our culture. Does not Western metaphysics originate as a reaction formation to that experience, most influentially with Socrates and Plato? Writers as different as Friedrich Nietzsche and Karl Popper have believed these early philosophers to have been deeply disturbed by change; Nietzsche even believed Socrates wanted to die to escape it.[10] Plato searched for the unchanging reality behind the world of appearance, flux and change, and, when he thought he had found it, was convinced he had found a better world. In the philosophical and religious tradition which thereafter develops the world of immediate experience (appearances) was said to be one of unreality, deception, loss, transience and death, to be contrasted with an ultimate, changeless reality, which was either deeper within, or entirely beyond, this one. This immanent or transcendent reality was also identified as the source of truth, whereas the world of appearances is the place of perpetual error or, at the very least, relative, as distinct from absolute, truth. Permanently alienated by the impermanence of the world of appearance, the human mind and soul profoundly identify with this domain of ultimate reality and unchanging truth.

Hardly surprising then that some of the greatest philosophers tell us that without death there would be no philosophy. Others go further: without death there would be nothing. A disturbing paradox then: death, which consigns everything to oblivion, is also what gives meaning to everything.

Stasis

The human skull as *memento mori* has a mesmerizing immobility that is more than stillness. It is the stasis which, in the Western imagination, promises absolute release. It suggests final freedom from all tension which is the aim of Freud's death drive;[11] more mystically, it is Eliot's 'the still point of the turning world'[12] or Shelley's Platonic One:

> The One remains, the many change and pass;
> Heaven's light forever shines, Earth's shadows fly;
> Life, like a dome of many-coloured glass,
> Stains the white radiance of Eternity,
> Until Death tramples it to fragments! – Die,
> If thou wouldst be with that which thou dost seek![13]

Shelley makes apparent what was always implicit: the desire for the eternal and the seduction of death are inseparable. Even orthodox Christian images of the afterlife have been resonant with the desire for ecstatic oblivion, the release from pain, the peace of God which passes all understanding. All very different conceptions of the stasis which is beyond life, yet connected by their promise of the end of Time – which is to say, more immediately, the end of desire and the escape from the pain of individuation:

> O, for the time when I shall sleep
> Without identity –
> And never care how rain may steep
> Or snow may cover me!

> No promised Heaven, these wild Desires
> Could all or half fulfill –
> No threatened Hell, with quenchless fires
> Subdue this quenchless will![14]

For the alienated modern consciousness adrift in a meaningless world, the *memento mori* is the stillness latent within all sound and all movement, and even in discarded objects after they cease to have a function within human praxis. For us, today, it is a stillness that is perhaps most hauntingly apparent in the photograph. Roland Barthes is not alone in seeing in the photograph's 'intense immobility' a modern *memento mori*:

> ... however 'lifelike' we strive to make it (and this frenzy to be lifelike can only be our mythic denial of an apprehension of death), Photography is a kind of primitive theatre, a kind of *Tableau Vivant*, a figuration of the motionless and made-up face beneath which we see the dead.[15]

The photograph seems, in its very immediacy, the certainty of future loss. Barthes describes and reprints a photograph of a young man waiting to be hanged.[16] We realize both that he is going to die and that he is already dead; we are both before and after this catastrophe; we anticipate it in horror and look back on it as that which happened long ago. Another old photograph of two little girls: 'How alive they are! They have their whole lives before them; but also they are dead (today), they are then *already* dead (yesterday)'. Whether or not its subject is already dead, every photograph tells of death in the future.[17] And beyond this death is nothing but 'indifferent nature', the sense of which involves, says Barthes, 'a laceration so intense, so intolerable'.[18] This indifferent nature is Coleridge's 'inanimate cold world'[19] and Tennyson's 'blank day':

> Dark house, by which once more I stand
>   Here in the long unlovely street,
>   Doors, where my heart was used to beat
> So quickly, waiting for a hand,
>   A hand that can be clasp'd no more –
>   Behold me, for I cannot sleep,

> And like a guilty thing I creep
> At earliest morning to the door.
>
> He is not here; but far away
>   The noise of life begins again,
>   And ghastly thro' the drizzling rain
> On the bald street breaks the blank day.[20]

Eliot's 'still point of the turning world' makes stasis signify an ultimate reality which is immanent rather than transcendent, a stillness that is 'not fixity'; an image of mystical release rather than eternal life:

> At the still point of the turning world. Neither flesh nor fleshless;
> Neither from nor towards; at the still point, there the dance is,
> But neither arrest nor movement.[21]

And yet some of Eliot's most powerful lines are of land- or seascapes where the ultimate reality is closer to Coleridge's inanimate cold world. They too evoke an oblivion that is a welcome release from the 'lacerating pain' which accompanies the experience of loss in the face of Barthes's indifferent nature; an oblivion denied to, but ambivalently desired by, those referred to in Coleridge's next line: 'that inanimate cold world allowed/To the poor, loveless ever-anxious crowd' ('Dejection: An Ode').

Escape from the pain of individuation – from anxiety – is so often imagined in terms of the same cosmic stillness which causes it. In the following lines from *Four Quartets* (ll. 46, 34–40) Eliot describes, and precisely evokes, in the repetition of 'time', the sound of a sea-buoy's bell being rung by 'the ground swell, that is and was from the beginning':

> And under the oppression of the silent fog
> The tolling bell
> Measures time not our time, rung by the unhurried
> Ground swell, a time
> Older than the time of chronometers, older
> Than time counted by anxious worried women
> Lying awake, calculating the future

Anxiety, for Eliot and for Coleridge, is the experience of consciousness imprisoned in time.

It is only partly true to say that such views are uniquely modern and attributable to 'the death of God', Darwinianism, the second law of thermodynamics and so on. A comparable sense of oblivion in immobility has earlier antecedents. Consider, for example, the deliberately non-heavenly sense given to 'eternity' in the lines quoted above from Shakespeare's Sonnet 77, and compare it with Marvell's famous lines from 'To his Coy Mistress':

> But at my back I alwaies hear
> Time's winged Charriot hurrying near:
> And yonder all before us lye
> Desarts of vast Eternity.

'Death's incessant motion'

But there is another, very different perception of death in the early modern period. Not so much death as ending, stasis, oblivion, non-being, but rather death as vicious energetic mutability. A couple of lines by the poet George Herbert brilliantly capture this. He had in mind perhaps the way that dust, or maybe leaves, collect in a corner (for us, in the corners of car parks and other concrete spaces, driven there by eddying winds). Herbert writes in 'Church-monuments' of 'this heap of dust;/To which the blast of death's incessant motion,/ ... /Drives all at last'.[22] Within this inert heap of dust death is present as a blast, an incessant motion, a driving force. The writer(s) of Ecclesiastes could sense oblivion in the aimless movement of the wind and the ceaseless flowing of rivers;[23] Herbert could see and feel it within a handful of dust.

I imagine that this perception of death as fiercely active influences the appearance, in visual representations of death, of the decomposing corpse, or *transi*. Ariès finds the *transi* appearing as early as 1320, but becoming most visible in the fourteenth to sixteenth centuries.[24] It represents *active* decomposition; death is at work, disarticulating and disintegrating the unity and the beauty of the individual form. The subterranean work of death is, as it were, brought to the surface. Thus Hamlet at the graveside. He wants to know death not as a metaphysical abstraction but as material reality. He remembers kissing Yorick, riding on his back, close to his head. And so he asks the gravediggers how long it takes for

the body to rot in the grave. Sometimes, in the *transi*, worms are
visibly at work, devouring the corpse. There was a word for this:
vermiculation. The incessant motion of death: it is as if the real
material energies of the universe reside not in the generative life
force but the *unbinding* potency of death. Some such idea motivates Hans Baldung Grien's *Love and Death*[25] or Nicolas Deutsch's
Death and the Young Woman, where the decaying corpse becomes
sexually active.[26]

Mutability was always much more, then, than a literary 'con-
vention', and never more so than in this conception of death as
incessant motion. It entails a contradiction. On the one hand mutability is the absolute enemy of desire because it always cheats it.
This is why mutability comes to mean not only this process of
ceaseless change but also the sense of loss which it creates
within, and which so profoundly affects, the human psyche: that
inconsolable sense of loss which is somehow always in excess of
the loss of anything in particular (man is in love and loves what
vanishes). On the other hand movement, motion, change, incon-
stancy are the very stuff of desire. In other words, this force of
*mutability, which is the enemy of desire, is also the inner dynamic of
desire*. As T. S. Eliot put it in *Four Quartets*, 'Desire itself is move-
ment/Not in itself desirable' ('Burnt Norton'); or, in the words of
Shelley, desire is 'that unrest which men miscall delight' (*Adonais*,
l. 354). Such lines epitomize a deep ambivalence towards the idea
of movement as it affects desire: it is an elemental condition of life
which nevertheless promises pain rather than pleasure. More
often than not evil is conceived in terms of an energetic, aberrant
movement, whereas good takes the form of restricted movement
(sticking to the straight and narrow) with the ultimate goal of
fixity and stasis.

Why is it that Western spirituality idealizes fixity and stasis,
yet actively promotes their opposite: unrest, lack, striving – and
anxiety? The answer lies partly in this conception of human
desire being driven by the same forces of mutability that deny it
fulfilment. I believe this contradiction becomes profoundly important in the formation of identity and gender in Western intellectual
culture – theological, philosophical and artistic – not least in the
way it renders desire seemingly impossible, destructively insatiable,

self-defeating and linked to death: 'Thy decay thou seekst by thy desire'.[27] The attempted fulfilment of desire is at once the destiny of the self and what destroys it, leading the poet to cry, in Shakespeare's Sonnet 147, 'I desperate now approve/Desire is death'. For Ralegh, Donne, Herbert and Shakespeare, death does not merely end life but disorders and decays it from within. Not just an ending, but an internal undoing which begins at birth. The moment we are born we begin to die. And if death is this inner dynamic – this 'incessant motion' of life itself – death is always already inside desire. What is being referred to here is human desire generally; sexual desire is often the actual focus, but never the exclusive, obsessive concern it has become for us. Deutsch's *Death and the Maiden* is hardly comprehensible to us unless we recognize this.

Arguably the death/desire dynamic is most vividly expressed in the literature and philosophy of the period I have been describing, which can loosely be called the Renaissance and which is widely regarded as the most artistically productive of all. Time and again we encounter a connection between that dynamic and intense artistic production. What many would now regard as a pathological way of thinking and feeling nevertheless inspires great aesthetic and intellectual achievements. However, the death/desire dynamic is not new to the Renaissance. By then it is already old. We associate it most obviously with early Christianity, but it is significantly present in Hellenistic philosophy, especially stoicism. Some would now argue that it was influential even in ancient Greece. But it is Christianity that intensifies and internalizes it. Man (or rather woman) experiences a transgressive desire for what is forbidden *because* it is forbidden. This tree of knowledge is also the tree of death. In Eden death did not exist. This transgressive desire, generated from the fact of prohibition, brings sex and death into the world simultaneously and henceforth makes them inseparable.

So the most remarkable aspect of our religion is not that it invented God and eternal life to lessen the trauma of death, but that it intensified the trauma by making Man/Woman responsible for death. Unforgettably, original sin epitomizes that inextricable blend of abjection and hubris which is the essence of Christianity.

As Elaine Pagels remarks, the power of the idea of original sin lies partly in the fact that there are times when we would rather feel guilty than helpless.[28] It is one of the earliest examples of the human mind hubristically seeking to identify with, and even internalize, what threatens it. One result of that hubristic internalization is that the individual who desires is never still but always driven forward by conflict and unrest. And sexual desire is where the unrest is felt most acutely. To what extent is all this gendered? Some feminists would argue that what I have been describing is very much a masculine structure of desire. Camille Paglia would agree, even while dissenting from the feminist agenda that has been inferred from this difference: 'Men know they are sexual exiles. They wander the earth seeking satisfaction, craving and despising, never content. There is nothing in that anguished motion for women to envy'.[29] Yet other feminists will say that to think it *is* specifically masculine is itself a gender prejudice: they say women can be just as restlessly obsessed with loss and death as men, even if that obsession does not necessarily take a sexual expression. They can point to the writing of, among others, Emily Dickinson, Emily Brontë, Virginia Woolf, Simone de Beauvoir, Sylvia Plath, Melanie Klein and Julia Kristeva.

Death and individualism

Modern theories of identity – especially as they have culminated in postmodernism – tend to be heavily gendered. They tell a story of the recent disintegration of Western humanism. The argument is all too familiar: once Western culture was underpinned by a confident essentialist ideology of subjectivity. The individual experienced 'himself' as unified, self-determining and stable. It was this conception of subjectivity which fed the predominantly masculine Western ideologies of individualism and its universal counterpart, 'Man'. But – so the argument continues – these ideologies were relatively short-lived. Often the full subject was said to have emerged in the Renaissance, become ideologically consolidated in the Enlightenment and experienced his high point in the nineteenth century, before collapsing in our own time, and collapsing in a way corresponding to the crisis of the West, of empire, of masculinity – or anything else we don't much like (and only what we don't like). This collapse is by no means necessarily a cause for regret; in some postmodern versions of the theory a new 'decentred' and multiple subject is also fantasized as the subversion of, or at least the radical alternative to, the oppressive ideologies which the individual, Man and Humanism once served.

In fact, some postmodernists seek empowerment in a quest for perpetual instability. Hardly surprising, then, their preoccupation with the death of man, the death of the author, the death of the subject – all allegedly obsolete and mystifying ideologies which postulated stability and fixity where there was none. Far from being radically innovative as their adherents claim, such recent ideas are mutations of older ones. Devotees of postmodern theory, often ignorant of intellectual history, remain unaware of the extent to which earlier ways of thinking, which the postmodern claims to have entirely superseded, remain active within it. Even more to the point, the mobile, decentred subject of postmodernism is often only a facile appropriation of the history of mutability. This is one problem with a certain kind of postmodernism. It takes something like subjectivity, cuts it free of its metaphysical history, and then inverts its significance: the mobile restlessness of desire and the contingency of self are flipped into their opposite, and what was once negative becomes positive. The delusion is in thinking that merely to recognize a past way of thinking is sufficient to be free of it. But it is not, and soon the old metaphysics of pain and loss, quest and quietism will stir inside the 'new' experience as never before. Of course, when it does it will be announced as something radically new – the after of the beyond of the postmodern.

Julia Kristeva avoids this facile celebration of fragmentation. For her, as befits someone indebted to Freud, we remain afflicted by a crisis of identity characterized by trauma, pain and loss. She found, in the 1995 'death-haunted' *Rites of Passage* art exhibition at the Tate Gallery in London, ample evidence for her view that 'we have never been in such a state of crisis and fragmentation'. Though wary of medicalizing the modern condition and its art, she agrees that psychosis is a fit description of our present malaise: 'I think the crisis we are living through is deeper than anything since the beginning of our era, the beginning of Christianity'.[30]

Perhaps, and yet as my too brief account of the early modern period suggests, the crisis of subjectivity was there at the inception of individualism and, far from corresponding to the end of Western cultural influence in our own time, it was crucial in achieving it.

The neurosis, anxiety and alienation of the individual-in-crisis are not so much the consequence of 'his' demise but the very stuff of 'his' creation and the culture which he (and now, increasingly, 'she') sustains – Western European culture – and never more so than in its most expansionist phases, of which the 'Renaissance' was undoubtedly one. If Man is wrecked by mutability, and in a way that leads him inevitably deathward, it is this same mutability which imparts to him an agonized energy. We find in Western culture a strange symbiosis between aggrandizement and the individual riven by death and loss, between quest and a metaphysics of pain. The individual has always been aspiring to stability but just as surely always been in crisis, energized and driven forward by the same inner divisions and deprivations that threaten disintegration.[31] As John Webster put it (in *The Duchess of Malfi*, 2.5.60–62.32):

> You have divers men, who never yet express'd
> Their strong desire of rest but by unrest,
> By vexing of themselves

It is a paradox dramatized in Spenser's *The Faerie Queene,* where the knights are beleaguered by temptations which threaten not simply to lead them astray but to unravel their arduously constructed and precariously maintained identities – including the seduction of death. Here indeed is Nietzsche's compulsion to rest (below, p. 97), that profound desire for rest prefigured as sleep. For example, Despair promises to restore the Red Cross Knight to an *original* (innocent?) condition of 'eternall rest' which the living 'want and crave' but 'further from it daily wanderest'. The 'little paine' of dying 'brings long ease,/And layes the soul to sleep in quiet grave', just as 'Sleepe after toyle, port after stormie seas,/ Ease after warre, death after life does greatly please' (1.9.40). Here too is Freud's death drive, the idea that somewhere inside consciousness is a regressive desire not just for death *per se* – the escape from consciousness – but for the oblivion of that more perfect state of non-being which preceded consciousness – which, in Spenser's world, we crave but are daily forced to wander further from. Yet those knights quest on for ever. Even the ingenuity of Penguin paperback packaging can't stuff this epic into a binding of less than 1,055 pages (1,247 with notes). And even then it breaks off with, significantly enough, an unfinished account of mutability.

Or consider Donne writing feverishly on his sick bed, convinced that he is dying. He wrote not random jottings but a book running to many pages. More remarkable still, this meditation on death, disintegration and the futility of desire was ready for publication even before he had left his sick bed. And even at the time the book was actually published he was still under doctor's orders neither to read nor write. Writers today are increasingly under the injunction to publish or perish. But the truer description of the Western tradition we are inheriting might be: publish while you perish, or, in Donne's case (and all we literate neurotics who come after), perish in order to publish. For Donne, suffering, mutability and death exhaust, disintegrate and ruin him, yet he responds *indefatigably*; to know and to express the truth about his own and the human condition as one of absence, loss and dissatisfaction become the source of an immense intellectual energy, a kind of praxis of death. A submission to death that is also an identification with it.

And then there is Ralegh in the Tower. What he writes on death while imprisoned there is, as we saw, in a long tradition which insists that decline, ruin and oblivion are the fate of everything, especially human effort. And yet he too works indefatigably in the face of the ruin of death: what I did not say earlier is that his meditation on death comes at the end of his *History of the World*. Under conditions of imprisonment, Ralegh had achieved nothing less than the writing of a monumental world history. In modern printed form it covers around 3,000 pages and extends to six volumes. And it might be said, admittedly rather unkindly and with mythic exaggeration – this being precisely the point – that the reason he was in prison in the first place was for failing in his aggrandizing brief to conquer, if not the entire world, then a significant part of the New World. We learn from death the futility of endeavour only to redouble our efforts.

We could say that, in their manic productivity, Ralegh and Donne are trying to disavow their mortality. This is a familiar argument: we repress death through work; workaholics, especially American ones, are really trying not to die. But this very explanation, though not without truth, is itself a disavowal of the significance of death for those like Donne and Ralegh, for their culture and, still, for ours. Donne is, after all, famous for writing the first published defence of suicide. In it he confesses to the experience of what we might call suicidal depression, if not a death wish. Far from fearing death, his writing is steeped in its seductions, the paradoxes and the profundity of its meanings. In the case of Ralegh, we might also say that his thoughts on death and human futility were a late rationalization of the experience of failure. Again I think this is wrong, or less than half true. The preoccupation with death, loss and futility is there in Ralegh's earlier writing. With him as with his culture more generally, this preoccupation with death does not set in when the impulse to an energetic centrifugal expansiveness falters; on the contrary, it is an integral aspect of that impulse from the very beginning.

Return one last time to that passage with which I began, from Ralegh's *History of the World*. It is the more conventional section of a remarkable meditation on death. Even as he discerns in death the defeat of all human aspiration, Ralegh deifies and adulates it – and to a truly blasphemous degree. He conceives death as a parodic, perverse tyrant even more powerful than God. Its awe-full power is revered from a position of abjection:

> [Death] puts into man all the wisdom of the world, without speaking a word, which God, with all the words of his law, promises, or threats, doth not infuse. Death, which hateth and destroyeth man, is believed; God, who hath made him and loves him, is always deferred.... It is therefore Death alone that can suddenly make man to know himself.
>
> O eloquent, just, and mighty Death! whom none could advise, thou hast persuaded; what none hath dared, thou hast done; and whom all the world hath flattered, thou only hath cast out of the world and despised. (p. 396)

Submission to, and an adoring identification with, a ruthless omni-potence is made from an experience of impotence; he who is powerless, becomes, precisely because of that state, beholden to the effortless, stupendous power of a superior force. Ralegh also derives a vengeful consolation from the obliteration of all dif-ferences which death promises, including that between human failure and human success.

As for Donne, he preached his most famous sermon, 'Against the Dying Life', when he was literally and visibly dying. According to Izaak Walton's account, written in 1640, his congregation inferred that he was preaching his own funeral sermon and, in a sense, dying for them, appearing as he did with 'a decayed body and a dying face'.[33] Some two weeks before his death he covered himself in his winding-sheet and in that garb had his portrait painted and then hung by his bed. Finally, he adopted the posi-tion in which he would be buried – requiring, Walton tells us, 'not the least alteration' (*Lives*, p. 82). In that last sermon Donne is once again obsessed with mutability, that inverted eternity, 'the everlasting flux of time' which brings decay and death. He tells his congregation that in the grave the motion of our dissolution con-tinues, and even beyond it, since one day the grave itself will decompose and we shall again be in motion, our dust blown on to the highway. And so the sermon continues, with Donne literally dying while speaking from the position of death. All the while sub-mitting to, and identifying with it (*Selected Prose*, pp. 310–26).

Modern readers are tempted to pathologize this kind of sensi-bility or at least look for a 'psychological' explanation of it. This is partly because we find it so difficult to empathize with the theo-logical, metaphysical and religious factors that influence it. But those factors, even as they 'mystified' the experiential realities of death, change and loss, and the ways in which they inflected the confusions of desire, also confronted them. A religious belief in redemption and transcendence means that the experiential encounter with the contradictions of desire and the pain of loss can be anatomized and felt on the pulses so relentlessly. In fact it is easier to get back to those realities from an early modern religious perception of them than it is to escape from a modern pathologizing view of the same. In other words, to pathologize the past entails an evasion even greater than the past religious 'mystifications' we struggle to release it from in the move from the 'religious' to the 'psychological' explanation of it. Especially when we realize that, for intellectual writers at the time, religious faith stimulated, licenced and cloaked attitudes that contradicted it. That is one reason why for Donne, just as for Ralegh, God is clearly less impressive and less engaging than death.

The radical elements in humanism inherit from these aspects of religion a strain of anti-humanism whereby consciousness identifies with what threatens it, and especially with what it submits to, thereby empowering and destabilizing itself both at once. The potency of death becomes irresistible to the consciousness rendered impotent by it. To a degree, artists like those I have been describing empower themselves through writing about death. But what I have been describing is an identification that goes further. It is, for example, apparent in Donne actually performing death for his congregation.

One further aspect of this: if the individual in Western culture is driven by a fear of failure, a crucial strand in the Western theology of subjectivity also provides the reassurance that failure is inevitable. If that sounds paradoxical, we need only recall that Western culture has, during its most expansionist periods, celebrated tragedy as the most profound of all aesthetic genres. And it is in the modern philosophy of tragedy (not necessarily in tragedy itself) that the metaphysics of failure is merged with the very creation of a questing individual whose destiny is death. Maybe tragedy works in the same paradoxical way as this metaphysic of death: even as it preaches the inherent futility of mortal existence, it keeps its adherents reluctantly forward-looking; savaged internally by loss, the individual is also driven forward by it: 'On through the houses of the dead past those fallen in their tracks/Always moving ahead and never looking back' (Bruce Springsteen, 'Blood Brothers').

In short, in Western intellectual and creative endeavour submission to death should never be taken at face value. It is never quite what it seems. Alongside or inside an abject, renouncing submission to death there is often an arrogant, questing identification with it. Similarly, while the instabilities, anxieties and contradictions to be found in subjectivity can be truly self-destructive, they are also the precondition, the incentive, for such identifications. From Christian theology to postmodernism, a desiring identification with death runs crucially through our culture. Nor is it confined to the religiously morbid or the artistically melancholic. Modern European thought, rigorous and speculative, philosophical and psychoanalytic, internalizes and identifies with death as never before. Most controversially, perhaps, with Freud and those of his followers like Jacques Lacan, for whom the death drive is what unbinds and disintegrates identities. But there are others, no less influential: Hegel, Schopenhauer, Heidegger, Bataille, Kojève all make death central to their philosophy, to modernity and issues of identity. And with them, too, it is less death as the event that ends life than the contradiction which energizes it. And with the exception perhaps of Schopenhauer – though he was influential for Freud's theory of the death drive – all these writers figure as important influences for the various strands of critical theory so central in recent decades. So much so that, while fully recognizing the radical intellectual breaks which some of these writers inaugurate, I believe it is appropriate to discern what I can only call, with deliberate awkwardness, radical continuity. By this I do not mean tradition – that slow, more or less conscious process of selective development. Rather I mean the way something can seemingly disappear, yet actually be mutating in the form of its (apparent) opposite or successor. In other words, the two things are strangely complicit, the radical break both disguising and facilitating the radical continuity.

My argument has led me on several occasions into unkind remarks about postmodernists. This may serve as the occasion for me to confess that writing about death is a good way to lose friends and have others regard one with genuine concern and suspicion. This was brought home to me recently when I had to go to hospital for some x-rays. Lying on the x-ray table I remarked to the radiologist – such conversational openings coming naturally to me these days – 'I guess you see lots of people who are going to die'. Looking startled he replied: 'I suppose I do; I've never thought about it'. Having been immersed in a way of thinking that made an encounter with the *memento mori* the sanest way to start any day, it was my turn to be surprised: 'Never thought about it! You must do!', I exclaimed. The radio-logist probably thought he had on his hands a highly distressed patient who was convinced he was going to die. And so, with averted eyes and in the neutral tones of the professional whose first law of survival is 'keep your distance', he said 'Why do you ask?' Suddenly I was apprehensive: he might refer me for coun-selling. At all costs I must correct the misunderstanding. I replied briskly: 'Death is my current research brief; I'm an academic you see'. 'Ah', he responded, visibly relieved; and then: 'And has your data yet admitted of any firm conclusions?'. I replied thought-lessly: 'Only that we don't think about death half enough'. It was not meant to sound rude, but to one who had just confessed he'd never thought about it at all despite dealing with the dying on an almost daily basis, it had to. From behind his protective screen he gave me a long, cold stare. And when he pressed the button I'm sure the machine buzzed interminably, or at least far longer than was necessary. Suppose, I suddenly thought, that, upset by my innocent question about death he'd given me, unintentionally or otherwise, a huge radiation overdose? What an exquisite irony; quite perfect for my research. I could hardly wait to get home to write it up. But before leaving I wanted to make amends. 'The thing is you see' – I was lingering by the door, naked but for that rather camp, inverted frock worn for x-rays – 'The thing is you see, without death there'd be no philosophy.' All communi-cation had by now broken down; this was the two cultures stand-off with a vengeance, and my gem of Western wisdom fell on deaf ears. On the way out I was stopped by someone undertaking a patient satisfaction survey on behalf of the Hospital Trust (when you don't have the resources it's important to spend what you do have on PR). First question: had I found the staff polite – yes, no or 'other'. Well I replied, I asked an innocent question about death and was given a lethal dose of radiation. 'I am sorry sir.' Her pen hovered. 'Shall I put that down as a no?' Under 'sugges-tions for improvement' I recommended a hospital plaque reading 'Live every day as if it was your last' and, under her bemused gaze, I at last realised that my postmodern friends' concern for my sanity was justified.

Nietzsche

One writer conspicuously absent from my list of those modern European philosophers who were preoccupied with death and yet, if anything, were even more influential for modern theory is someone who quite literally lost his sanity – Friedrich Nietzsche. (Thomas Mann believed it was syphilis that sent him mad, whereas Wagner was convinced it was excessive masturbation. I don't see why it couldn't be both.)

Nietzsche sought to revalue – or transvalue – the death/desire dynamic. He believed that Western culture was built on a kind of intellectual death wish stemming from the traumatic experience of change and loss. He described this as *décadence*. He found it supremely in Christianity but also in the dominant philosophical tradition as far back as Socrates.[34] Even when one strongly disagrees with Nietzsche, his charge of *décadence*, which included more than I can represent here, is deeply insightful. But one thing is crucial to this *décadence*: a cultural, psychic and physical exhaustion behind which is a kind of death wish. He notes that the very concept of 'sleep' is deified and adored in all pessimistic religions and philosophies and he sees this as 'only a symbol of a much deeper and longer *compulsion to rest* – In practice it is death that works so seductively behind the image of its brother, sleep'. But this exhaustion is more deeply at the heart of our culture than even this would suggest, since all the supreme value judgements that have come to dominate mankind derive from the judgements of the exhausted.[35]

Nietzsche hated this *décadence* and wanted to oppose it with every fibre of his intellectual will. But he was also fascinated by it, especially in the philosophy of Schopenhauer and the music of Wagner, both of whom were, by Nietzsche's own admission, two of his most formative influences. So he was reacting against something he had already powerfully internalized and never entirely escaped. As late as 1888, shortly before he lost his sanity, Nietzsche is still telling us that he had never encountered a work of such 'dangerous fascination' as Wagner's *Tristan and Isolde*, adding, 'The world is poor for him *who has never been sick enough*' to respond to such music.[36]

Because in what follows I shall be critical of Nietzsche, I want to say now that he is one of my intellectual heroes, and central in the sub-text of this article (a defence of intellectual history against contemporary postmodern theorizing). Nietzsche undertook a profound intellectual and existential engagement with the history of thought. He had a passionate wish to break with the past and a profound understanding of the difficulty of doing so. He knew that you do not make that break simply by recourse to 'wishful theory'.[37] The irony then is that so much wishful theory claims his influence.

For a start he truly understands the condition he condemns, and is so perceptive about its influence, even or especially in those who repudiate it, including himself:

> It is a self-deception on the part of philosophers and moralists to imagine that by making war on *décadence* they therewith elude *décadence* themselves. This is beyond their powers ... they *alter* its expression, they do not abolish the thing itself.[38]

To oppose *décadence* one has to embrace it; there is no chance whatsoever of going back: 'One *has* to go forward, which is to say *step by step further into décadence* (– this is *my* definition of modern "progress")'.[39] Nietzsche even endorses a conception of the human condition resembling the *décadent* one, seeing it as intrinsically sick and driven by a mutable, questing, restless desire:

> Man is sicker, less secure, less stable, less firmly anchored than any other animal; he is the *sick* animal ... eternally unsatisfied ... still unrealized, so agitated by his own teeming energy that his future digs like spurs into the flesh of every present moment.[40]

If Nietzsche's greatest work is energized by his vehement repudiation of *décadence*, it is also never free of its seduction, and he acknowledges precisely this when he denounces Schopenhauer and Wagner. Which means that the energy and brilliance of his work also comes from the tension, the conflict between the repudiation and the seduction. Nietzsche's writing is one of the most significant examples of that effort to transform or escape a way of apprehending the world which has already formed one's own intellect and sensibilities. As that last quotation makes clear, for

Nietzsche the heroic repudiation of death and mutability energize desire because they are already inside it as a sickness. Nietzsche's philosophy was forged in a struggle against the death wish. Perhaps this too was a factor in his mental breakdown. In certain unavoidable respects it was a deeply erotic struggle. Both the *décadence* which Nietzsche was struggling to escape and his alternative to it were steeped in different but complementary kinds of sexual desire.

So what did he advocate instead? Nietzsche insisted that we stop regarding change and loss as anti-life. The melancholy absorption with mutability was anathema to him. He insisted that we must break with the entire philosophical tradition which found the fundamental fact of transience unacceptable and which tried to posit a more enduring reality beyond or within change with the help of concepts such as unity, identity, duration, essence and universal. But this was the route of the exhausted. Only when we make an urgent identification *with* change as the essence of life will we transcend the decadent world-weariness of the Western tradition. Never regret change, transience and loss. Celebrate and immerse yourself in them – ecstatically, even sacrificially. He argued for what he called 'a *strong* pessimism' whose effect would not be a withdrawal from the pain of loss but an heroic going with it, a risking of everything in the name of life's Dionysiac excess – at least for the truly great men who, 'like great epochs, are explosive material in whom tremendous energy has been accumulated'. The great human being essentially '*expends himself* ... he uses himself up, he does not spare himself'; in such individuals 'the instinct of self-preservation is ... suspended; the overwhelming pressure of the energies which emanate from him forbids him any such care and prudence'.[41]

Of course it all remains highly self-conscious, so much so that we must speak here of an aesthetics of energy. But it is indeed a momentous shift. Nietzsche was not the first, and even then his was not the only radical reassessment of change. In a completely different way Feuerbach, Marx and Engels would also make change the new dynamic principle of the human as well as the social. But it was Nietzsche's aesthetics of energy that have been profoundly significant for the culture of modernity, and even more for the postmodern. But again, like many radical breaks it both disguises and facilitates equally 'radical' continuities. Nietzsche repudiates the traditional philosophical quest for transcendent being (stasis, duration, identity, perfection), celebrating instead becoming (energy, flux, change, loss, transience, imperfection). In this he sources the postmodern. But for him the desire for true being remains, along with a fear of change, and it is played out in this world, and with a vengeance. Most obviously in that the masochism of sacrifice remains underpinned by sadism. We need only recall how, within his fantasies of heroic self-sacrifice, are even stronger fantasies of mastery, control, repudiation and purification, and an urgent desire to fight the degenerates who are the beleaguering enemies of the 'highest types'. Because this is an *aesthetics* of energy it is never energy *per se* which is celebrated. In fact, the unrestricted energy of life's lower forms is itself usually regarded as deeply disgusting: this is a degenerate and corrupting energy and in urgent need of being controlled by its superior and higher forms. Nowhere is this more necessary than with the inferior races – in relation to whom we also encounter a glaring paradox, namely that fertility is a sure sign of degeneracy; as a character puts it in D. H. Lawrence's novel, *Aaron's Rod*: 'I can't do with folks who teem by the billion, like the Chinese and Japs and Orientals altogether. Only vermin teem by the billion. Higher types breed slower.'[42] The 'purer' forms of energy are beleaguered and threatened by their 'degenerate' – more energetic, more mutable – lower forms.

Similarly, Nietzsche's sacrificial immersion in mutability and loss produced an aesthetic of energy which is anti-Christian, anti-socialist, anti-democratic, sometimes recognizably fascist, anti-woman, and prepared to administer rather than submit to death.[43] Hence the fascistic fantasies of punitively cleansing the world of all weakness, of engaging in 'the remorseless destruction of all degenerate and parasitic elements' in the name of 'a tremendous purification … of mankind'.[44] Nietzsche thought of himself as one of the great men of history, recklessly expending himself. But one thing that distinguished him from a predecessor like, say, Ralegh, was the nature of the expenditure, and it suggests a certain irony which resonates through modernism into postmodernism via academic departments: Nietzsche celebrated sacrificial, heroic immersion in the omnipotent flux of life but did so from a position of erudition, withdrawal, chronic sickness and relative impotence; his philosophy and his fantasy identifications precisely epitomize the modernist man of *in*action, with the emphasis here falling fairly equally on modernist, man, and inaction.

Nietzsche celebrated the Renaissance as 'the last great age'.[45] But, as we have seen, that period was shot through with what Nietzsche despised as *décadence*. Those like Walter Ralegh, who would presumably qualify as Nietzsche's ideal type of great man, full of the will to power, were often those who expressed the mutability aesthetic most strongly. Nietzsche's view of the Renaissance is a simplistic reconstruction which eliminates an obvious paradox about it, namely that the mutability aesthetic emerged not from a *décadent* turning away from 'the real' but from an energetic encounter with it – precisely what Nietzsche would later call the will to power. Now the will to power is supposed to be the answer to *décadence*. But long before even the early modern period the will to power and the death wish go together. Nietzsche is surely right in believing that religion and philosophy derive, at least in part, as a reaction to change and loss, and thereby express a turning away from the world. What he cannot see is that the profound melancholy which change and loss may induce is equally derived, in part, from worldly engagement. Such engagement, far from being the answer to the problem of *décadence*, was in part its cause. We need only recall that two of the greatest advocates of a philosophical renunciation of a world governed by change and loss – Seneca and Marcus Aurelius – were also, quite literally, two of the most powerful men in the world. One was an emperor, the other an emperor's right-hand man. Of both it has been said that their philosophy was rooted in a death wish. *Décadence* was what their will to power produced, not what it left behind; more generally, what Nietzsche identified as the Western decadent tradition, going back through Christianity to Plato, represents not a faltering of the Western expansionist enterprise but a crucial strand of it. So it is not the antithesis of the will to power but its precursor, and the Nietzschean embrace of change is an evolution of that tradition, not a breaking with it.

Nietzsche, like Ralegh and Donne, continues to identify with death. Only now, much more than before, a fatalistic submission to death is replaced by fantasies of wreaking death. Thus the vitalistic celebration of life is most powerfully a fantasy of destructive energy: the 'joy in *destruction*' – which finds expression in war: 'there will be wars such as there have never been yet on earth'.[46]

The aesthetics of energy was fused with an aesthetic of war and death most notoriously by the Italian futurist, and fascist, Filippo Marinetti (1876–1944). Under the influence of diverse contemporary philosophers, but especially Nietzsche, Marinetti idealized violence. In 1914 he described the first world war as '*the most beautiful futurist poem which has so far been seen*'. And now, far from being debilitating, ceaseless change is the source of all energy, progress and the very excitement of the future itself: 'To the conception of the imperishable, the immortal, we oppose, in art, that of becoming, the perishable, the transitory and the ephemeral.' There is no need to yearn for the absolute because we already have created it ourselves in the form of 'eternal, omnipresent speed'.[47] Surely, again, a fantasy of self-sacrificial identification with the potent that is more fundamentally a reaction formation to impotence.

What is evident, and what postmodernists should consider, is that the trauma of mutability is not cancelled in the identification with change; rather it mutates into something else, and historically that something else has included fantasies of violent purification: annihilation not of the self but of the other.

Notes

1 This article was undertaken to oblige the student who, in a brief bookshop encounter with my book *Death, Desire and Loss in Western Culture* (London: Penguin, 1998), became convinced that its real message was that life was too short even to finish such a study, and so would I please summarize it in something much shorter. As usual, the summary also became a development.

2 W. Ralegh, *The History of the World*, ed. C. A. Patrides (London: Macmillan, 1971), p. 396.

3 W. Shakespeare, *The Sonnets and A Lover's Complaint*, ed. J. Kerrigan (Harmondsworth: Penguin, 1986). See Sonnets 12, 77.

4 See also Sonnet 126: 'O thou, my lovely boy, who in thy power/Dost hold Time's fickle glass, his sickle hour'. And *All's Well that Ends Well*, ed. R. Fraser (Cambridge: Cambridge University Press, 1985), 2. 1. 161–2, where the hour-glass takes the same 'thievish' metaphor as here: 'the pilot's glass/Hath told the thievish minutes how they pass'. Visually, death was sometimes shown holding a scythe on one hand and an hour-glass in the other.

5 By contrast, the divine mirror will 'reflect' the end of time: 'that eternal glass/Where time doth end ... /Where all to come is one with all that was'. F. Greville, *Caelica* LXXXVII, in *Selected Poems*, ed. N. Powell (Manchester: Carcanet, 1990), p. 99.

6 J. Donne, *Selected Prose*, ed. N. Rhodes (Harmondsworth: Penguin, 1987), p. 99, my emphasis.

7 F. Bacon, 'Of Death', in *Essays*, intro. M. Hawkins (London: Dent, 1972), p. 7.

8 Bacon 'The World's a Bubble', in *Poets of the Seventeenth Century*, ed. J. Broadbent (New York: Signet, 1974).

9 W. B. Yeats, 'Nineteen Hundred and Nineteen', in *Collected Poems* (London: Macmillan, 1971).

10 K. Popper, *The Open Society and its Enemies* [1945] (London: Routledge, 1995) (single volume edition), pp. 11–34; F. Nietzsche, *The Birth of Tragedy*, in *The Birth of Tragedy* [1872] *and The Genealogy of Morals* [1887], trans. F. Golffing (New York: Doubleday, 1956), pp. 85–86; and *Twilight of the Idols*, in *Twilight of the Idols* [1889] *and The Anti-Christ,* [1895], trans. R. J. Hollingdale (Harmondsworth: Penguin, 1968), p. 34; Plato, *Apology*, p. 75, and *Phaedo*, pp. 107–8, 111, 113, in *The Last Days of Socrates*, trans. H. Tredennick (Harmondsworth: Penguin, 1969). Nietzsche's views of Socrates are not shared by Popper, for whom the real villain is Plato.

11 In 'Beyond the Pleasure Principle' Freud comments: '"*The aim of all life is death*"'. See *The Penguin Freud Library 11: On Metapsychology: the Theory of Psychoanalysis*, trans. J. Strachey, ed. A. Richards (Harmondsworth: Penguin, 1984 [1920]), p. 311; both the emphasis and the quotation marks are Freud's.

12 T. S. Eliot, *Four Quartets* (London: Faber, 1954 [1944]). 'Burnt Norton', II.

13 P. B. Shelley, *Shelley*, ed. Kathleen Raine (Harmondsworth: Penguin, 1974). *Adonais*, ll. 460–5.

14 Emily Brontë, 'The Philosopher's Conclusion', in Brontë, *Wuthering Heights and Poems*, intro. Margaret Drabble, ed. Hugh Osborne (London: Everyman, 1993).

15 Roland Barthes, *Camera Lucida: Reflections on Photography*, trans. Richard Howard (New York: Hill and Wang, 1981 [1980]), pp. 31–2.

16 Barthes, *Camera Lucida*, p. 95.

17 For Barthes, all the young photographers at work in the world, industriously attempting to capture actuality, are in fact 'agents of Death'; it is in the photographic image that our time 'produces Death while trying to preserve life'. See *Camera Lucida*, p. 92.

18 Barthes, *Camera Lucida*, pp. 96, 94.

19 S. T. Coleridge, 'Dejection: An Ode', l. 51.

20 Alfred Tennyson, *Poems*, ed. Christopher Ricks (London: Longmans, 1969). 'In Memoriam', VII.

21 Eliot, *Four Quartets*, 'Burnt Norton', II.

22 G. Herbert, *The English Poems*, ed. C. A. Patrides (London: Dent, 1974).

23 'Blowing toward the south and veering toward the north, ever circling goes the wind, returning upon its tracks. All the rivers flow continually to the sea, but the sea does not become full; whither the rivers flow, they continue to flow. All words fail through weariness, a man becomes speechless; the eye cannot see it all, nor the ear hear the end of it'. *Ecclesiastes*, I. 6–8).

24 Philippe Ariès, *The Hour of Our Death*, trans. H. Weaver (Oxford: Oxford University Press, 1991 [1977]), pp. 113–14.

25 Reprinted in G. Bataille, *The Tears of Eros*, trans. P. Connor (San Francisco: City Lights Books, 1989 [1961]), p. 90.

26 Ariès, *The Hour of Our Death*, p. 258.

27 Edmund Spenser, *The Faerie Queene*, ed. T. P. Roche, Jr (Harmondsworth: Penguin 1978), p. 1054

28 E. Pagels, *Adam, Eve and the Serpent* (London: Weidenfeld and Nicolson, 1988), p. 146.

29 C. Paglia, *Sexual Personae: Art and Decadence from Nefertiti to Emily Dickinson* (Harmondsworth: Penguin, 1992), p. 19.

30 J. Kristeva, 'Of Word and Flesh: an interview with Charles Penwarden', in *Rites of Passage: Art for the End of the Century*, ed. S. Morgan and F. Morris (London: Tate Gallery Publications, 1995), pp. 21, 27; the description of the exhibition as 'death-haunted' is Stephen Greenblatt's, from p. 28 of the same book.

31 Eventually this feeds into the 'uninterrupted disturbance of all social conditions, [the] everlasting uncertainty and agitation' which Marx identifies as a definitive feature of the bourgeois epoch and capitalist production. See K. Marx and F. Engels, *The Communist Manifesto*, intro. A. J. P. Taylor (Harmondsworth: Penguin, 1967), p. 83.

32 See John Webster, *Three Plays*, ed. D. C. Gunby (Harmondsworth: Penguin, 1972).

33 Walton, *Lives*, intro. G. Saintsbury (London: Oxford University Press, 1927), p. 75

34 As early as *The Birth of Tragedy*, Nietzsche speaks of Socrates's 'corrosive influence upon instinctual life', p. 85.

35 F. Nietzsche, *The Will to Power*, trans W. Kaufmann and R. J. Hollingdale, edited with commentary by Kaufmann (New York: Vintage, 1968), pp. 134, 34.

36 F. Nietzsche, *Ecce Homo: How One Becomes What One Is*, trans. R. J. Hollingdale (Harmondsworth: Penguin, 1979 [1888]), p. 31.

37 I describe this elsewhere: 'Bisexuality and Wishful Theory', *Textual Practice*, 10.3 (1996), 523–39.

38 Nietzsche, *Twilight of the Idols*, p. 34.

39 Nietzsche, *Twilight of the Idols*, pp. 96–7.

40 Nietzsche, *Genealogy of Morals*, p. 257.

41 Nietzsche, *Twilight of the Idols*, pp. 97–8.

42 D. H. Lawrence, *Aaron's Rod* (Harmondsworth: Penguin, 1968 [1922]), p. 119.

43 Nietzsche, *The Anti-Christ*, pp. 186, 178–9

44 Nietzsche, *Ecce Homo*, pp. 51, 53.

45 Nietzsche, *Twilight of the Idols*, pp. 91, 98.

46 Nietzsche, *Ecce Homo*, p. 97; cf. p. 52: 'the harshest but most necessary wars'.

47 F. Marinetti, *Marinetti: Selected Writings*, ed. R. W. Flint, trans. R. W. Flint and A. A. Coppotelli (London: Secker and Warburg, 1972), pp. 41–3; *Fascism*, ed. Roger Griffin (Oxford: Oxford University Press, 1995), p. 26, emphasis original.

6

Freud's metapsychology of the drives and the transmutability of death

SUHAIL MALIK

Technoscientific research in the 1990s on the parameters and conditions of life mean that its traditional determinations cannot be maintained in any unified or stabilized way. Correlatively, the fact and meaning of death and what is dead have mutated beyond stable or unified traditional determinations (for example and in the first instance, as that which is simply not alive). The unity of life is *technically* loosened in at least three registers:

- the life of heredity, which is molecular life, the life of (*phylo-*) *genetics*. Such life is the operative condition for the implanting of the DNA of a differentiated cell into a fertile reproductive cell for the former's genetically identical reproduction through gestation and parturition (the 'Dolly' case). Furthermore, the work of Stuart Kauffman[1] and others on self-organizing systems revokes the uniqueness of organic life as the only stable mode of transgenerational transmission.
- the life of the body, which is animal or organic-vegetal life, the life of biotic or somatic *ontogenesis*. Such life is directly supported not only between, but also at, its birth and death. Organic life may now be supported from before its birth (foetal scanning and surgery) and after the arrest of bodily functions (life support). These two aspects are coordinated in the *factum* of after-death births: sperm may be stored and used to impregnate a woman who can then give birth to a child after the death of the father/donor; equally, the 'comatose' and otherwise dead pregnant mother may be artificially kept alive until the foetus-child is able to be removed at a medium stage of its antenatal development and also artificially supported.

- the life of experience, which is human or animal life, the life of the soul or the *psyche*. This life is massively mediated by technically organized production and representation on a planetary scale, the horizon of which at the time of writing is the universality of the internet.

Though the immediate point is that this tripartition of life is techno-scientifically implemented, our primary concern here is rather the *condition* for such historico-technical alterations, which is to say the historicity of the actuality and meaning of *what* life is. To be clear: the historicity at issue here is that of the condition of life in its transmutable facticity.

The critical elaboration of the historical and technical transmutations of life is not *simply* a matter for evolutionary or developmental biology since what is also at issue is technoscientific development and the historicity of the actuality and meaning of death.[2] A precedent for such a critical undertaking is, however, presented by Freud in 'Civilisation and Its Discontents'.[3] Freud summarizes the essay by noting that the 'struggle between Eros [that is, the sexual/life drives] and the death drive' characterizes three processes, which duplicate the registers of life's technical mutation just specified. These processes are 'the civilisation-process (*Kulturprozeß*) which humanity undergoes', which is the historical life of a human experience, 'the development of the individual [ontogeny], and, in addition, it reveal[s] the secret of organic life in general [phylogeny]' (p. 333). We do not take up the 'general characteristic of life' in the terms of Freud's argument here since its focus is not the fact of life but the reciprocal effect of the development of culture on the organization of the individual psyche. The 'struggle' of the life and death drives is instead taken up in terms of its initial theorization in the 1920 paper 'Beyond the Pleasure Principle'[4] together with the theoretical insight it gives on aspects of the development of the human ego in the 1923 paper 'Inhibitions, Symptoms and Anxiety'.[5]

The notion of the death drive and its struggle with the sexual drives famously marks a turning point in Freud's metapsychology of ego and id processes. Its rearticulation of psychoanalytical concerns in explicitly biological terms nonetheless marks the continuity of Freud's earliest and abiding interest in characterizing the concerns of psychoanalysis – the life of a human experience in whatever register it happens – together with the primary processes of living organisms, such as their onto- and phylo-genetic development.[6] Our interest in this aspect of Freud's metapsychology should then be evident. It should also be made clear that since we do not consider the factor of repression in ego–id formation, our concerns here are not directed towards psychoanalysis but to the *meta*psychological theorization of the development of the fact and concept of life. Our argument is only that Freud's metapsychology of the drives proposes a theory of the development of life whose condition is the cortical development of the organism. Such a development of the cortex in the 'struggle' of the drives is in certain circumstances also the loosening of the unity of life as it is the diversification of death in its historicity. The development of the human is in particular (but not exclusively) not that of the organism alone but also of its external supports or, as Freud suggests in the quotation above, culture. Death, then, is transmutable in its facticity and meaning for the human correlative to its transorganic development.

Freud's principal question in 'Beyond the Pleasure Principle' is why does the psyche – the 'mental apparatus' (*seelischen Apparates*) – repeat *unpleasurable* experiences, as in war neuroses. Unlike inhibited, 'diverted' or repressed drives, which are obstructed by 'obstacles' or are 'sublimated' but which nonetheless yield pleasure by another route or source, Freud's interest here is in unpleasures which can 'never' be experienced as pleasurable yet are incessantly relived (pp. 281–3). The repetition of unpleasurable experiences is a puzzle because pleasure is not just a *state* of the mental apparatus but its very *principle*. The pleasure principle is an economic regulation by the mental apparatus of motile excitations that tends to a decrease of excitations 'present in the life of the mind' (*Seelenleben vorhandenen*) (p. 276).[7] The 'excitation' here is a 'free', mobile quantity, which is 'not in any way bound' (p. 276).[8] Unpleasure is attributable to an '*increase* in the quantity of excitation' and pleasure to its '*decrease*'. It is not the absolute levels or amplitudes of the quantity of excitation but only and 'probably' the *rate* of its increases and decreases that Freud 'relates' to the feelings of pleasure and displeasure. Freud leaves it open whether the pleasure principle functions to reduce the quantity of excitation to a *constant* state or just as *low* as possible (p. 277) or to a *zero* level (p. 336).[9] As will be seen, life and death are correlative to these quantitative determinations.

The initial questions are straightforward: how and why does the psyche repeat what contravenes its organizing principle? Freud's 'hypothesis' is that the countertendency of the 'compulsion to repeat' unpleasurable experiences points 'beyond the pleasure principle' to a 'tendency more originary (*ursprünglicher*) and independent of it' (p. 287). That is, its ætiology is beyond the pleasure principle and is not primarily psychological.

The countertendency to the pleasure principle is attributable for Freud to the fact that the mental apparatus is itself a dynamic system of a living body. The compulsion to repeat therefore requires an investigation into the *corporeal* dynamic organization of differential excitation: namely, organic life. This is not far from our concerns: for Freud it *alone* is the source and origin of death.

Freud initially considers a 'living organism in its most simplified possible form[,] as an undifferentiated vesicle of a stimulable substance' (p. 297). But this most basic because undifferentiated life is not feasible: a living organism *must* be differentiated since if it is not to be destroyed by the stimulation of its environment the external surface or skin of the 'vesicle' has to withstand the external excitations, energies and forces which are generally much more powerful than it. The protective ectoderm 'provides a *stimulus-shield*' (p. 298) for the living organism and the 'cortical layer next to it must itself be differentiated as an organ for receiving stimuli from the outside' (p. 300).

However, in its differentiation from the living substance 'the outer surface gives up its living structure' and dies (p. 298). The condition for the life of the living organism is, then, the death of its protective ectoderm though it 'is supplied with its own store of energy and must above all endeavour to preserve the special forms of energy transformation operating in it against the ... destructive influx of enormous energies working outside' (p. 299).

Freud notes that this ectoderm is the phylo- and onto-genetic precursor of the brain: embryology indicates that the 'grey matter of the cortex is even yet a descendent of the primitive surface layer and may have taken on some of its essential properties through inheritance' (p. 297).[10] Moreover, in 'highly developed organisms' this cortical layer has 'withdrawn into the depths of the interior of the body, though portions of it have been left behind on the surface immediately beneath the general stimulus-shield' (p. 299). The latter are the sense organs and skin of more complex organisms, which are as primary to the constitution of their life as the neural cortex.

The pleasure principle functions once the protective ectoderm has been established and external excitations are regulated. Quantitative considerations in the constitution of the living organism mean that the 'excitations coming from within are ... more adequate to the system's way of working' than the external stimuli (p. 300). Feelings of (un)pleasure, which are an 'index to the processes inside the apparatus', then 'predominate over all external stimuli'.

Beyond the pleasure principle, then, are the stimuli *external* to the living organism and of excessive power with respect to it. This order of stimuli is, however, of no consequence to the organism unless they are *inside* it. The compulsion to repeat increases of excitation is concerned exclusively with the excitations which this 'sensitive cortex ... receives from *within*' and towards which 'there can be no such shield' since it protects the living organism against *external* stimuli (p. 300). This entry, which must broach and surpass the organism's cortical ectoderm, is what Freud calls 'trauma' (p. 301). It is an excitation of the living substance that is not small enough to be felt as pleasure or unpleasure nor large enough to kill it, and it excites that substance from *within*.[11] With such a 'disturbance' the living organism is no longer able to freely circulate unbound energy. Specifically with regard to its cortical operation the pleasure principle is 'pushed to the side' (p. 294). Consequently, the living differential organization continues to live but does not function as it should in that it maintains a state of unpleasure.

Freud proposes that the organism reacts to traumatic excitations by treating them as coming from the outside so that they can then be protected against. This is the 'origin of projection' (p. 301). Physical pain or preparation for anxiety both reduce traumatic excitations according to the pleasure principle in this way. Pain localizes the excessive stimulation so that it can be 'anticathected' and 'all other psychical systems ... impoverished', thereby lessening the general psychic excitation (pp. 301–2). Preparation for anxiety reduces excitation by the 'hypercathexis of the receptive systems', which can then bind incoming stimuli of greater quantities (p. 303), thereby lessening the *increase* of excitation in the system (though as a projective reaction to a stimulation it is too late to prevent the excitation).

To return then to the experiences that increase unpleasure: Freud remarks that, although dreams that reinvoke traumas, for example, are not functioning according to the pleasure principle,

> [w]e may assume, rather, that they are placed at the disposal of *another* task which must be accomplished before the pleasure principle can begin its mastery. These dreams attempt the governing of the stimulus (*Reizbewältigung*) by the *retrospective* development of *anxiety*, the omission of which was the cause of the traumatic neurosis. (p. 304, my emphasis)

Beyond the pleasure principle, then, is a retrospective wish for anxiety. With the completion of this 'task' by the psyche – by the compulsion to repeat, for example – the living organism will be able to follow the pleasure principle and, with that, function.

The crucial *metapsychological* point, however, is that 'the manifestations of a compulsion to repeat ... exhibit to a high degree a driven (*Triebhaft*) character' (p. 307); its 'power' is greater than that for reducing excitations. By generalizing the effects of traumatic excitations on a living organism Freud specifies the relation between the *somatic* excitations of a living organism and its *psychocortical* operation:

> the most abundant sources of such an internal excitation are the so-called drives of the organism, the *representatives* (*Repräsentanten*) of all the actual forces stemming out of the interior of the body and transmitted to the mental apparatus. (p. 306)

As for traumatic excitations, these 'forces' are '*freely mobile* nervous processes which press towards discharge' (p. 306). Freud then asks the primary question about any 'beyond' the pleasure principle insofar as it determines the psychocortical processes: 'in what way is the driven connected to the compulsion to repeat?' (p. 308). The question is a complicated one, not least because it asks about the relation between the forces and excitations 'stemming' from within the living organism and their representation, and this is no less than the relation between the psyche of a living organism and its cortical organ.

The elaboration of the constitution of the drives as such follows directly from the organism's primary condition for sustaining life. Since the living substance still lives despite its once small capacity for withstanding excitations, the initial process of differentiation of the cortical ectoderm is itself formed by what can be characterized as 'traumatic' stimulations. The constitution of the differentiated living organism as such therefore involves somatic excitations impacting on the (proto-) cortical organ in its development – that is, drives. Drives, then, can be said to be 'natural' and are a general attribute of the living.

Insofar as drives serve to restitute the organism from traumatic excitation, they are representations which allow the biopsychic organism to preserve and protect itself against *internal* stimulations and so can be characterized as 'conservative'. The pleasure principle is the psychic 'expression' of this general tendency of biopsychic life (p. 329), which Freud articulates in the following way:

> the idea imposes itself upon us that we may have come upon the track of a universal ... character of drives, and perhaps of organic life in general. *A drive would be an urge inherent in organic life to restore an earlier state of things* which the living [thing] must give up under the influx of external disturbing forces; that is, ... the expression of the inertia inherent in organic life. (pp. 308–9)

The 'urge' of the drives on the psyche is to reduce their driven character, which is in fact only the *internal* excitations of the organism, its life.

Freud famously calls the organic-representational 'urge' of the drives the 'death drive' (p. 316) since the absolute 'earlier state of things' is zero excitation, inanimate *dead* matter (pp. 308–9). Freud's naming here may, however, be too hasty since, *ex hypothesi*, the organism's state before its differentiation is only the *undifferentiated* and 'open' 'living substance', which is what is killed by its environment. Later, in 'Beyond the Pleasure Principle' and elsewhere, Freud also takes up Barbara Low's phrase 'the Nirvana principle' to characterize the 'mastering tendency of mental life, perhaps of nervous life in general: the effort to reduce, to keep constant or to suspend internal stimulus-tension' (p. 329). This wider formulation is the more prudent one insofar as it speaks of a living organism without external or internal biopsychic stimulation and leaves open whether such a condition is life or death.[12]

In any case, two crucial points follow:

- since 'all the organic drives ... are acquired historically', Freud remarks that 'in the last instance what has left its mark on the development of organisms must be the developmental history of our earth and of its relation to the sun' (p. 310).[13] All such biopsychic development is 'stored up for further repetition' by the organism because of its death drive, which is, therefore, the condition for the onto- and phylo-genetic development of life.[14]
- the self-preservative drives of the living being (p. 311) are but 'component drives (*Partialtriebe*)' of the death drive. If organic–somatic life is conservative it is only because it tends – is internally driven – towards its death. Such is the driven of the drive. Such is the drive of life.

This sketch of Freud's initial hypothesis of the death drive has maintained the generality that Freud attributes to it with respect to organic and biotic development. The death drive characterizes the development of life *as such*. However, for any living system *as such* this *purely* organic 'conservation' is not tenable. If it lives, the organism is differentiated from its surroundings and in itself by the (partial) death of its ectoderm (it is a body with organs). This (partially amortizing) differentiation of the living organism is the condition of its differentiation from death as the state of inorganic matter. By virtue of the organism's psychocortical differentiation and external circumstance, life is however nowhere else but here: between death. Although this is the case for the organic development of *life*, our argument now is that this biotic determination does not *alone* characterize the specificity of *cortical* onto- and phylo-genesis, and it is this *complex* order of biopsychic development to which we we now turn. This is of direct interest to our concerns: it will be seen that the condition for the transmutability of death is the transorganic development of the psychocortex.

In the 'systematic/dynamic' terminology adopted from the time of the 'Pleasure Principle' essay, Freud calls the differentiated *and* differentiating organization of excitations of a living system the *ego*.[15] It is a dynamic organization since it is both conscious and, in its resistances, unconscious. It is to be distinguished ('differentiated', as Freud says) from the repressed or the id, which is unorganized.[16] Freud's argument in 'Inhibitions, Symptoms and Anxiety' – recapitulating the case studies of 'Little Hans' and the 'Wolf Man' – is that egoic organization of the boy's biopsychic life develops with a 'castration anxiety'. There are two immediate questions: first, why *castration*? Second, why is it the *principal* organization and anxiety of the boy's development? Concomitantly, why does Freud privilege the boy in the discussion of biopsychic development? The debates are well known and extensive and will not be reviewed here. The questions will instead be taken up here in terms of the relevance of anxiety to biopsychic development.

As proposed in the 1920 paper, anxiety is a reaction to 'danger', which is itself attributable to an 'economic disturbance caused by a growth of quantities of stimulus which demand dealing with'.[17] If in the earlier developmental history of the living organism this 'economic disturbance' was occasioned by a traumatic stimulation, Freud's interest now is rather in the *human* biopsychic system, which, even for the infant, has developed and achieved a complex enough differentiation so as to *prepare* for such excitations. However, in its *prospective* anxiety the psychic system is stimulated to a degree which is unpleasurable and, as Freud says, *this* economic disturbance is the 'proper core of "danger"'.

Even if it comes from within the biopsychic organization of the human infant, this anxious disturbance is not traumatic. It is still economic, bound. The *cause* of its anxiety *and its avoidance* are, however, not *internally bound* for two reasons: first, the human infant is psychodynamically 'helpless' against the increased excitation of 'a growing tension from need' (p. 294), which may be a somatic need, as in hunger;[18] and second, in its limited motility the baby is 'biologically' helpless (p. 295). Since the human infant is, then, *biopsychically* helpless against its anxiety, the excitation remains free and grows. If the excitation is not externally abated it becomes traumatic; if it is too great the infant dies.

However, as seen, Freud proposes that increases in the excitation of the biopsychic system are projected to originate *outside* the body, as for a traumatic stimulation.[19] The infant can thus bind this excitation due to need by psychocortical processes – but only if the *external* danger is removed. The point here – from which the rest of the argument follows – is that the human infant exteriorizes the occasion of its anxiety and has to be *externally* helped to lessen the excitation. That is, the tendency of the child's death drive and the pleasure principle has to be supported.

Because of its prematurity, the development of the child does not then depend *principally* on the protection of the differential psychocortical *organ* but coevally on external supports, as psychoanalysis has been saying since its inception. It is precisely the helplessness of the human infant which stimulates its development – but only insofar as it is supported. The principal issue of the onto- and phylo-genetic development of *human* life is then the relation of the death drive to its external supports. If excitation is lessened and maintained in early human development by an external support, then every organic drive of the human living organism is inhibited-diverted in its constitution, as then is the 'urge' of the differentiated human biopsychic life to 'return' to its organic death.

This *deferral* of the death drive via the exterior support of the biopsychic organism divorces the onto- and phylo-genesis of the human from the *organic*-cortical development of the regulation of excitations. For the human, then, the differentiation of the living organism is diverted and displaced by its external supports. Human biopsychic development is thus one of the *differantiation* of the organic drives. That is, the life, ego and development of the human are differantially organized by its external supports, as then is the binding of excitations and, with that, all ego organization by the human biopsychic system.

Human biopsychic development *in particular* is then inherently and constitutively differantially organized with and since its external supports. The 'particularity' is emphasized here to stress that human biopsychic development is *not exclusively* dependent on external supports. Although the onto- and phylo-genesis of other living organisms are also dependent on external supports for their (early) development (at whatever order of organic complexity), it is the *degree* of the organism's biopsychic dependence on external supports and the provision of those supports that determines the differantiation of its death drive, and so the influence of external factors on the onto- and phylo-genetic development of its psychocortex.[20]

The differantiation of biopsychic development does not just disturb all later attempts at *economic* restitutions by the psychic or organic drives.[21] It means, moreover, that the onto- and phylo-genesis of the human in particular (but not exclusively) *must continue* to depend on external supports for its maintenance and development, at whatever stage of biopsychic organization. The onto- or phylo-genetic development of the human psychocortical ego cannot then be identified with the development of the *organism*, though neither is it independent of it.

Although the differentiation of the death drive is attributable to the biopsychic 'helplessness' of the *human* infant and the adequacy of its external supports, the latter themselves in turn preserve and maintain the differantiation of the death drive for the human *in particular*. That is, the externally supported human biopsychic development maintains the biopsychic prematurity of the human infant. But, with that, the self-preservative drives of the human biopsychic organism continue to be constituted by and directed to its *external* supports as much as to its organic maintenance and reproduction.

In the theoretical speculations of 'Beyond the Pleasure Principle' Freud remarks that it is the 'conservative' but externally directed drives of living germ cells, standing for the earliest and minimal development of life, that are the 'true life drives', or the sexual drives. Such drives 'provide [the elementary organisms] with safe shelter while they are defenceless against the stimuli of the external world, [and] bring about their meeting with other germ cells' so as to perpetuate each one's life. Altogether, sexual drives 'preserve life itself for a comparatively long period' (p. 313). The differantial development of the human psychocortical ego in particular means that its sexual drives towards its *external* supports serve the 'self-preservative' function of the death drives and *vice versa*. Human sexuality, then, is the differantiation of its death drive.

The sexual and death drives of the human are therefore indissociable from one another.[22] It follows that insofar as human death drives are not only externally directed but also supported, the human sexual or life drives are also generalized beyond the functions of biotic drives. Furthermore, since the former serve the death drive in its developmental binding of excitations, the psychocortical development of the human, of its ego and its anxieties, and of what it inherits, is itself constituted in the differance of its sexuality.[23]

The transmutability of death in fact and in its symbolic–affective meaning follows from the differantiation of the death drive. To elaborate how, two aspects of the aneconomy of biopsychic development need to be expanded: the differantiation of the death drive in its relation to the onto- and phylo-genesis of life and, second, the centrality of anxiety, castration and sexual difference for human biopsychic development in particular. These aspects will be considered in turn.

First, then, if for the human in particular the organic restitution from excitation is differantiated by its external supports, the *pleasure* of the sexual drives for the human needs to be further specified. It has been seen that pleasure is the psychic 'expression' of the death drive's successful 'conservation' of the biopsychic organism by its binding of stimuli. For the externally directed *sexual* drives of organic life (of whatever order of development) the diminution of excitation indexed by pleasure requires 'fresh amounts of stimuli' so as to conserve them. Commenting on experiments that examined the conjugation of protozoic cellular organisms, Freud remarks that such stimulation, which can 'be taken as typical of the effect produced by sexual union', 'introduces what may be called *vital differences*' for all living organisms 'which may then be "lived off"' (p. 329). Although this may be unequivocally the case for the well-differentiated organism, the differantiated development of *human* biopsychic life in particular means that the effect of an external stimulus on the human psychocortical ego depends on the stage of psychocortical development *and* the external supports for that stage of organic development.

In its early development, the human ego is characterized by the effort to reduce external stimulation in the way the *organic* death drive does:

> the child repeats unpleasurable experiences since through this activity it gains a still more basic [governing] power over strong impressions than would be possible by its merely passive experiences. Each fresh repetition seems to strengthen this sought after mastery. Nor can the child get enough of having the pleasurable experiences repeated and is inexorable in insisting on an identical impression. (p. 307)

The differential development of the human psychocortex means that 'this character trait disappears later on'. With its maturing the 'vital differences' by which human biopsychic life develops are effectuated as much by its external supports (which may be non-organic) as its organic functions. Freud characterizes the general condition for pleasure for the human ego in its differentiated maturity:

> a joke heard for a second time remains almost without effect; a theatrical production never arouses so great an impression the second time as was left the first time; indeed, it is hard to move *an adult* who has very much enjoyed reading a book to read it once again at once. *Novelty is always the condition for enjoyment.* (p. 307; my emphasis)

The examples here propose that the 'novelty' which Freud determines as the *condition* of pleasure for the mature human ego is from the realm of culture (*Kultur*), suggesting in turn that the pleasure and 'vital differences' by which it develops, its sexual drives, are not just those of its *organic* self-preservation. We return to this point in the closing argument below.

The second aspect of the differantial constitution of the sexual and death drives, which will return us more immediately to the transmutability of death, is the affect of anxiety. The aspect of anxiety which is important here is that it is, as Freud suggests in 'Inhibitions, Symptoms and Anxiety', 'a particular state of unpleasure with acts of discharge along determined paths ... [for which] we are tempted to assume the presence of a historical factor (*Moment* ['element', 'moment']) which firmly binds the sensations of anxiety and its innervations together' (p. 289). This is of *particular* importance to the psychocortical development of the human since its internal or external excitations are not reduced by the differential organic development alone but also by its external supports (which are symbolic and technical as well as biotic).[24] In the terms of the present discussion, the 'historical moment' central to anxiety suggests that it is an affective state constituted in the differance of biopsychic development. That is, if the organically constituted drives serve to 'master' the 'historical factor' correlated with anxiety, the reliance on an external support to reduce excitation means on the other hand that the degree of anxiety *and its reducibility* in biopsychic development depend on 'historical factors' as much as its organic drives. Just as the external support can reduce excitations (and so the drive of an organic restitution from generating anxiety), so in the differantiation of psychocortical development must it contribute to anxiety. If, furthermore, anxiety is generated by a danger if the 'historical factor' in the development of the biopsychic system is present in the comparatively later 'state of unpleasure', then a differantiated biopsychic development is more susceptible to anxiety and the feelings of danger than the biopsychic organism which is not so 'helpless' in the early stages of its development. This is particularly (but not exclusively) the case for the human.[25]

The characterization of egoic development by a castration anxiety can then be clarified. Psychoneurotic anxiety is egoic insofar as it is correlative to a 'judgement about situations of danger' and judgements are processes of the ego (p. 298). The excitation and unpleasure occasioned by the *exteriority* of the support can be lessened by the ego organization's judgement on the danger of that exteriority and the projection of it to be *instead* about the removal of what is in some way external to it but not independent of, or separated from, it. Excessive excitations are not only lessened by attributing them to the absence of the external support (the mother, for instance), but the anxiety of this latter danger is itself reduced by attributing it to the removal of an organ, the penis, which the boy has yet is in some way external to him, and towards which the sexual drives are therefore directed. That is, castration anxiety lessens as it is derived from the boy's anxiety at the absence or removal or insufficiency of his external supports (which, insofar as they are supports, are a way for excitation and anxiety to be reduced).[26] It is a preparation for anxiety.

The boy's ego and sexual drives are then genitally organized because of the differantial ontogenesis of his biopsychic life. Accordingly, he is compelled to repeat the unpleasure of his castration anxiety. Pleasure as the diminution of these excitations is to be gained by attendance to the external sexual organ (genital sex or masturbation). Insofar as the girl child (in contrast to the woman) also develops because of dangers which are external (as projected as these dangers may be), her biopsychic development is different to the boy's. With Freud, the infant girl cannot suffer a castration *anxiety* but only a castration *complex* (p. 278) because, first, the danger situation is far more complicated and non-specific since there is no organ which can be differentiated by the girl's biopsychic organization as clearly external yet attached to her; and, second, the excitations of the danger situation can then only be attributed by the girl to the external support, which *is* independent of her body. The girl's anxiety and (un)pleasure, and her repetition of it, are therefore of another differantial organization than the boy's ego organization. Freud writes that for women 'the danger-situation of loss of object seems to have remained the most effective': the determinant of anxiety is not the 'want or loss of the real object but the loss of love on the part of the object' (pp. 300–1). If, then, the ontogenesis of the boy and girl are differantiated by somatic and historical factors, it follows that there is no (organic or conceptual) unity or identity of life *as such* for the human in particular but only a differantially sexualized biopsychic development.

The fact and meaning of death for the human in particular (but not exclusively) can now be elaborated in terms of her or his biopsychic/egoic development. Although all biopsychic organisms have a dead protective ectoderm as the condition for maintaining themselves, and a tendency to return to a state of inorganic matter, which is the *fact* of death, the human biopsychic organism in particular *also* encounters death in the affective sense constituted by the sexual/life drives – that is, through the differantiation of its death drive.[27]

Freud remarks that in human experience death is feared; it is a danger that provokes anxiety (p. 284). As obvious as this is, what is proposed thereby is that the fear of death is an affective state of the ego–id system. But, as Freud continues to say, there cannot in fact be an anxiety about *death as such* since anxiety revives an 'available mnemic image', yet 'something similar to death can never have been experienced; or if it has, as in fainting, it has left no detectable traces' (p. 285). Death itself cannot then be a source of anxiety since there is no affective mnemic state corresponding to it in the development of the human biopsychic organism. To explain the fear of death (one's own or, differently, another's), Freud 'adhere[s] to the view' that 'the fear of death should be regarded as analogous to the fear of castration, and that the situation to which the ego is reacting is one of being abandoned by the protecting superego ... so that the protection it has against all dangers is at an end' (pp. 285–6). That is, the fear of death is a projection of the danger of 'abandonment' by the external supports necessary for the development of the human in particular.

Thus, the fear of death – which is its symbolic–affective meaning – is correlative to the external supports for the onto- and phylo-genetic development of the human. However, as seen, these supports may be non-organic and even cultural as well as living. As death may be the *factum* of the 'return' of life to inorganic matter, so its symbolic–affective meaning is then culturally conditioned. That is, the meaning of death transmutes with the specific actuality of the development of human biopsychic supports.

We conclude by elaborating the transmutability of death in terms of the development of the external supports. This involves not just the transmutation of the meaning of death, as suggested above, but also the historicity of the *fact* of death. That there is a historicity of death for the human in particular is a consequence of the indissociability of the sexual and death drives. The differantiation of the death drive means that the organism's external support not only alleviates the organism's excitations but is also *at once* a stimulus generating what Freud calls the 'vital differences' of its development. The external supports of human onto- and phylo-genetic development therefore serve the 'conservative' urge of the death drive and the biopsychic development of the psychocortex. Since these supports may be non-organic or biotic, the development of the psychocortical ego is not then simply that of its *organic* development but, for the human in particular, is also occasioned by what may be dead matter. That is, for the human in particular the development of the psychocortical ego is transorganic. Culture is the *life-death* of this transorganic development.

   The external supports of biopsychic development, be they biotic or not, cannot then be described as 'secondary' to its development (or primary) without reintroducing a principally organic (or, correspondingly, non-biotic) determination of them and, with that, de-differantiating the development of the human psychocortex. In other words, the development of the human psychocortex is transorganic. Two points follow directly: first, it is not then clear that 'life' is the best term or even suffices to characterize the transorganic development of the human psychocortex; and second, since the 'novelty' of the 'first time' of its external supports itself occasions and is occasioned by the development of the psychocortex, such novelty is not then just the historicity of that development but is, moreover, itself historical.

The 'condition of pleasure' and the stimulation of the 'vital differences' which constitute the conserved development of the human psychocortex in particular is therefore hard pressed to be characterized as occasioning the development of *life* (in any simple or intraorganic sense). Moreover, that condition–stimulation is at once novel *and* historical. It is then not so much a process of life as it is *invention* (in the modern sense of production and the premodern sense of discovery).

Invention therefore accords with the drive of life (*qua* death drive) as it is counter to it. In occasioning the vital differences which 'counter' and accord with the death drive's conservation, the transorganic differantiation of psychocortical development historicizes the actuality of what death is in terms of the actuality of invention. For human biopsychic development in particular (but not exclusively), death is then not merely an organic *factum* but also has a historico-affective meaning occasioned by invention *qua* external support; or, put the other way, invention transmutes the meaning and actuality of death in the transorganic development of the psychocortex.

Notes

1 S. Kauffman, *The Origins of Order* (Oxford: Oxford University Press, 1993).
2 The historicity at issue here is not to be confused with the existential–ontological sense it has in Heidegger's *Daseinsanalitik*, where it is appropriated in the totality of *Dasein*'s resoluteness towards its own death. It is precisely the singularity and punctuality of this primary condition which is weakened (if not undone) by the transmutation of the fact and meaning of death discussed here (M. Heidegger, *Being and Time*, trans. J. Macquarrie and E. Robinson (Oxford: Blackwell, 1962 [1927]), §74).
3 S. Freud, 'Civilisation and Its Discontents', in *Penguin Freud Library 12*, trans. J. Riviere, ed. A. Dickson, (Harmondsworth: Penguin, 1985 [1930]). Unless otherwise indicated all citations in the main text are from Freud. For the most part translations have been slightly modified.

4 S. Freud, 'Beyond the Pleasure Principle', in *Penguin Freud Library 11*, trans. J. Strachey, ed. A. Richards (Harmondsworth: Penguin, 1984 [1926]).

5 S. Freud, 'Inhibitions, Symptoms and Anxiety', in *Penguin Freud Library 10*, trans. James Strachey, ed. A. Richards (Harmondsworth: Penguin, 1979 [1920]).

6 F. Sulloway, *Freud – Biologist of the Mind* (Cambridge, MA: Harvard, 1992 [1979]).

7 The pleasure associated with the *increases* in biopsychic tension in sexual excitement to orgasm later leads Freud to propose that (un)pleasure is not correlated to quantitative considerations but is rather a *qualitative* attribute of biopsychic life (Freud, 'The Economic Problem of Masochism', in *Penguin Freud Library 11*). It will be seen that this is an unnecessary hypothesis arising from Freud's overly opposing the life and death drives.

8 As Freud says later in the essay 'Beyond the Pleasure Principle', it is not known *what* the excitation is a quantity of (p. 331). Freud's warranted circumspection means that it would be a mistake to articulate the excitation at issue here in simply symbolic, physiochemical or thermodynamic terms.

9 The formulation of living processes in terms of equilibrial energetics was initiated by Helmholz's adoption of thermodynamic doctrines to physiology in the mid-nineteenth century. Freud directly acknowledges in 'Beyond the Pleasure Principle' that the more immediate influences are Breuer and Fechner, though his theory diverges from both in significant ways. See, for example, J. Laplanche, *Life and Death in Psychoanalysis*, trans. J. Mehlman (Baltimore: Johns Hopkins University Press, 1970).

10 Freud here follows a well-established (and principally German) recapitulationist thesis established in its proto-Darwinian evolutionary form by Haeckel in the mid–late nineteenth century, which germline inheritance theory discredits. Freud's remarks are however not incompatible with 'weak' recapitulationism, formulated by von Baer in the early nineteenth century, wherein embryonic development passes through the *embryonic* states of phylogenetically 'earlier' organisms (D. Depew and B. Weber, *Darwinism Evolving* (Cambridge, MA: MIT, 1995)). This is the process of increasing cellular and then organismic differentiation of which Freud speaks. Nor is Freud's theory incom-

patible with the complex articulation of Haeckel's theory of the acceleration and retardation of phyletic development in ontogeny, the latter of which is crucial for the biology of human neoteny and which, in
turn, determined the particularity of the human in the development of
life (S. Gould, *Ontogeny and Phylogeny*, Cambridge, MA: Harvard, 1977).

11 It is to be noted then that a trauma is not simply the impact of an
external event directly on to the psychocortical or an egoic organization via the sense organs. Even if the stimulus which occasions a
traumatic excitation is not itself somatic but external, it is for Freud
nonetheless somatically mediated.

12 In *Life and Death in Psychoanalysis*, Laplanche attempts to render
coherent Freud's varying accounts of the energetics of excitation and
its diminution. By so doing, he removes the ambit of psychoanalysis
from that of other sciences as well as the theories of Breuer and
Fechner. It will suffice here to note that for Freud excitation is in any
case reduced to a relative or absolute equilibrium.

13 Morowitz presents just such an account of biogenesis in terms of contemporary 'reductionist' chemical physics in which, most pertinently
for the present discussion, the 'major event' for *bio*genesis in the
strict sense is the formation of 'closed vesicles' by the stabilization of
a membrane barrier. It is from these protocells that genetic codes are
chemically and energetically stabilized. Artificial life theories which
attempt to 'reproduce' the genesis and/or development of life
processes in formal terms (analogized from genetic algorithms) cannot in principle characterize this material condition of biogenesis
(H. Morowitz, *Beginnings of Cellular Life* (New Haven: Yale University
Press, 1992)).

14 We do not pursue Freud's considerations of the death and life drives
in terms of Weismann's 'soma' (or phenotype) and 'germ' (genotype)
distinction (pp. 318–22). Suffice it to say that for Freud the latter is a
morphological theory of 'living substance' and the metapsychology of
the drives a dynamic theory since it concerns the 'forces acting in it'.
Freud suggests that the drives of the dynamic theory of life may only
'come to be recognised in higher animals where they have generated
a morphological expression'.

15 Freud, 'Inhibitions, Symptoms and Anxiety', pp. 249–50; S. Freud,
'The Ego and the Id', in *Penguin Freud Library 11*, trans. J. Strachey, ed.
A. Richards, (Harmondsworth, Penguin, 1984 [1923]).

16 Freud, 'Inhibitions, Symptoms and Anxiety', p. 249.

17 Freud, 'Inhibitions, Symptoms and Anxiety', p. 294.

18 Klein notably stresses the coupling and diverging of somatic functions and phantasmatic projections as central to biopsychic development even in early infancy (M. Klein, 'Weaning', in *Love, Guilt and Reparation* (London: Virago, 1988 [1936]).

19 The factor of projection cannot then be underestimated in considering the ætiology of post-traumatic reactions. Freud's (controversial) abandonment of the 'seduction theory' is coherent with the realization of the primacy of pre-egoic 'projection' as an irreducible if not primary factor in the ætiology of traumatic neurosis.

20 To then propose that differance occasions/is the history of life as such is a primarily anthropic determination of life, even if it is presented in terms of the transhuman genesis and development of writing (J. Derrida, *Of Grammatology*, trans. G. Spivak (Baltimore: Johns Hopkins University Press, 1976 [1967])) or memory (B. Stiegler, *Technics and Time I: The Fault of Epimetheus*, trans. R. Beardsworth and G. Collins (Stanford: Stanford University Press, 1998)).

21 Derrida stresses the conservation of the death drive in reappropriating and 'governing' the 'detour' of the organism's life in its (thus differantial) return to death (J. Derrida, *The Post Card*, trans. A. Bass, (Chicago: Chicago University Press, 1987 [1980], pp. 353–64). Since the movement of life 'comes back' to death in the death drive, life is but an 'exappropriative' economy of death involving heterology. However, such an economy can itself only be maintained if either the sexual drives are other to the death drive or the sexual drive *does* serve the death drive; if, that is, the sexual drives do not transmute the organism's propriative principle in its effectuation. But if the life and death drives *are* coeval for the organism, the 'economy of death' is no more or less primary than its exteriorizing heterogeneity, and its development is aneconomic.

22 Freud's metapsychology of the drives is neither a monism nor, despite his insistences, a dualism of 'opposition' between the drives ('Beyond the Pleasure Principle', p. 326; 'Civilization and Its Discontents'). To borrow a description of Deleuze's philosophy, the metapsychology of the drives can instead be characterized as a 'monodualism' (F. Zourabichvili, *Deleuze: Une philosophie de l'événement* (Paris: PUF, 1994)). There is, however, no compatibility between Freud's metapsychology and Deleuze's identification of the constitutive primacy of the 'passive contraction' of life's development with the life/sexual drives. For Deleuze the latter are constituted around 'virtual centers' drawn up from the 'pure past' of a fecund repetition, and are never realized as such (G. Deleuze, *Difference & Repetition*, trans. P. Patton (New York: Columbia, 1994 [1968])). Pleasure achieves the status of a principle only with regard to these imaginary objects (which synthesizing of multiplicity comes to be called in the work with Guattari the 'body without organs' (G. Deleuze and F. Guattari, *Anti-Oedipus: Capitalism & Schizophrenia*, trans. R. Hurley, M. Seem and H. Lane (Minnesota: University of Minnesota Press, 1983 [1972], pp. 322–7)). For Deleuze the sexual drives exist in another series to the base 'material repetition' and 'active synthesis' of a death drive that is itself only the derivative 'desexualisation of Eros'. Freud's argument suggests however that the death drive is a passive synthesis which is at once material and symbolic, and is acentered in its primary projection. In Deleuze's terms the death drive is then the second order of synthesis (Eros and Mnemosyne) in its first order (Habitus).

23 Laplanche stresses this point exhaustively – and too much so in seeking to refound the dimension of human psychosexual experience in *primarily* non-biological terms (*Life and Death in Psychoanalysis*; J. Laplanche, *New Foundations in Psychoanalysis*, trans. D. Macey (Oxford: Blackwell, 1989 [1987])). On the other hand, Sulloway's characterization of Freud's project as a 'genetic *psychobiology*' (*Freud – Biologist of the Mind*) systematically misses the *non-organic* constitution of human sexual and death drives. The complexity of biopsychic development is accordingly reduced to *primarily* biological determinants and, like genetic determinism, cannot speak to the sexual co-constitution of biopsychic development (in its contribution to human neoteny, for example).

24 The epigenetic aspect is important in Freud's argument with Rank, who attributes the model of all anxiety – and thus all neuroses – to the *birth-trauma* of the human infant (Freud, 'Inhibitions, Symptoms and Anxiety', §X). Such an argument would revert to considering the biopsychic organization as one dominated primarily and perhaps exclusively by presexual drives. Jung's generalization of all instincts as sexual or libidinal on the other hand forsakes the 'inertial' organic drives of the biopsychic system. This not only reduces the complexity

of human biopsychic life in its originary dependency but moreover collapses the differantial ontogenesis of the sexual drive into organic differentiation ('Beyond the Pleasure Principle', p. 325ff.).

25 As Freud remarks, anxiety may then be common to all life, though it would be 'differently contrived in different organisms' ('Inhibitions, Symptoms and Anxiety', p. 290). Following Freud's and Morowitz's theories, for early cellular life such protoanxiety would be a prege-netic determination in biogenesis.

26 Lacan abstracts this lessening of anxiety by the castration complex/ anxiety as characterizing a 'lack' or hole at the centre of human sub-jectivity. Such a determination, however, blanks the specific and his-torical actuality of the 'danger' that is reduced by castration, turning it into an absolute past about which the subject pivots. Even the brief outline of the factor of castration in the main text is enough to suggest that insisting on *or* negating castration as primary to human biopsy-chic development misses the more originary constitution of human sexual difference and prevents its theoretical (or clinical) recognition. Castration theory is in other words an organic idealism in that it is a reduction of the differantial ontogenesis of human sexualities. It reduces human sexuality to an organically determined symbolic for-mation while simultaneously unifying human sexuality and biopsychic development by a trans-historical scheme (J. Lacan, 'The Signification of the Phallus', in *Ecrits: A Selection*, trans. A. Sheridan (London: Routledge, 1977 [1968])). With that, the transorganic development of the human psychocortex/ego can only be a derived rather than a constitutive process.

27 By contrast, Laplanche's proposal of the 'enigmatic signifier' explains the constitution of the child's sexualized ego on the basis of the *exte-riority* of the care of its vital body functions (*New Foundations in Psy-choanalysis*). For the adult involved such care is sexual (the mother's breast in feeding, for example) and this dimension of (unconscious) meaning is transmitted to the child in attending to it, instituting thereby the properly psychosexual dimension of human experience for the infant. The inauguration of the psychosexual ego from external factors follows for Laplanche because *any* 'biological' determinants in the constitution of the dimension of human intersubjective and sexual experience for the infant, such as the 'self-preservation' of the death drive, have been ruled out. Likewise, Boothby's commentary on the

death drive resolves its inherent dualism by disassociating it from the 'vital functioning of the biological organism' and considering it *instead* as a challenge to the 'psychological integrity of the ego'. Boothby accordingly turns to Lacan's suggestion that the 'death' of the death drive is not that of the organism but of the imagining (and imaginary) ego (R. Boothby, *Death and Desire* (New York: Routledge, 1991)). Such clear discriminations between the biotic (and the death drive) *in contradistinction to* the psychical (and the sexual drives), however, de-differantiates the biopsychic development of the human in particular.

7

Liebestod: sex, death and Wagnerian androgyny

STEVE SWEENEY-TURNER

We must imagine androgynes as happy creatures.[1]

Jean-Jacques Nattiez

> *ertrinken,*
> *versinken –*
> *unbewußt –*
> *höchste Lust!*
> *(Isolde sinkt, wie verklärt...)*[2]

In opera to love is to wish to die ...[3]

Catherine Clément

Sex and death, opera and death: these conceptual associations have, no doubt, been well rehearsed since the nineteenth century. But one opera in particular seems even now to stand at a crucial point of articulation. Wagner's *Tristan und Isolde*, premièred in 1865, is for some the moment at which the crisis of musical modernism is inaugurated in the dissonant structure of its very first chord – the famous and oft-cited Fm7b5, also known as the 'Tristan chord'.

Indeed, this single sonic event has come to represent the conceptual milieu not only of the whole opera and of Wagner's work in general but of the entire point of articulation between musical romanticism and modernism, a milieu of sex and death, focused through the opera's intense libidinal investments in the transgressive body and its erotic annihilation.

As Theodor Adorno writes (in a section of *Aesthetic Theory* entitled 'Aesthetic hedonism and the bliss of knowing'),

Dissonance (and its counterparts in the visual arts) – the trade-mark, as it were, of modernism – lets in the beguiling moment of sensuousness by transfiguring it into its antithesis, that is, pain. This is an aesthetic phenomenon of primal ambivalence. Dissonance has had a momentous and far-ranging impact on modern art since Baudelaire and Wagner's *Tristan*; it has almost become a kind of constant in modernism.[4]

Here, the whole conceptual and technical field of *Tristan und Isolde* is invoked: the notion of aestheticism coupled with a sensuous hedonism, and more specifically, the idea of dissonance resulting in a 'primal ambivalence' between pleasure and pain. Indeed, it is this very ambivalence, present in the famous Tristan chord, with its harmonic ambiguities so neatly inscribed within a mere four notes, which infects the entire opera.

But the ambivalence of the Tristan chord also takes on a specifically sexual meaning. The French theorist Serge Gut, amongst others, has referred to it as 'this androgynous chord', a chord that sits ambiguously between the keys associated with the figures of Tristan and Isolde's desires.[5] Certainly, the theme of ambiguity suffuses the entire opera, and the question of identity is central – specifically, the trope emerging from the loss of one's Self in the identity of the Other. As Isolde sings in her *Verklärung* or *Liebestod* section at the end of the opera:

> In the surging swell,
> in the ringing sound,
> in the vast wave
> of the world's breath –
> to drown,
> to sink –
> unconscious –
> highest pleasure!

As Isolde sings herself to death, wills her death as a union with the already dead Tristan, it is a death that brings about a melding of identities – for many commentators, a mythic union of opposites.

And between the first chord of the opera and this, Isolde's dying breath within 'the vast wave / of the world's breath', the whole complex of intoxication and dissipation traces an intense terrain which Nietzsche once read under the sign of Dionysos, the phallic and yet androgynous, twice-born god of Ancient Greece.

From the very beginning we find Dionysos associated with certain forms of dissonance, his cult emerging from lands such as Lydia and Phrygia, whose wild musical styles gave concern to the moralizing Pythagoras, amongst others. As Iamblichus relates, Pythagoras condemned the intoxicating affectivity of Phrygian music, its dissonant construction whipping up young men into drunken frenzies and criminal violence. In opposition to such influences, it is said that Pythagoras devised music that soothed and healed its listeners, opening them up to the rational order of the Music of the Spheres. And in this opposition between a foreign, transgressive, dissonant music and a homely, law-abiding, consonant music, we can discern the emergence of a trope that Nietzsche was to expand upon in his Dionysian writings.

For Nietzsche, of course, the opposition lies between the Apollonian concept of art, based on order and sobriety, and the Dionysian concept, based on disorder and intoxication. In musical terms, Apollo is manifested through consonance, and Dionysos through dissonance. Dissonance represents, then, the destruction of established harmonic rules, which in Greek terms is always also the destruction of social and moral structures – the death of good forms. For the Nietzschean Dionysos, dissonance is the most reliable way to score a fix of musical intoxication:

> For art to exist, for any sort of aesthetic activity or perception to exist, a certain physiological precondition is indispensable: intoxication. Intoxication must first have heightened the excitability of the entire machine: no art results before that happens.[6]

Here, in almost proto-Deleuzean terms, Nietzsche highlights the importance of Dionysian intoxication suffusing itself throughout 'the entire machine' before the aesthetic experience can be fully affective. Indeed, for Nietzsche, affectivity is governed by the processes of intoxication, as if the affect is in fact an *in*fection, raising the possibilities both of overdosing, and of succumbing to a hostile disease. Music, for Nietzsche, is a deeply corporeal, and often dangerous experience – in a strange echo of the Pythagoreans, it is almost a medical event. Music can cure or kill. One must be careful what one listens to. As Jacques Attali has written:

> Of course, in sacrifice and representation, the body is already contained in music: Ulysses' companions risked dying of pleasure by listening to the song of sirens, and the duos in *Così fan tutte* and *Tristan und Isolde* express a real erotic drive. Music, directly transected by desires and drives, has always had but one subject – the body.[7]

Indeed, one must be careful what one listens to. And for the early Nietzsche, one listened to Wagner – *Tristan und Isolde* in particular, for here, intoxicating dissonances, mysterious narcotics and transgressions of socio-sexual laws abound. Indeed, they are the focus of the whole opera, and it is for this reason that Nietzsche takes as the defining moment of Dionysian music the *Liebestod* section of *Tristan und Isolde*:

> how can anyone experience the third act of *Tristan and Isolde*, apart from either word or image, simply as the movement of a mighty symphony, without exhausting himself in the overstretching of his soul's pinions? How is it possible for a man who has listened to the very heartbeat of the world-will and felt the unruly lust for life rush into all the veins of the world, now as a thundering torrent and now as a delicately foaming brook – how is it possible for him to remain un-shattered? How can he bear, shut in the paltry glass bell of his individuality, to hear the echoes of innumerable cries of weal and woe sounding out of the 'vast spaces of cosmic night,' and not wish, amidst these pipings of metaphysical pastoral, to flee incontinent to his primordial home?[8]

For Nietzsche, then, the dissonance of the *Liebestod* section in particular induces in the listener a certain 'overstretching', a 'shattering', and, ultimately, a primordial 'incontinence', a cosmic shitting-oneself, which represents the loss of rational selfhood and the need to return, like Isolde, to the ecstatic flux of 'the world's breath'. These three stages of tension, rupture and dissipation form the Dionysian affectivity of Isolde's swansong, mirroring the transfiguration (*Verklärung*) which she herself goes through in her intoxicated and intoxicating death. And make no mistake as to the ritualistic aspect of Isolde's death – it is there for the audience to witness, to enjoy as a sacrifice, to become intoxicated by. As Catherine Clément writes: 'In opera to love is to wish to die; it is to count our steps in the sandy path leading to death, for the sake of our collective joy. And in *Tristan and Isolde*, whose plot is reduced to its simplest form, this is perfectly demonstrated.'[9]

The simple reduction which Clément identifies as the catalyst for 'our collective joy' echoes once more Nietzsche's theories of the social function of the tragic sacrifice of Dionysos: at once a moral warning and an incitement to pleasure in abandon. Isolde's death – more than Tristan's – is the most intoxicating moment of the entire opera, the ultimate narcotic fix which is the real score we make as we buy our tickets from the dealers and pimps in the foyer of the opera house. And if Isolde is in actuality the more Dionysian figure of the two, this merely reminds us of Dionysos' own androgyny, the anarchic youth with long blonde curls and wine-red lips whose songs and dances drive the people (male and female) into an ecstatic frenzy. As Pentheus relates, in Euripides' *Bacchantes*: 'They say there came a stranger hither, a trickster and a sorcerer, from Lydia's land, with golden hair and perfumed locks, the flush of wine upon his face, and in his eyes each grace that Aphrodite gives.'

Of course, Isolde herself is a dissonant foreigner, the Irish princess who is also versed in the arts of sorcery, a chromatically voiced feminine figure, whose song exceeds the normative rules of Apollonian harmony. And just as Dionysos himself is an androgyne, so too Isolde takes on the mantle of a certain phallic power at various key moments in the opera, despite effectively being the prisoner of a patriarchal marriage suite deriving from the spoils of war.

As a token of symbolic exchange between a defeated patriarchal kingdom and a victorious one, nevertheless, through the media of Celtic sorcery and Dionysian intoxication (both sexual and narcotic), Isolde evades the patriarchal marriage which the Cornish king has defined as her destiny. As an exotic, erotic, dissonant, androgynous figure, she transgresses the patriarchal. In fact, for Jean-Jacques Nattiez, Isolde 'actuates the lovers' androgynous union',[10] and, moreover, he claims that 'the androgyny of

Tristan und Isolde is a female-dominated androgyny.'[11] For most theorists, Isolde is the prime, dominant figure, a fact noted in 1911 by Sâr Péladan when he wrote (rather bluntly): 'Isolde is the man and Tristan the woman'.[12] And as has often been noted since, Tristan, of all operatic heroes, is a highly feminized character, perhaps the most feminized of them all – a feminine Dionysos, beautiful, boyish, but weak and increasingly ineffectual. For much of the opera, and its preceding narrative, he lies prone and wounded, vulnerable and dying. Most resonantly, of course, this feminization of the conventionally phallic hero is signified by the sword-wound in his torso. And this is not the only moment in Wagner's operas when the phallic warrior is dephallicised and transformed into a vaginal figure – in *Parsifal* (Wagner's other 'Celtic' opera), too, we find Amfortas, the King Arthur figure, nursing his 'eternal wound', this time caused by a highly phallic spear. And, as with Tristan, this wound is in his torso, an opening to an absent womb, a symbol of the non-phallic and yet ultimately unfemale masculine.

Yet, as Nattiez makes clear, there are two forms of androgyny operating in the space between these two operas. Nattiez writes that 'the androgyny of *Parsifal* is no longer the same as that of the *Ring* or of *Tristan*: it is an asexual androgyny'.[13] This perhaps explains the shattering critical shift which Nietzsche underwent on hearing *Parsifal* – its highly asexual forms of ambiguity belong not to the pagan, Dionysian androgyne, with its libidinal investments in excess and intoxication, but to the Christian androgyne, with its libidinal reserve and logocentric concepts of redemption. For Tristan, his vaginal wound is a constant source of erotic charge and his death is the ultimate orgasm, but for Amfortas, the vaginal wound represents his loss of manhood without a purely erotic twist; it represents the fallen state of his kingdom and his ineffectual powers of government. For Tristan, being overcome by his vaginal wound is a release only in its intensity and the possibility it gives of an intense *jouissance*, but for Amfortas, it represents redemption from the pain of the world, a return to his father and forgiveness by the patriarchal order.

But these vaginal masculinities, of course, bear little relation to the realm of the actually vaginal – Wagner's masculine vaginas are wounds, signs of lost phallic power, ailments that threaten the death of the masculine figure. And of course, in the cases of both Tristan and Amfortas, the vaginal male longs for his wound to lead finally to his death. In both cases, there is the figure of death as a release from terminally feminized illness. For Tristan, this moment of what we might call the 'masculine *Liebestod*' comes in Act Three, where, in a state of delirium, he finally attempts to rise and greet the returning Isolde. Tearing the bandage from his wound, and bleeding copiously as a result ('Ha, my blood! / Flow joyfully!'), he prays for Isolde to 'close / [his] wound forever'. In this, it is clear that while Tristan has become a vaginal male, Isolde is a phallic female – an exchange of androgynous composition. And if this is true, it is quite clear that of the two figures, Isolde, and not Tristan, is the fullest embodiment of the Dionysian ethos which Nietzsche outlines.

Nevertheless, this fuller Dionysian power of Isolde over Tristan stems from the very fact that Wagner inscribes androgyny within both of the figures. For Deleuze and Guattari, 'Wagner-voices are reterritorialized upon man and woman'.[14] In other words, there is a deterritorialization of conventional gender constructions, followed by a reterritorialization on a new plane. This is simple enough to claim, but for Deleuze and Guattari, it happens specifically on the plane of the voice, a specifically musical, technical feature of the songs of the two ambiguous figures.

Of course, the theme of androgyny emerges in Wagner's own writings, too. In a fragment from 1882 entitled 'On the Masculine and Feminine in Culture and Art', Wagner, perhaps the most phallic of superstar composers in the nineteenth century as far as his obsessively documented personal life is concerned, surprises us with the following:

> So long as we can see only the division of the sexes in its various manifestations when we judge natural and human things, the genus is bound to remain far short of the ideal. Culture and art, too, could be perfect only if a product of the act of suspending the divided unity of male and female.[15]

Perhaps even more surprising to read for the first time is the other famous passage, from *Oper und Drama*, in which, in the middle of holding up the final, choral movement of Beethoven's Ninth Symphony as the prime inspiration for his own concept of the music-drama, Wagner writes the following: 'In order to become a human being, Beethoven had to become a whole person, a social being subject to the conditions of both male and female'.[16]

So for Wagner, Beethoven as a composer is intimately connected to the figure of the androgyne as the ideal form of the artist. This is, no doubt, a reading of Beethoven which would be interesting to compare with those prevalent in the New Musicologies, which tend to characterize Beethoven as one of, if not *the* phallic Viennese master.

In many ways, these two quotations stand at the head of the strain of critiques which have considered the question of the androgyne in Wagnerian opera. Indeed, the first of them stands as the epigraph to Jean-Jacques Nattiez's book *Wagner, Androgyne*, more on which shortly. Initially, notice the alignments of the androgyne concept that Wagner establishes. There is first a primordial unity between the masculine and the feminine, followed by a figural Fall into a state of division, differentiation, between the two. In this context, the reunification of the two opposing-yet-complementary mythic 'principles' represents a return to an originary order, a return that suggests completion, closure. Origin – division – return – closure. Of course, if this closure does represent a death of sorts, then, as a recovery of the primordial state, it is necessarily a transfiguring death, possibly even a transcendent one. Here, we have the shadow of dialectics cast over the proceedings. Throughout the following argument, it will be useful to recall that Isolde's *Liebestod* is also called her *Verklärung*, her transfiguration – a concept which does not immediately or necessarily lead us towards Hegelian idealism but which could potentially also be taken in the direction of a transgression of sorts. The question is, in which direction are we to read the text of the *Liebestod* – the direction of a dialectical closure, a death of redemption or an ecstatic death in Dionysian *jouissance*? As we will see, this will become an increasingly Nietzschean problematic.

For many traditionalist musicologists writing on Wagnerian opera, these quotations from Wagner himself open up the possibility of a psychoanalytic reading. However, unlike most other dis-

ciplines in the humanities, musicology in its psychoanalytic mode
tends to take its cue from Jung rather than Freud. Jung, it seems,
can be applied to opera with a perfect fit: the aesthetic and metaphysical ideal of totality, the concepts of the symbolic and the
mythic, all translate perfectly between Jungian theory and traditionalist musicology, both, of course, sharing a common root in
German idealist philosophy.

No doubt the pre-eminent psychoanalytic reader of Wagner
is Robert Donington, whose *Wagner's 'Ring' and its Symbols: The
Music and the Myth* (1963) applies Jungian theory in liberal measure. In Donington, the Jungian alchemically derived figure of the
hermaphrodite connects closely to the already quoted sections
from Wagner on the relationship between the 'principles' of the
masculine and the feminine. Significantly for our current reading
of *Tristan und Isolde*, Donington extends the Wagnerian idea of an
originary unity towards the theme of incest. In a section entitled
'Mythological Incest as a Ritual Marriage', he writes:

> The unconsciousness of nature is often presented symbolically
> as a hermaphrodite whose male and female principles are un-
> differentiated. This is a primordial incest of opposites which
> are not yet distinguished, still less reconciled ... But when our
> consciousness has developed far enough for life's opposites to
> be seen apart, the possibility arises of reconciling them in a her-
> maphroditic union which on the contrary is differentiated and
> regenerative.[17]

Here, we have two faces to the idea of 'mythological incest as a
ritual marriage': on the one hand, the undifferentiated, 'primordial incest', which results in what Donington calls the 'primordial
hermaphrodite',[18] and on the other, the differentiated, 'regenera-
tive' hermaphrodite, which represents a dialectical return of the
origin at a higher register. One might, of course, question the
status of the primordial incest if it occurs prior to differentiation –
how can the two 'principles' be identified as distinct entities prior
to their separation?

However, other problematics emerge in the Jungian reading of
Wagner, which have been identified by Nattiez. He criticizes
commentators such as Donington on the grounds that their
interpretations are 'quintessentially allegorical'[19] compared with

his own 'philological' hermeneutics[20] and asks 'why should the psychoanalytic interpretation not be based on a simple philological fact?'[21] The problem for Nattiez is that Jungian interpretation is too closed a system, too concerned with its own terms and concepts to open itself up to the specificity of the text:

> The essential problem, from a semiological point of view, is that in reducing the multiplicity of symbolic manifestations to a single set of archetypes, we are depriving ourselves of the chance to interpret each individual symbol once it is incorporated into the syntax of the narrative ... Jung's symbol is asyntactical.[22]

Although this may be a pertinent point, and although Nattiez's philological insistence on finding allegorical connections between the operas and Wagner's biography and critical texts may satisfy methodological conditions for empirically minded musicologists, the fact remains that at a different level of method – specifically within theory – Nattiez's concept of the androgyne is structurally very similar to Donington's concept of the hermaphrodite.

For Nattiez, it is once more a question of the return of a primordial unity – this time at the level of gender rather than biology. Just as the Jungians claim that the union of Tristan and Isolde in the *Liebestod* is a mythic repetition of the 'primordial hermaphrodite', so too Nattiez claims that their union is in and of itself an 'androgynous union'.[23]

What needs to be answered here is why we should consider the union of a male and a female opera character to be either hermaphroditic or androgynous. On a certain symbolic level, it may be possible to make a case for these viewpoints, assuming we grant a specific semiological status to the concept of the symbol – a status that, in part, our Jungian and semiological critics both grant. Further, this evidently involves recourse to the idea that two different characters are merely provisionally differentiated manifestations of aspects of a larger unity – an inherently psychoanalytic strategy of reading opera which, it seems, even Nattiez fails to escape. But reading opera more literally, so to speak, and less psychoanalytically (possibly even less mythically), why should we accept the symbolization of two characters as complementary (or even dialectically aligned) components of a greater unity? This, it seems, is the main claim that allows us to see Tristan and Isolde's love as being productive in and of itself of a certain androgyny. Is it not enough here to realize that both characters are in and of themselves androgynous?

Of course, there is the famous exchange between the two in Act Two, Scene Two, when Tristan sings: '*Tristan du, / ich Isolde, / nicht mehr Tristan!*', to which Isolde replies: '*Du Isolde, / Tristan ich, / nicht mehr Isolde!*' – and this exchange appears to form a major part of the view that their mutual loss of self in the *Liebestod* represents a form of hermaphroditism on the one hand, or androgyny on the other. Yet even with the evidence of this exchange, one must resort to a specifically transcendent concept of symbolism before the claim can hold.

Tristan und Isolde is, above all else, an opera about fucking. Or rather, the desire to fuck, the desire for a totally overwhelming *jouissance* which fractures and dissipates all identity of self; a desire which, as a fully libidinous desire, is never brought to closure, never consummated in actuality, never as such. In other words, it is also about not fucking at all. Throughout the unresolved harmonic tensions which sonically inscribe this longing so profoundly, teasing our ears for a full four and a half hours, the figure of *coitus reservatus* is perpetually invoked. At least in *Die Walküre*, the sibling lovers Siegmund and Sieglinde actually consummate their incest, albeit in the narrative lacuna between Acts One and Two – behind closed doors, so to speak. But in *Tristan und Isolde*, the lovers – constantly risking, yet deferring, two forms of incest – only achieve something like a consummation in the act of a drug-fuelled double suicide. And even here, the two climax apart from each other – Tristan's exposure of his bleeding wound allows him, once more an androgynous figure, to existentially dissipate in the arms of his beloved, while Isolde, subsequently enraptured by the beauty of Tristan's corpse, only then swoons herself into 'the surging swell ... of the world's breath'. Only at this point, a double and yet spaced death, does the sonic plane of the opera take us to a harmonic unity on the ostensibly tonic major. But no phallically pumping perfect cadence here; this is a resolution only of sorts – a resolution which flows, as the previous suspensions and dissonances do, in a potentially perpetual continuum. No unequivocally stated dialectic of tonic and dominant here – merely the coming to rest of a liquid, almost formless process. No masculine cadence, for sure, but for Susan McClary, Isolde's *Liebestod* does suggest a certain feminine power, as the summation of her dominance throughout the preceding narrative:

> Of course, Isolde is not presented as a dominatrix ... Still, she does befuddle and seduce poor Tristan by means of her chromatic excess, and she too (like Lucia and Salome) achieves transcendence in the absence of the phallus. Isolde gets the last word in this most unconventional opera: *Tristan und Isolde* has a feminine ending of sorts. Yet she does not survive the frame, for after her climax she expires through a spectacular effusion of irrational bliss.[24]

Yet if Isolde is to an extent phallicized, just as Tristan is vaginized, might we not see the final cadential sequence of the opera in a similar light to the ambivalence of the opening chord? Certainly, there is no doubt that the last few bars represent no masculine cadence, but also, perhaps, not a feminine ending either – at least not figuratively. Traditionalist musicology offers us two alternatives: the masculine cadence and the feminine cadence. But could it be that the final bars of *Tristan und Isolde* represent the emergence of the *androgynous cadence* in music, an androgyny framed by, driven by the uncontrollable desire for a form of death that is in actuality a sublimation of the desire for an illicit, perhaps sublime, sexual act? – a cadence that is still, despite its major triad, suggestive of (to invoke Nietzsche once again) a certain deferral, a certain shattering, a certain dissipation, or a cosmic incontinence? For in the affective incontinence that Nietzsche identifies within the Dionysian moment we do not find ourselves, and we are not saved or redeemed, but rather, we lose ourselves, shatter and become multiple.

This chapter may have seemed to be aligned to the general field of the New Musicologies and their subterranean influences from French post-structuralism in particular. However, there is a serious problem to be addressed by the proponents of the New Musicologies in their readings of nineteenth century operas along basically Dionysian lines of desire, excess and transgression: it is, that Nietzsche's reading of *Tristan und Isolde* shifts radically as he himself becomes more fully Dionysian as a writer. Of course, the later Nietzsche, who turns viciously against Wagner, the Nietzsche who rereads *Tristan und Isolde* after the shock of hearing *Parsifal*'s ultimately Christian usage of the chromatic, this Nietzsche begins to see too much of the idea of Christian, rather than provisionally Schopenhauerian redemption in the text of *Tristan und Isolde*. For the later Nietzsche, Wagner is merely 'the heir of Hegel', another example of the dialectic that is to be shattered by Dionysian fury.

If the later Nietzsche begins to see the shadow of Hegel cast over even *Tristan und Isolde*, and, moreover, if Wagner himself saw a certain mythic dialectic within his own conception of androgyny, what is the basis upon which the Dionysian reading of the concept of *Liebestod* is made? For Deleuze and Guattari, who have read their later Nietzsche with consummate skill, Wagner is, finally, a proponent of a 'passional delusion',[25] which, as for Nietzsche, remains Christian rather than pagan and Dionysian. Certainly, Nietzsche himself was acutely aware of the Hegelian shadow that is cast across Wagner's work:

> Foreigners are astonished and drawn by the enigmas that the contradictory nature at the bottom of the German soul propounds to them (which Hegel reduced to a system and Richard Wagner finally set to music).[26]

No doubt, in Nietzsche's mind, the possibility of a Hegelianism within Wagner's music coincides with his deep mistrust of speculative dialectics in general. If, then, the *Liebestod* signifies a redemption rather than a shattering and dissolution, a dialectical return to the originary state of oneness rather than a Nietzschean incontinence of cosmic proportions, a transcendence rather than a transgression, a merely spiritual copulation rather than an explosive moment of *jouissance*, where might this leave theorists of the New Musicologies such as Attali, Clément, and McClary? In attempting to re-Dionysise *Tristan und Isolde*, are the New Musicologists taking the same risk that deconstruction does – that of retaining too much of the structure which it inhabits? If so, they have yet to fully implement a reading of the later, more faithfully Dionysian Nietzsche.

Notes

1 Jean-Jacques Nattiez, *Wagner, Androgyne: A Study in Interpretation* (Princeton: Princeton University Press, 1993), p. 301.

2 'To drown, / to sink – / unconscious – / highest pleasure! (Isolde sinks, as if transfigured ...)'.

3 Catherine Clément, *Opera, or the Undoing of Women* (London: Virago, 1989), p. 54.

4 Theodor Adorno, *Aesthetic Theory* (London: Routledge, 1984), p. 21.

5 Serge Gut, 'Encore et toujours: "L'accord de Tristan",' in *L'Avant-Scène Opéra*,1981, 34–35 (*Tristan and Isolde*), 151.

6 Friedrich Nietzsche, *Twilight of the Idols* (Harmondsworth: Penguin, 1985), p. 71.

7 Jacques Attali, *Noise: The Political Economy of Music* (Minneapolis: University of Minnesota Press, 1985), p. 143.

8 Friedrich Nietzsche, *The Birth of Tragedy and The Case of Wagner* (New York: Vintage, 1976), p. 127.

9 Clément, *Opera, or the Undoing of Women*, p. 54.

10 Nattiez, *Wagner, Androgyne*, p. 144.

11 Nattiez, *Wagner, Androgyne*, p. 297.

12 Sâr Péladan (1911) *La Science de l'Amour*, quoted in Nattiez, p. 141.

13 Nattiez, *Wagner, Androgyne*, p. 171.

14 Gilles Deleuze and Félix Guattari, *A Thousand Plateaus: Capitalism and Schizophrenia* (London: Athlone, 1988), p. 307.

15 Nattiez, *Wagner, Androgyne*, p. 169.

16 Richard Wagner, *Oper und Drama*, 3, 1851, 312.

17 Robert Donington, *Wagner's 'Ring' and its Symbols: The Music and the Myth* (London: Faber, 1984 [1963]), p. 121.

18 Donington, *Wagner's 'Ring' and its Symbols,* p. 254.

19 Nattiez, *Wagner, Androgyne*, p. 226.

20 Nattiez, *Wagner, Androgyne*, p. 227.

21 Nattiez, *Wagner, Androgyne*, p. 228.

22 Nattiez, *Wagner, Androgyne*, p. 230–31.

23 Nattiez, *Wagner, Androgyne*, p. 144.

24 Susan McClary, *Feminine Endings: Music, Gender, and Sexuality* (Oxford: University of Minnesota Press, 1991), p. 100.

25 Deleuze and Guattari, *A Thousand Plateaus*, p. 127.

26 Friedrich Nietzsche, *Beyond Good and Evil* (Harmondsworth: Penguin, 1982), p. 156.

8

The last hours

ALPHONSO LINGIS

In Balconcillo, a working class barrio of Lima in Peru, a youth has arrived at the threshold of manhood. He has the still vertiginous sense of how much his body – his size, his voice, his hirsuitness, his musculature, his genitals – has developed by contrast with that of his brother two years younger than him. He was vividly aware during his time through school how much his knowledge, his know-how, his thinking changed each year so that he found it awkward and uncongenial to associate with students two years or even a year below him in school. New efforts, new undertakings, new escapades, new thrills, beckon him each week. He has an intense sense of his past as a succession of stepping stones he has crossed, and of his present as open upon the paths of a future whose next stages are already visible and beckoning.

Then the President abruptly shuts down Parliament, arrests hundreds of opposition leaders and journalists and launches an all-out military campaign to exterminate the armed opposition. For this young man, the horizons widen abruptly and he sees the field of his life inserted into the broad expanse of his prostrate country. Everything he thinks of doing begins to take account of the changes affecting his country. He knows someone in the neighbourhood who has contacts with the Resistance. Impulsively he determines to join the underground army. He will fight with all his strength for the overthrow of the oppressor, for a renewed birth of his country delivered to a stronger, nobler future by the arms of his united comrades.

He learns how to exist and operate in clandestinity; he does everything possible to conceal his activities and those of his comrades; he does everything possible to escape from a raid unharmed and unidentified, for his fundamental obligation to his cause is, even when undertaking the most dangerous of subversive activities, to preserve that precious and invaluable agency of the resistance, his life.

But he is captured. He is tortured; he has done everything to hold strong, lest in a moment of weakness and syncope he involuntarily betray his comrades. When his torturers finally come to think they will get nothing from him, they tell him he will be executed at dawn. They tell him he still has this one night to save his life and decide to cooperate.

He could try to gain his life, but only at the cost of betraying his comrades. To live then is inconceivable to him; he cannot imagine that such a life would be, could be, anything other than repugnant – to others, but more deeply to himself. Were he to try to imagine himself surviving, living by collaborating with the secret police, betraying his countrymen one after another, forever distrusted and despised by the secret police themselves, he could not identify that image with the one, in the deepest core of himself, he feels and knows as himself. He will die. It is not that he suddenly gives up the will to live and wishes to die, but rather that, confronted with the inevitability of his execution, he no longer struggles to push off his death. He assents to his fate.

Now, as he is led to the prison yard where he will be tied to a stake and shot, he feels a strange lightness. He is not standing on a scaffold where the people have assembled to hear his last words of courage and defiance and witness how he dies; it is dark, and all about him the thick walls of the prison will muffle the shots so that they will not be heard even by his fellow prisoners. He will be 'disappeared'; his mother will never be told by the police that her son was captured. Yet, in the dark, he feels something like exultation; he is floating on light. It is as though the future and the past, with all their weight, had fallen from him and left these last moments disconnected, buoyant, and with all their energies intensified on them – a strange, miraculous buoyancy and lightness, a miraculous elation as he feels himself falling, falling upward into the sky.

'Love your enemies', Jesus said. To do evil to them, to seek to exterminate them, is to hate them. Hypocrites give themselves

permission to hate by claiming to love the sinners while eradi-
cating their deeds. But when the enemy is defeated, there is no
one who so arouses passion in us – erotic passion – than someone
condemned to death. It is true that there is an element of pity, and
also of power, in our attraction for men and women waiting for
their death sentence to be executed. The pity feels that we too are
living under death sentence. The total helplessness of the condemned man or woman makes us feel the exultation of power
over him or her. But there is also the transport of erotic abandon
in what we feel. We cannot think of the condemned human being
without feeling a subterranean yearning to denude ourselves
before that person and cover him or her with all we have of kisses
and caresses. Erotic passion is the exultation of a moment of time
without resources or goal, without past or future.

Men and women on death row, convicted murderers and
traitors, guerrillas awaiting execution in the dungeons of Peru,
Colombia and Indonesia, what violent surges of passion they
arouse in us! Because we do not bribe our way into their cells on
the night before their execution, tear off our clothes, opening all
our orifices to them on the stiff cots or cement floors of their
cells, our sensuality is constricted, asphyxiated, and ashamed.

It is true that civilized sensuality is not frenzied at all. It is
limited, modest and controlled. It is not driven by a suicidal and
criminal craving for communication. It is driven simply by the
desire for pleasure. This pleasure comes in the physical contact
with a body and its orifices that excites your own, and gives you
release. It comes in the contact with a person who looks up to
you, admires your achievements, your personality and your body,
and thus confirms you in a sense of sufficiency and fullness.
Civilized sensuality is not passionate, vertiginous: it is only a
means of pleasure, of gratifying, satiating the body and confirming
your sense of yourself. How understandable that it does not count
very high in our estimation; we feel a kind of aversion for this
pleasure that makes us sink back into the heaviness of our bodies
and the opacity of our sense of ourselves.

An episode in the life of Saint Catherine of Sienna is known
through a letter she addressed to her confessor. The year is
around 1377 and she is about thirty years old. Niccolo Toldo, a

dissolute young nobleman from Perugia, had given voice to some utterances that the authorities deemed to be blasphemous and treasonous. He was condemned to be beheaded. While awaiting execution, he cursed the authorities and cursed God for his fate. Then Catherine visited him in his cell and brought it about that he consented to die. Here is her letter:

> Most beloved and dearest father and my dear son in Jesus Christ, I, Catherine, servant and slave of the servants of Jesus Christ, write to you, commending myself to you in the precious blood of the son of God, with desire to see you inflamed and drowned in this very sweet blood which is churning with the fire of his most ardent charity. This is what my soul longs for: to see you in this blood, you and Nanni and Jacopo, my sons. I see no other means by which we may reach those chief virtues which are necessary to us. Sweetest father, your soul which has become my food (and there is no day that I do not take this food at the table of the sweet Lamb, who was slaughtered with such ardent love) – your soul will not reach the modest virtue of true humility if you are not drowned in this blood. This virtue will be born from hate and hate from love. In this way will the soul come forth with perfect purity, as iron issues purified from the furnace.
>
> I wish then that you shut yourself in the open wound on the side of the Son of God, which is an open shelter full of such fragrance that sin itself there becomes fragrant. There the sweet spouse rests in the bed of fire and blood; there the secret of the heart of the Son of God shows itself and is seen. Oh flowing wine which drenches and fills every spirit that gives itself to it such that that spirit can retain nothing, understand nothing, love nothing but this sweet and good Jesus! Blood and fire, inestimable love! Because my soul will be filled with happiness to see you drowned thus, I wish you do as does he who draws water with a bucket and pours it over something else: that you pour the water of holy desire on the head of your brothers, who are our members united in the body of the sweet spouse. And take care that the artifice of demons (which, I know, have created and will create obstacles for you) or what some creature may say never makes you turn back! But persevere always in the hour when things look most cold, until we may see blood shed with sweet and enamoured desires.

Up, get up, my very sweet father; let us sleep no more! For I hear such news that I wish no longer bed nor rest. I have just received a head in my hands, and it was for me a sweetness such as my heart could not conceive, my tongue express, my eye see, nor my ear hear. The will of God went on through other mysteries which took place, about which I shall not speak, for it would be too long to recount. I went to see him whom you know and from this visit he received so much comfort and consolation that he confessed and prepared himself very well. And he made me promise, for the love of God, that when the time of the sentence should come I would be with him. Then in the morning, before the bell rang, I went to him, and he received great consolation. I led him to hear Mass and he received holy communion, which he had never before received. His will was accorded and submitted to the will of God. There remained in him only a fear of not being strong enough when the moment came. The measureless and glowing goodness of God surprised him, creating in him so much affection and love for the will of God that he could no longer do without it. He said: 'Stay with me, and do not abandon me! and all will necessarily turn out well and I shall die content.' And he laid his head on my breast. I then felt a great joy and smelled his blood, which was mingled with the smell of my own, which I long to shed for my sweet spouse Jesus. And as desire swelled in my soul and I felt his fear, I said: 'Take courage, my sweet brother, for we will soon be at the wedding. You will go to it, bathed in the sweet blood of the Son of God, with the sweet name of Jesus, which I want to no longer leave your memory. And I will wait for you at the place of justice'. Imagine then, Father and Son, that his heart then lost all fear, and his face changed from sadness to joy. He rejoiced, he exulted and said: 'How does so great a grace come to me, that you, the sweetness of my heart, await me at the holy place of justice?' (You see that he reached such an enlightenment that he called holy the place of execution!) And he said 'I will go joyous and strong. Until then, impatiently thinking that you will be waiting for me there, the time will seem to me to stretch out to a thousand years'. And he then said words so sweet as to break one's heart, of the goodness of God.

I then went to await him at the place of justice. I waited in continual prayer, in the presence of Mary and of Saint Catherine, virgin and martyr. But before he arrived, I knelt down and extended my neck on the executioner's block, and did not have any thought for myself. There I prayed and with all my forces cried out: 'Mary!' How I wanted this grace, that at this moment she would give him light and peace of heart and that I would then see him reach his goal. So overfull was my soul because of the sweet promise that had been made to me that there in the midst of the crowd that had gathered I saw no one.

Then he arrived like a sweet lamb, and upon seeing me broke out laughing, and asked that I make the sign of the cross over him. When he received this sign, I said, 'Fall on your knees, my sweet brother, soon you will be at the eternal wedding feast'. He knelt down with great gentleness, and I extended my neck to him, and bent over and recalled to him the blood of the Lamb. His mouth said only 'Jesus' and 'Catherine'. And then, saying those names, I received his head in my hands, its eyes fixed on divine goodness and saying 'I wish it'.

Then I saw the God-man, like we see the brightness of the sun! In his side was the wound that had been opened with that lance [of the Roman soldier], and he received blood into his blood, and a fire of holy desire, given by grace and hidden in his soul. He received that blood into the fire of divine charity. When [the God-man] had received [Niccolo's] blood and desire, he also received his soul, which he, full of mercy, put in the open shelter of his cut-open side. The supreme Truth showed that he received it only by grace and mercy and not by some other operation. Oh! how sweet and inestimable it was to see the goodness of God! With what tenderness and what love he received this soul separated from the body! He turned toward that soul the eye of his mercy when it entered into the open side, bathed in his blood, rendered precious by the blood of the Son of God. Thus he was received by the power of God – powerful enough to do so. The Son, the Word and the Wisdom incarnated in him, gave him his crucified love and made him participate in it, that love by which he received painful and infamous death in obedience to the Father, for the utility of the human race. And the hands of the Holy Spirit closed over him [Niccolo] to shut that crucified love within him.

As for him [Niccolo], he had an expression so sweet as to break a thousand hearts, and I was not surprised, for he tasted already the divine sweetness. He turned around, like the bride who has reached the door of the bridegroom turns her eyes back and bows to those who accompanied her to show her gratitude.

When he was buried, my soul rested in peace and tranquillity, and in such an odor of blood that I could not endure the idea of cleansing from me his blood that had drained upon me.

Alas, unhappy and wretched am I! I can say no more. I who have remained on earth do so with very great regret. It seems to me that the first stone [of my tomb] has been laid. And that is why do not be surprised if I order nothing else for you than to be drowned in the blood and fire which flows from the open flank of the Son of God. No more negligence, my very sweet son, for the blood has begun to flow, and to receive life. Sweet Jesus, Jesus Love.

That a young man condemned to die at the start of his manhood could suddenly know the last hours before his execution in buoyancy and lightness and exultation is what filled Catherine – and fills us – with dumbfounded wonder. That a cocky and luxurious young aristocrat suddenly faced with the certainty of his death could live the last hours with composure and the bliss that radiates good will fills her, and us, with stupefaction – and with wild flames of erotic passion!

The execution of a man or woman who has violated the fundamental taboos of the world of work and reason – the prohibitions on incest, the prohibitions on the corpse and on murder – or who has led a raid on, or an insurrection against, a society of work and reason, declares the condemned person to be incorrigible, irredeemable. The execution is an expulsion by the society of one who was born and raised in that society; he or she is now expelled as a waste product and as excrement.

But the execution of the guilty or of the just, even if it is decreed as an act of surgery on a cancerous growth on the body of the society and carried out by the rational machinery of the judicial system, induces the notion of sacrifice – in the primal sense of *sacrum-facio*, to make separated, to make sacred. Sacrifice makes something sacred by using destruction to separate it definitively from the world of work and reason.

What is thus separated is delivered over to its own violence. Once delivered to the realm of the demonic and sacred, the executed person becomes a spectre that haunts the laborious and rational citizens. There he or she remains in storms of blood and fire. We cannot think of that person without thinking what he or she would do; we are haunted by deeds of violence shaking again and again the walls of the society from which this body has been expelled. In our society today the execution of capital offenders maintains about the confines of the ordered daylight world of work and reason an underworld of the irrational and the incorrigible, the monstrous and the demonic.

Making sacred – *sacrum-facio* – is also an effort to enter into collusion with the outer zone of sacred and demonic forces. The notion of sacrifice induces the notion of an exchange. Humans have killed and kill other animals – and sometimes humans – in blood sacrifices to ensure an abundant harvest. The practice of sacrificial rituals, and the sacrificial death of Jesus on the cross, are taken to be necessary for the moral order. Small everyday acts of separation and exclusion – of goods from use, of pleasures that are disallowed – are taken as the price one pays for a morally functioning order.

Sacrifices of lives, of one's best citizens and one's most virile youth, are required by the political and military authorities to ensure wealth and empire. The high command of the world of work and reason calculate the gains to be made if thousands of young men are sent to die on a desolate outcrop of rock like Iwo Jima.

It is possible that these young men assent to the sacrifice being made of their lives, that they assent to die in the belief that they are sacrificing the good of their lives in exchange for the good of those who will live in the victorious nation or empire. Many also die to prevent that nation or empire from being victorious; and many die in order that their land be freed from external or internal oppression.

Socrates convinces himself that he is renouncing the superficial and perishable goods of this life to secure the possession of a beatitude independent of all human vicissitudes. This conviction produces in him a state of serenity in his last hours, among friends who cannot contain their outbursts of grief, indignation, sense of abandonment and resentment.

No doubt those who go to die could form the idea that their

very deaths, as martyrs, would serve the cause of the Resistance. How many cases have there been in history when the sheer numbers of resistants executed forced the tyrant to recognize the hopelessness of his policy of terror?

We also know that victory does not arise as the outcome of the accumulated number of men who sacrificed their lives for it. History has shown – and continues to show – that the most noble causes, which inspired the noblest youths to fight for them and which resulted in the greatest number of martyrs, have failed and continue to fail.

At the end of Ernest Hemingway's *For Whom the Bell Tolls*, Robert Jordan, gravely wounded, pushes away his comrades that they might try to save themselves. He lodges himself above the path, with his sub-machine gun, and determines to use the last of his strength to shoot at the Fascist patrol. Yet it is most unlikely that his comrades will be able to elude the army bearing down on them. He knows that several of them have been killed and he himself mortally wounded in an operation to blow up a bridge as part of a strategy that he knows has failed. And he has concluded that the Republican cause will either be defeated by the superior armies of the Fascists or be betrayed and corrupted by the leaders he has obeyed and come to know.

While the condemned person waits in the trenches for the invincible assault of the enemy or, in the cell on death row, for the footsteps of the warden and guards, or for the imbibed hemlock poison to take effect, the time of waiting can be filled with an intellectual exultation over the idea of an exchange. But whether one can believe in the reality of this exchange or not, the last hours, the time of waiting for the inevitable and the irrevocable, is a floating time, disconnected from the time of the enchainment of acts.

When a human being is condemned to death and has the certainty that the sentence will be carried out within the time decreed – whether by the judge who orders a prisoner to be executed, or a doctor who announces the inexorable progression of the fatal disease – a black wall and an abyss of impossibility abruptly eliminate the finalities by which a future had structured that person's acts. With the same stroke, the death sentence severs from the condemned the momentum, direction and sense their present state had derived from the past. They have yet to live their last hours, under the effect of this disinsertion from the time of the enchainment of acts.

These hours may be lived in the paralysed despair of their meaninglessness. Whatever explosive forces surge in the midst of this paralysis break out as curses: curses hurled upon one's judges and executioner, curses hurled upon one's fate.

But this paralysis has also been lived as a strange state of buoyancy and lightness. This buoyancy and lightness may be caught up in the exultation of those who consent to die, believing that in this consent they are exchanging the transitory and perishable good of their life for the imperishable good of celestial life, or for the more lasting or more extensive terrestrial good that will come when the cause for which they stake their life triumphs. Such is the exultation of those who die as martyrs to a religious confession or of a revolutionary struggle to overthrow a regime of oppression. The exultation they live through is shaped by the significance of bearing witness. This significance exists for the condemned in the measure that there are survivors for whom it will exist – a God who sees their comrades in the struggle and in coming generations who will learn how they died.

But the last hours may know this same strange state of buoyancy when those condemned to die do not, or cannot, believe in any afterlife, and when they know that the cause for which they stake their life has been lost. In Auschwitz, by 1943, Jews who were informed (by their clandestine radios and by incoming prisoners) of the progress of the war could well believe that it would end in a Nazi victory and the thousand-year Reich, that they would in any case all be lost in the Night and Fog and that all trace of how they died and of their very existence would be effaced irrevocably. They had never believed in a personal afterlife, and if they had been able to believe that Jahweh had once made them his chosen people, he had now visibly abandoned them. But we know that many of them with this conviction nonetheless walked to the gas chambers in dignity, even in buoyancy and lightness.

Indeed, does not every guerrilla who enters into clandestinity and struggle against a regime of oppression know that they may end up before the firing squad and that their cause may end in defeat? They know that strange, extraordinary lightness of entering into the struggle against all odds.

All the activity of the mind – identifying, relating, judging – is inserted in the course of laborious activity, where each thing has a meaning by reference to a further thing, is a means to an end and a cause of a result. Each operation of our intellect has meaning only in the operations that follow it, which it makes possible. We form clear and distinct concepts in order to use them in statements and in reasonings. We think about confused matter in order to come to some conclusions; these conclusions we will retain so that we may think clearly about further confused matters.

The state of mind that thinks of one's imminent death as a witness and an exchange subordinates, subjugates these last hours to a future – a future of individual bliss in an afterlife, or else a future that is not one's own future but the future of the better lives of those who will benefit from one's struggle to death against the present oppression.

There are feelings – hope, fear, craving, appetite, arrogance, remorse – that serve to launch actions and thoughts. There are feelings – satisfaction, contentment, pride, disdain, shame – that result from, and seal, actions and thoughts. But sensuality is a wholly distinct order of feelings.

Sensuality is a feeling of abandon to the moment. It may long to prolong this moment, but it does not launch anything further. It does not seal and ratify the actions and thoughts that may have preceded it. Far from bearing witness to them, sensuality forgets them. When one is aroused voluptuously, the intensity of the voluptuous feeling smothers thoughts and evaluations of the actions that led to it. Sensuality adheres to the moment it fills, without evaluating that moment or justifying it. The feelings of sensual abandon interrupt the subordination of means to ends, causes to results, the inexorable enchainment of acts in time. The intensity of sensual feeling serves nothing and no one, not even oneself.

There are other feelings that likewise break with the enchainment of acts in time – laughter, poetic emotion, ecstatic emotion.

Laughter interrupts discourse and breaks with the enchainment of thoughts in the coherent succession of words. The feeling of the poetry of the twilight illuminating the colonial town in the valley below breaks with the thoughts we had been elaborating about our itinerary or our task and causes us to interrupt our action for the moment. Ecstatic emotion is not only transported wholly into the ecstatic object or spectacle before us, but disconnects our thoughts and immobilizes our operations. It is true that we can ascribe meaning and significance to poetic emotion, ecstatic emotion, laughter and sensuality. We can, later, see the poetic emotion as an insight into the value of the old colonial town, see the laughter as a vitalizing release of tension, see the voluptuous abandon as a commitment to love or serve someone. But beneath that significance, or without that meaning, these feelings intensify themselves, for themselves, filling up the moment, losing sight of the moment before and the moments after. Their reality, which serves nothing and no one, not even the one who feels them, is sovereign.

Indeed, does not every duration that finds itself disconnected from a future and from a past give rise to a pulse and intensity of sensuality? The bus breaks down on the mountain road; while the driver is waiting for a mechanic to come with the spare parts, the time longs to be filled with laughter or with wandering in poetic reverie in the forest paths. The onward flights have been cancelled because of a hurricane; the night longs to be filled with a chance meeting with someone in whose arms to abandon ourselves in nakedness and passion.

When the death sentence has been pronounced, and its execution certain, the condemned live this sentence as a disconnection of every future and a disconnection of the momentum that comes from all that has come to pass in their life. They are left only with the present hours.

It is true that one can, in the time that is left, make the intellectual act of assent to one's death, an assent that is itself made possible by an intellectual act that assigns to one's execution the meaning of an exchange or of a witness. But the act of assent does not fill up these hours. The hours are hours one has to live through, hours that one cannot make pass, that one can only endure. These hours themselves are disconnected also from the future for which one proffers this life in exchange and from the future for which one's way of dying will be a witness.

These hours can expose themselves only to sensuality. Sensuality attaches itself to these hours, adheres to them, in all this disconnected buoyancy and lightness. Sensuality affirms them, intensifies them, for themselves. Then these hours and the sensuality that adheres to them are absolutely sovereign.

The sexual drive imposes the future on individuals. It would be, in the individual, a compulsive concern for the future of the species. Eroticism is a perversion of the sexual drive, which is deviated and employed entirely for the intensity of pleasure in the existing individual. Eroticism drives under the law of the repetition compulsion; it acquires nothing, accumulates nothing, synthesizes nothing, does not advance to a future and only repeats itself compulsively. Voluptuousness cares nothing for the consequences, as it sets aside nothing to repay those who or that which led to it. It disconnects the sexual subordination of the present to the future, as it disconnects the gratitude that subordinates the present to the past.

Erotic pleasure is distinctive in that it is an ecstatic pleasure, a pleasure in the other, a pleasure that surges towards the disparate, disconnected body of another. Voluptuousness is the voluptuous release from our integrity, our identity. Voluptuous craving is necrophilic, embracing, sinking into a body decomposing and cadaverous, already soaking the sheets and oneself with released inner fluids teeming with nameless and chaotic micro-organisms.

The genital organs are also the excremental organs, expelling the dead part of the body, the cadaverous part, which repels and disgusts. But we would never have seen our genitals to be less beautiful than our noses and mouths, were it not for the devious compulsions, the monstrous tastes and the brutal violences we feel when the locus of our sense of self migrates to them. The erotic compulsion is not only that which tears aside the adornments and fine clothes to plunge the blindly throbbing erect penis into the lubricating labia and vagina, and into the mouth and anus, releasing sweat, secretions, semen and blood, releasing the forces and compulsions from their confines in our integrity and identity. It is the compulsion that plunges all that is infantile, feral, violent in oneself in the other, seeking all that is disharmonious, predatory, bloodthirsty in the other.

The letter of Catherine of Sienna is addressed to her confessor, whom she addresses as 'Most beloved and dearest Father', and immediately inverts into 'and my dear son in Jesus Christ'. She confesses all the tumultuous emotions that have overwhelmed her since she last communicated with him – emotions which she nowise confesses as sins but, to the contrary, as sovereign, so that she advises him (nay, orders him) as her son – dear son in Jesus Christ – to join her in these emotions and go yet further. As her son and disciple he must reach the modest virtue of veritable humility. 'Up, get up, my very sweet father; sleep no more!'

'This virtue will be born from hate and hate from love', she says. She is writing to hold up to him the example of a worldly young nobleman, who cursed the authorities and cursed God, but, through her intercession, through her presence in his cell, this hatred was abruptly reversed into the most intense love.

Her letter recounts how love was born from hate, but she does not elaborate on how hate will be born from love. Yet it is no doubt the real reason for her letter: to forewarn the Father confessor that the intense love of this young man, Niccolo Toldo, for Jesus will be seen to be inextricable from the intense love Catherine of Sienna aroused in him when she caressed his head laid on her breast in the prison cell; this love will be despised and condemned by the Church. Her rapturous love for this young man, whose head she grasped out of the execution block and whose blood she cannot bring herself to wash from her hands, clothing and breast, will be condemned and abhorred as a necrophilic love for a criminal. 'Take care', she writes, 'that the artifice of demons … or what some creature may say never makes you turn [your] back [to me]'.

This letter is not the report of a missionary dedicated, in mind and heart, to the spread of the Christian gospel, reporting on success with a particularly difficult case. It is a letter of a woman under suspicion to her confessor. It is to be sure wholly formulated in the religious vocabulary, and the words never diverge

from orthodoxy. Is she using the vocabulary of salvation to trans-
pose her passionate and desperate love for this criminal and
render it justified in the eyes of her confessor?

The letter elaborates intelligible content for all the vehemence
and obsessiveness of her emotions: she had gone to this dis-
turber of the established order and blasphemer who now in his
prison cell uttered only cries of hate. Repairing the disorder, she
induced him to cease cursing the civil and ecclesiastical authorities and God, and to consent to his elimination from society. More
than that, he went to his death like a gentle lamb, under the sign
of the cross, his eyes fixed on divine goodness, saying 'I wish
[this death]'.

She saw with her own eyes the God-man himself receive the
blood of young Niccolo into the open wound in his side. She saw
Jesus not only receive young Niccolo with nothing but grace and
mercy and love but, she brazenly declares, she saw the God-man
himself identify the execution of Niccolo Toldo for rebellion and
blasphemy with his own crucifixion at the hands of the high
priests of Jerusalem and the Roman authorities. 'The Son, the
Word and the Wisdom incarnate ... gave him his crucified love
and made him participate in it ... And the hands of the Holy Spirit'
closed him up in that crucified love, that love for which Jesus himself 'received painful and infamous death'.

Is she then deceiving her confessor? Is she deceiving herself?
For those of us for whom the vocabulary of christology is only
mystification and cant, and for the celibate priesthood itself,
which has taken such anxious pains to separate sacred love
entirely from profane love, the mystical love of Jesus from the car-
nal love of a man, the answer could only be yes. We would subject
her letter to a deconstruction, a demystification, exposing her
deliberate wiles. Or else we would subject her letter to psychoanalysis, taking the sacred vocabulary to be the mythology written by her subconscious.

Let us drop all this deconstructionist and psychoanalytic clever-
ness, and respond to what we feel: the passionate outbursts, the
extreme emotions of a love-maddened and desperate woman.

Let us only deconstruct the notion, so instinctual in all our
contemporary conceptual schemes, that passion is a storm of

energies generated in us, in our bodies and in our minds – energies that generate only images, which for their part are located only on the inner screens of our own minds; and that the figure of Jesus – and of the godmen who have appeared in all religious art on all continents since Cosquer, Chauvet and Lascaux – are, as we so crudely put it, 'projections' of our own feelings.

The truth is that passion is quite unable to be this creative artist, fulfilling its wishes with fantasies generated out of its very longings and emptiness. Terror is the storm outside passing through us. Awe is the blazing white light gaping infinitely above the unending glaciers of the Andes and emptying our inner darkness of all its ideas and images. The man or the woman who suddenly appears, moving with the wild and free forces of a lion or the grace and power of a tigress, electrified with the most remote cosmic forces, makes erotic passion erupt within us. The erotic passion is the opening up of all the doors of our heart, so that our energies flood out towards this person, drowning our meticulous cerebral constructions, our ideas, intentions and decisions, our very sense of identity and separateness.

In the rapturous visions of Catherine of Sienna, Jesus is this sacred transfiguration seen, felt and experienced in the body of the nobleman Niccolo Toldo, at the same time as this demonic transfiguration seen, felt and experienced in the body of the criminal Niccolo Toldo. What she has longed to see, touch and hold in the figure of Jesus she abruptly, in one night of passion, sees, touches and holds in her hands and up against her breast in the body of Niccolo Toldo.

She writes that she began by taking his head in her hands, and it was for her a sweetness so great that the heart cannot conceive it, the tongue express it, the eye see it, the ear hear it. And young Niccolo, for his part, she says, received so much comfort and consolation that, in the raptures of passion his hatred of the authorities and of God were drowned in his love for her. He confessed and prepared himself to die bravely in her eyes and made her promise that when the hour of justice would come she would be there with him. She could not spend the night with him, but she came before the first bell of daybreak and, she writes, the ardent and infinite goodness of God surprised him, creating in him so much affection and love for the will of God that he could no longer do without it, saying, 'Stay with me, and do not abandon me!' But it is to her that he addresses this cry; it is in her that he was surprised by the will of God; it is in her that ardent and infinite goodness surprised him; it is for her that there welled up in him so much affection and love. He laid his head on her breast, she writes, and she felt great joy and inhaled the smell of his blood, intermingled with the smell of her own blood, which she so desperately longed to spill for the dear spouse – Jesus. In these words she can now no longer distinguish Niccolo from Jesus or Jesus from Niccolo, her god-man and saviour. When the guards come to take him away, he begins to shake with fear, and she tells him she will wait for him at the executioner's block, which will be their wedding-place.

Catherine waits for him at the place of execution, calling on the assistance of Mary the mother of Jesus and St Catherine – two virgins like herself and one of them, a saint from Roman times, bearing her name. Like her, Catherine now feels herself to be a virgin and a martyr. Before Niccolo gets there, Catherine kneels down at the executioner's block and extends her own neck upon it, having lost all sense of herself. 'So overfull was my soul because of the sweet promise [Niccolo had] made to me that ... in the midst of the crowd ... I saw no one.'

When Niccolo – a criminal whom she sees as a gentle lamb – gets there, he sees her and laughs with joy. She says to him: 'Fall on your knees, my sweet brother, soon you will be at the eternal wedding'. How passionately, how desperately she longs to be there too! He kneels with a great gentleness, and she extends her neck to him – how she longs his would be the axe that would fall upon her neck! His mouth said nothing but 'Jesus' and 'Catherine' – names confounded into one; his Catherine is Jesus, his Jesus is Catherine.

Niccolo, now on the block, turns to Catherine as though, she writes, she were the bride who had arrived at the door of the bridegroom. This line hallucinates what she so ardently wishes: he is the bride, she the bridegroom; she is on the block instead of him. She who did not receive him in the bleeding gash between her thighs saw with her own eyes the God-man receive Niccolo into the open wound in his side. She can no longer distinguish the blood of the God-man commingled with the blood of Niccolo from the blood that drained from his severed head upon her hands, clothing and breast.

On Niccolo's severed head, which she had seized as the axe fell and had pushed against her breast, she saw an expression sweet enough to break a thousand hearts and, she writes, 'was not surprised, for he tasted already the divine sweetness'. This line expresses the orthodox explanation that gives intelligible content to the heartbreakingly gentle expression on the face of the young nobleman as the axe fell, by seeing in it the bliss acquired from an exchange that has been made: that of the superficial and perishable life he was leading for a life of eternal bliss on the side now of Jesus.

It will be said that Catherine gives significance, can give significance, to the unearthly buoyancy and lightness, the disinsertion she knew one night and one terrible dawn in the company of Niccolo Toldo, only by projecting it into a time of the enchainment of activities, into an after when her passion for Niccolo, taken up into the deathless body of Jesus, will turn into a longing to join him through martyrdom at the unending wedding with which she extinguishes his fear at the sight of the executioner's block.

These words are indeed in her letter. But are they not the words a disconsolate, desperate woman has to utter to herself in order to hold back the suicidal tides of her despair upon losing a man she has loved so wildly? A mother whose child was killed by a hit-and-run motorist or a young woman whose lover was killed in crossfire by inner-city drug gangs has to say such words – he has gone to a better place – and believe them if she can in order to hold back her despair, to hold back from putting an end to her life, unable to live without this love. 'Alas, unhappy and wretched am I!' Catherine writes. 'I who have remained on earth do so with very great regret. It seems to me that the first stone [of my tomb] has been laid.'

In reality, the passion of Catherine and of Niccolo was a passion of one night only, doomed, without a future from the start. Niccolo Toldo is a nobleman from Perugia and Catherine is illiterate – she did not write her letter but dictated it. It was only after he had been condemned to be executed that Catherine, who had only been able to catch glimpses of him from afar, had been able to get close to him. She managed to get herself admitted to his prison cell that night, was able to hold his head against her breast, felt a great joy and smelled his blood mingling with her own. Nothing in her past, as a woman devoted to religious works, led to this encounter or justified it. Only the imminence of the executioner's axe made it possible. They had but a few hours together, hours without a future, hours that make it now impossible for her to live, to remain on this earth with anything but an immense, desolate, desolating regret. When the death sentence was pronounced, Niccolo abruptly found himself disconnected from all his past, wealth, noble ancestry and frivolous youthful pleasures. Up against the breast and pounding heart and blood of Catherine, he found himself separated from his words and acts of youthful, aristocratic rebelliousness and blasphemy. They faded away, vanished; he no longer felt any claim from them or commitment to reinstate them, to be true to them, to identify himself and the hours remaining to him with them. Life was reduced to these hours – hours without a past or a future; hours that surged in this strange, ethereal, unearthly buoyancy and lightness.

She nowise speaks of a final, eternal deliverance from this passion, this outpouring of blood, this fire. She nowise speaks to her confessor of Niccolo delivered now from the blood flowing from his severed head, his neck, his trunk; she nowise speaks of him healed now, his body whole once again and for eternity in the presence of the transcendent Godhead; instead she speaks of Niccolo's decapitated body lodged in the still open, still bleeding wound of the God-man.

Wildly, as the axe falls, her hands seize the head of Niccolo and push it again against her breast, its blood pouring upon her hands, her clothing, drenching her breast. She feels her heart bursting to pour forth her blood into his. She feels herself entombed under the stone laid over Niccolo's grave. Now, days, weeks later, she cannot endure the idea of cleansing his blood from her hands, clothing and breast. She sees and smells his blood pouring from on high, all her identity drowning in the coursing of this blood. She sees Niccolo bleeding on her arms and breast, unendingly bleeding, bleeding in the cosmic bleeding of the wound of the God-man. Niccolo is now the God-man whose blood is streaming from the firmament.

Exultant and wild, she writes to her confessor:

> Most beloved and dearest Father and my dear Son ... I Catherine ... write to you, commending myself to you ... with desire to see you inflamed and drowned in this very sweet blood, which is churning with the fire of his most ardent charity. This is what my soul longs for: to see you in this blood.

To her confessor – and to us – Catherine writes

> Because my soul will be filled with happiness to see you drowned thus, I wish you do as does he who draws water with a bucket and pours it over something else: that you pour the water of holy desire on the head of your brothers...

Part 3
Death and testimony

9

Execution and fiction

ALLAN STOEKL

Hugo Adam Bedau, a noted authority on the death penalty, has observed the return of the popularity of this most extreme form of punishment; for him, this signals a new instance of 'American populism'.[1] Whereas in the 1960s there seemed to be a general turning away from this harshest penalty, today, Bedau notes, more and more survivors and kin of victims are calling, in the harshest possible terms, for its imposition. Opinion polls in California, for example, show that 80 per cent of voters are in favour of its reinstatement;[2] indeed one of the major gaffes of Michael Dukakis in the 1988 election was his failure to affirm strongly the necessity of execution.[3] And this desire for vengeance, along with the emotions that have made possible the revival of the death penalty in the 1980s and 1990s, is, according to Bedau, 'regularly reported in the press and on television, and ... bit by bit these behaviors and attitudes are increasingly portrayed by the media (intentionally or not) as the appropriate ones for survivors'.[4]

What is behind this apparent bloodthirstiness, this sudden desire for retribution, if not revenge? Bedau, a veteran of the anti-death penalty crusade of the late 1960s, seems somewhat bemused by it all; on the one hand he is surprised, given the sheer numbers of survivors of violent crime, that more people are not howling for state sponsored killing;[5] but, on the other, he wistfully and rather inexplicably awaits the subsidence of these raw emotions, noting that, if the lust for execution of the 1930s passed and was replaced by the mildness of the 1960s, in thirty years' time, today's thirst for blood could well be replaced by a new compassion.[6]

Clearly we have arrived at a decisive moment in the history of execution when a – perhaps the – leading expert on the question finds himself unable to account for the mechanisms of the tenacity of its appeal. He, like so many others, had expected its seductiveness to wither in the face of an irrefutable logic: as society becomes more civilized and as it progresses, the harshness of its penalties fades.[7] For the death penalty to prove so resistant, there are two possible corollaries, both of which could very well drive to despair anyone who thinks (or once thought) that the death penalty will be eliminated, forever, with one stroke of the pen: first, society is not progressing – indeed, there may be no necessary larger social progression (even if the death penalty once again loses its popularity, that phase could very well be followed by another, harsher one); and, second, people are inherently unkind and vengeful (hence the ambiguity of the word 'populism' in Bedau's title, with all it implies of irrational and dangerous collective emotions unleashed through the democratic process).

Perhaps to understand the undying appeal of execution we need to go beyond naive optimism and quick fatalism. What *is* execution's appeal? Is it merely the desire to get back at the one who has caused the pain and the irreparable damage? But what is this desire, where does it come from, what is its logic? Can it ever be satisfied? If not, why not? Why do people think it *can* be satisfied? How could they ever be convinced that it cannot be?

First, we should note that the new popularity of execution goes hand in hand with the 'victim's rights movement'. This movement, or attitude, is not one that in itself is inherently narrow-minded, regressive or reactionary. Writers, such as Williamson M. Evers,[8] who have argued for the need to consider the rights of victims in the legal process, have noted a glaring omission in the legal process, especially in the United States, as it has developed in modern times. According to Evers, criminal justice from earliest times has been concerned with restitution – that is, the return to the victim of what has been taken. He cites the Bible (Numbers 5:6–7) as an example of an early model that mandates reparation.[9] But already in the Middle Ages 'feudal barons and medieval ecclesiastical powers', out of sheer greed, and to reinforce their own power, started demanding recompense from the wrongdoer;[10] in other words, the criminal act came to be seen as directed against feudal, and then state, power and not against the victim as an individual. The victim, if anything, was the property of the state or the king; he or she was nothing more than a tiny part of the king's body. Recompense was thus due to civil government first and to the victim, if at all, only thereafter. Today, according to Evers, we see the consequences: the victim is an invisible party at the trial of his assailant, often not even allowed to testify: 'The US criminal justice system currently pits the criminal against the government and leaves the victim on the sidelines'.[11] After all the pain of the crime and the trauma of the trial the victim is left with nothing – perhaps a plea bargain is carried out behind closed doors, and the victim is not even informed of the fate of the criminal. The result of this sort of thing, of course, is the victims' anger, their well-known feeling that they have been doubly mistreated – first by the criminal, then by the justice system itself. Eventually, the victim, the victim's friends and relatives and finally the entire population will come to distrust and despise the courts, the police and the government.

Evers suggests as a solution the return to a model that holds victims' rights to be paramount; he argues for a 'punitive restitution' that will not only punish the criminal but also ensure that the victim is given substantial monetary recompense for his or her loss and suffering.[12] Needless to say, this presents many problems, since most criminals have little money and few skills with which to earn it. But Evers's proposal is nevertheless potentially satisfying because it would return *something*. All the words used in debates over punishment, and in this debate in particular, imply a *return*: *re*stitution, *re*compense, *re*tribution, *re*paration. In each case something comes back that was lost, either to the state or, in the best of worlds, the victim (restitution) or to the criminal (retribution). For Evers, restitution is retribution: the goods that are lost come back to the victim, and the evil that is emitted by the criminal comes back to him or her as well. In fact there will be a kind of exchange (or chiasmus) of returns: victims will get back what has been lost and criminals will get back, at least on a metaphorical level, what they have administered. The victim's possessions, or wellbeing, will be exchanged in the act of judgment for the criminal's misery.

All this works very nicely, at least on a theoretical level, when one considers crimes such as burglary, extortion, perhaps even assault. There something *can* be returned. Evers's model means that the judgment can be more than a hollow, failed speech act: finding the criminal guilty actually means that something will happen in the world, something tangible from which the victim can benefit. For the failure indicated by Evers is the failure of language to *do* something, at least from the point of view of the victim and eventually that of the larger public as well. Perhaps the criminal is in jail, perhaps he or she is out – who knows? The sentence is an empty phrase, overheard in court, which effects nothing.

There is, then, nothing inherently sinister or retrograde in the recent emphasis on victims' rights. Just as one should be able to sue, say, the maker of a faulty product for damages and receive recompense for one's injury and losses, so too one should be able to get back, through criminal proceedings, what has been taken from one in the course of a crime. The convicted criminal is just as liable as someone who is negligent. But what happens when the crime is not theft or assault but murder? What will restitution mean in this case? How can the victim's family – for strictly speaking there is no victim, or no longer a victim – be recompensed? What will restitution mean, if the damages caused by the criminal are somehow to *return* to him or her? At this point a model that made perfect sense starts to seem sinister and primitive, at least to an observer like Bedau. For the only way for the violence of the crime to return to its author is through the death of the criminal; and the only recompense available to the victim's family is the satisfaction of watching the criminal die, since the criminal can hardly return to them the life that's been taken.[13] Restitution now becomes at best retribution, at worst revenge. Life cannot return, like money; it does not circulate as a purely abstract and quantifiable signifier. Paradoxically, it can only return as its reverse: violence and death, the witnessed spectacle of the death of the other. What can be exchanged – money, wealth – is now itself exchanged for what is least susceptible of exchange: life, death, terms that are not quantifiable, not even graspable in any conventional sense.[14]

Yet many victims' families do not perceive their desire to see or know of the execution of the murderer of their loved one as an act of revenge. Rather, for them it is a kind of restitution: what is given back, through the death of the perpetrator, is, in principle at least, their old life, or a life that resembles in some way their life as it was before the crime. David van Drehle, in his book *Among the Lowest of the Dead: The Culture of Death Row*, writes this of Wendy Nelson, the mother of a young victim:

> The death penalty was [Wendy's] solace, because it channeled her fury. One day she would get Mann [the murderer] out of her life forever, and it would be done in a lawful way. In her work with crime victims, she had met many people whose victimizers had received lesser sentences, and she saw what an ordeal it was to go year after year to parole hearings to plead with the State to keep a scourge behind bars. She would not have to endure that. The day would come when it would be all over.[15]

All over, of course, when the criminal is executed. So there is a sort of compensation, but it is not so much the return of a quantifiable element like money; it is, instead, the unquantifiable return of an absence: the lack of the presence of the criminal. It is not even the restitution of a former pre-crime life; that is gone forever. It is just an ending. Wendy Nelson tells van Drehle: 'The bottom line [is that] if they're dead, they can't commit more crimes. I want a finality. I'm tired of hearings and court proceedings. I want him out of my life, and I really see only one way to do that'.[16]

Note that Nelson starts her remark by arguing, at least implicitly, that the death of the murderer has a positive result: no more crimes. But very quickly she shifts to the essential: he will be not only out of society, even out of prison society, but, more important, out of her life. The endless complications, the trauma and fear will be over.

There is a certain paradox in this demand for 'finality', or – an equivalent buzzword – 'closure'. The demand now is not for anything at all: it is for an end, an absence. One receives in compensation from the criminal, when he or she dies, nothing, or a nothing that is something in that it ends a traumatic history. It gives, in other words, an order to a series of events that otherwise is not only meaningless but horrifying. Wendy Nelson's young daughter has been murdered, senselessly; now her death takes on a certain meaning by virtue of being placed within a story with a beginning, middle and end. It is still a senseless death, to be sure, but it nevertheless takes on a kind of ghostly sense because it is an element in a larger story, or plot: one of a criminal who got his due. 'Hearings and court proceedings' are just another term for all the uncontrollable and aimless events that cluster around the crime. Now, with the execution of the perpetrator, they too take on meaning within a story.

It would seem, then, that the compensation the family of a murder victim receives is not so much monetary as it is narrative. The 'nothing' they get in return for the loss they have suffered – the death of another – is necessary because it gives meaning and coherence. 'Closure' is narrative satisfaction. But it is a very unusual kind of satisfaction, since, unlike the action of a novel or fiction film, it depends on an actual murder, a very real loss for which, as I've noted, there is no compensation. What would have been pleasure at the end of the end of the story in the case of the victim's family is a non-pleasure, the simple removal of affect. In principle at least, it is not positive; it is simply absence – of pain, of confusion. Retribution is not vengeance. But the structure on which this absence depends is the same kind of structure that normally gives us pleasure when we read a novel or see a film: the satisfaction of the *dénouement*. The same structure now instead produces a zero-degree of satisfaction: the victim's family is not satisfied, content when the criminal dies; nor is it unsatisfied. The victim's family would certainly not want to be associated with the crowing hooligans standing before the doors of the prison, cheering when the death of the criminal is announced. And we cannot speak of catharsis in an Aristotelian sense here: there is no moment of the purging of emotions through identification. No one is, after all, identified with – least of all the criminal; there is no king or sacrificial figure who takes on the violence of the world in order to expiate it, to cast it out.[17]

If the catharsis model involves a movement towards renewed health, the model of execution entails only a void: death, which produces a retrospective ordering and meaning, but which in itself is empty and projects nothing into the future. The victims of a robbery can actually do something with the money they receive in compensation; the family of the murder victim 'receives' nothing that leads outside itself, not even a pleasure to be remembered.

This, as I have said, would seem to be, and would have to be, the characterization of the 'victim's rights' in the model of execution put forward by its proponents. There is no satisfaction – at best there is only what is often characterized as 'grim satisfaction', a satisfaction that is the absence of conventional satisfaction, and that can be defined by negatives: it is not pleasure, not contentment, certainly not happiness. If, after all, the victim's family were satisfied in the conventional sense, content with the end of the story, there would be a certain valorization of the crime that initiated the sequence of events leading to the execution. Such a thing must, however, be unthinkable. 'Grim satisfaction' is therefore an oxymoron, which can have meaning only in the context of capital punishment and in related cases of retribution. (No doubt many Americans felt 'grim satisfaction' when, in 1945, they learned of the bombing of Hiroshima.) Something of this kind of satisfaction can be seen in the remarks of the parents of the murdered Faith Harvey, immediately after the execution of her killer, Robert Willie (as recounted in the celebrated book by Sr Hélène Préjean, *Dead Man Walking*):

> Vernon says he wishes every victim could have the opportunity he had tonight. Lizabeth says that since Robert Willie saw Faith die, her parents should see him die ... Vernon says he feels it was too easy and quick for Willie [because] 'he didn't suffer no pain, and my daughter had to'.[18]

Vernon and Lizabeth want exact retribution, and this alone will end the story of their daughter's murder; they want their 'rage satisfied', as Sr Préjean puts it.[19] Satisfaction is the end, but it also embodies a pleasure that dare not speak its name: this desire to see Willie not just die but die exactly, or as closely as possible, the death of their daughter, marks Vernon's and Lizabeth's satisfaction with a certain guilty pleasure. For the end entails an exchange of roles: now Faith's parents will be the witnesses to Willie's death, thereby doubling Willie's witnessing of Faith's. In other words, the satisfaction of the end which they demand will reproduce the killer's pleasure in witnessing – but only in order, at least theoretically, to extirpate that pleasure. After Willie's death, the story will be over, the emotions will be quieted, if not purged, the tension and horror will be replaced by calm. Or so they hope.

Now we shall consider further the question of plot. If the families of murder victims are seeking an end, they are, as I have argued, trying to create a coherent story out of the disparate events through which they have lived. They want narrative satisfaction, the satisfaction of plot. This story will provide, at least in principle, 'closure' – and 'closure', in turn, will generate the story, since any coherent story must end and must derive its larger meaning from that end. The end, in other words, will retrospectively order, and give meaning to, all that comes before it. But what is the nature of this ending? How definitive is it? In other words, can capital punishment really provide an ending when it is considered from the perspective that really counts – that of the story? Or, put another way, since execution is a function of storytelling, can the ending it provides be definitive, given the nature of narrative ending in general? If it cannot be definitive, what does this tell us about the practice of execution?

When we consider the relaxation longed for by the Harveys – the lessening of tensions resulting from an awareness of the execution of the murderer of their daughter – we inevitably think of Sigmund Freud's *Beyond the Pleasure Principle*. In that work, according to Freud, an instinct is

> *an urge inherent in organic life to restore an earlier state of things* which the living entity has been obliged to abandon under the pressure of external disturbing forces; that is, it is a kind of organic elasticity, or, to put it another way, the expression of the inertia inherent in organic life.[20]

The pleasure principle and the death drive, at first seemingly opposed, are seen, finally, to be very closely related if not identical; both are movements whereby the organism seeks to move from a state of greater complication, greater internal force, to a lesser one. But not just any relaxation will do: for the 'earlier state' to be returned to, a well defined series of movements and actions are necessary. Freud, writing of the 'instincts of self-preservation', states:

> They are component instincts whose function it is to assure that the organism shall follow its own path to death, and to ward off any possible ways of returning to inorganic existence other than those which are immanent in the organism itself ... What we are left with is the fact that the organism wishes to die only in its own fashion.[21]

The pleasure principle, as it is tied to sexual release and reproduction, goes to postpone death – but in a sense it already presupposes death (through the necessity of reproduction) and therefore points the way, so to speak, to the death of the individual. But the desire for pleasure, for the 'little death', is also a way of postponing death; we live, as Georges Bataille once wrote, mainly for the 'violent pleasure of coitus',[22] but in order to experience that pleasure we must live, not die. So our entire life is a movement towards death, but through a series of crucial detours; we resist as strongly as we can simple death. Unless there is something profoundly wrong, we fight as hard as we can against the killer who would throw us off a cliff. And yet the end of the story, the end which will give our lives meaning, the end to which our instincts and pleasures are tied ('the organism wishes to die only in its own fashion'), is, inevitably, death.

What is, after all, the difference between a meaningful and a meaningless (or 'senseless') death? The meaningful death will be arrived at through the correct set of detours and complications, the appropriate collection of pleasures and satisfactions – what we call 'life'. The anger of the victim's family comes from the awareness that this movement has been violated; the drama of trial and execution is therefore often seen as a way of restoring meaning to death by joining to the interrupted story another, finalizing one. But at this point life becomes not so much a question of organic survival – for, as we know, that can never be returned – but rather one of plots, stories: in a sense the interrupted life is a story that can be completed only through a kind of link with another, prosthetic, one.

Peter Brooks, in his book *Reading for the Plot*, makes the point that Freud's theory is as much about plots and story-telling as it is about 'organic instincts'.[23] Brooks displaces Freud somewhat by situating the pleasure principle and the death drive not in the realm of some organic system hard-wired in the body, but rather in the logic of plot; in this way the instincts are a function of plot, and not vice versa. In the same way too, reading – and enjoying – a story becomes a model for human existence itself. The detours and complications of a story are the same as the movement outlined by Freud in which the organism seeks death 'in its own way': the satisfaction and the pleasure of the story only come about through the postponement of the end in the tensions and lesser pleasures of the plot. Brooks, writing of the movement of the plot, states that there is

> a delay, a postponement in the discharge of energy, a turning back from immediate pleasure, to ensure that the ultimate pleasurable discharge will be more complete. The most effective or, at the least, the most challenging texts may be those that are most delayed, most highly bound, most painful'.[24]

Tough love, in other words. The final pleasure of the plot, of the consumption of the text, is inseparable from the agonies of delay. Brooks's metaphors are clear enough: the act of reading is a kind of sexual play in which delay, foreplay and sustained arousal are necessary for a truly pleasurable end. The metaphorics of the end – the end as meaning – is possible only through a string of metonymic connections and postponements. Brooks in fact writes of the 'middle as detour, as struggle toward the end under the compulsion of imposed delay, an arabesque in the dilatory space of the text'.[25] The twists and turns of the plot are 'repetitions serving to bind the energy of the text so as to make its final discharge more effective'.[26] There is, at least for Brooks, clearly something kinky in all this: the act of reading, of following the ins and outs of a plot, is a sweet torture that involves the 'hard labour' of desire and interpretation.

We think, inevitably, of the 'final discharge' of the Harveys, watching the execution of Robert Willie – their satisfaction, their grimness, their pain. But where is the pleasure in their witnessing? We think of the double meaning of execution: killing someone in a legal fashion and completing a task, a work, reaching an end.[27]

But these two varieties of execution both seem somewhat removed from the Nietzschean and even Sadian pleasure that Brooks would find in the elaboration and interpretation of the plot. We could even say that, for the victim's family, the plot of crime and execution works in exactly the opposite way from that sketched out by Brooks, via Freud. For the Freud–Brooks model implies a retrospective and anticipatory pleasure: without the teasing suffering of delay the silence and/or death of the end is nothing. With it the end is the supreme pleasure. In the model of execution the reverse is the case: the victim's family wants the death of the guilty one precisely so that the 'middle,' the detour of the complications of the plot, can be evacuated. The pleasure, such as it is, comes from termination, execution, not from detours. To argue otherwise is to hold that somehow the Harveys *wanted* the death of their daughter, indeed revelled in the delays and postponements of Willie's case.

But there is more at stake than pleasure. If the pleasure of the plot is tied to the uncertainty and willingly affirmed constraint of narrative repetition (the twists of plot that seem to double back on themselves before ending), then the 'grim satisfaction' of victims' families is necessarily without pleasure, since all uncertainty, all delightful delay and delicious surprise, is necessarily eliminated from the plot of apprehension, trial and execution (and, hopefully, the witnessing of said execution). If plot in literature involves hypothesis, hesitation, speculation and many provisional versions that are repeated (and subverted) in the final end, plot in execution requires certainty, righteousness and immediacy – the quickest movement possible between beginning (the murder of the victim) and end (the execution of the victimizer). And if the plot of a text – 'literary' or otherwise – involves a certain ambiguity concerning who or what actually ends – does the story end? Does the pleasure of the reader end? Is the end of the experience of the reader – of the act of reading – necessarily tied to the end of the story *per se*? The end of execution is quite clear: the criminal dies, ends in the most definitive way, while the victim's family lives on, fully compensated, sated in their compensation but certainly not enjoying it – God, no – not satisfied in the usual sense of the word.

For the proponents of 'victim's rights', the end cannot be ambiguous; an exchange must take place, death for death, and with the second death, that of the criminal, the story will end – for good. And presumably, on a larger scale, the very existence of the death penalty will serve as an example and will 'deter' others from committing the crime of murder. Execution, in other words, will end, will execute, murder itself. It may not do so completely (we do not live in a utopia), but in the best of all possible words we would see the decline in the number of murders, an asymptote leading to zero, as a consequence of the imposition of death. In principle, execution stops murder and therefore abolishes itself: execution executes execution. It is pure end, without the typical narrative satisfactions of ending.

If, however, we see the execution drive as a fundamental need to end a story, then, following the model sketched by Brooks, we note some difficulties in what might be called the certainty of execution – that is, in the version of execution that would see it as an acceptable response to a societal problem, murder. Certainty means that execution itself does what it is supposed to do (end crime, end itself) and, thus, that the meaning of execution is simple. The victim's family is the victim's family; the guilty one is the guilty one; society is right in executing the guilty; and the exchange of death for death between two clearly demarcated parties does indeed take place. Here, though, we start to see the problems involved in this model. Are the two parties so clearly separable? Who, or what, in effect, dies in a story? Brooks's model of erotic discharge as story-telling (and ending) seems to propose death as the realm of the consumer of the story. Reliving the story, reading it, we anticipate our own deaths: we vicariously partake of life not only of the characters of the story but of the life of the story itself. We are stimulated by it, we are its detours, its moments of procrastination: its climax is the excitement that we ourselves lend it and receive from it. Without us, without our participation, the story is nothing but sound-waves, or blots of ink on paper. The death – the end – of the story is our death.

Yet in the story of execution the death is not ours but solely that of the guilty one. Our grim satisfaction in witnessing his or her death comes from the fact that we are not the condemned;

indeed we are the recipients of an exchange, where the death we suffered (through the death of our loved one) is 'paid back' to the one who committed the crime. The payment we receive is only the movement by which death is sent back to its author. We get back only the end, without real pleasure, without the cathartic purge offered by satisfying sex or great drama.

Someone might respond that there are two kinds of death at stake here: 'real' death, the physical death of the condemned, and the 'little death' of the story-teller, the story consumer, the victim's family. But this in itself signals a significant change from the model of story-telling proposed by Brooks. Once again we have a change in the model: death is separated from itself, so to speak, and now the significance, the real meaning of the story, is not in our (the reader's) 'little death' but in the death of the other, of the prisoner. There are now two deaths: one definitive, the other play, simulation, a provisional enactment – the death of the other and the death of the self.

This radical distinction is nevertheless clouded by the fact that some identification between victim's family and the condemned must still take place for there to be execution. For any exchange to be possible there must be some identification between the two parties. (Vernon Harvey, for example, wants to see what the killer saw.) If there were no fundamental similarity, if there were not two parties in an exchange, the transfer of death could not take place. And yet the accomplishment of that transfer assures the family that the murderer is indeed different: he is ejected from existence through the exchange. He is or will be dead and, therefore, not a party in an exchange.

So on the one hand we have play, the provisional identity between two radically opposed parties; this play, this ambiguity, makes possible definitive dissimilarity, which is death. One does not execute, for example, a pit bull terrier that has caused the death of a child; it is instead put to sleep and destroyed. One executes a person who murders a child. The difference is that the murderer is human like us; the dog is not. Part of our horror before a serial killer lies in our identification with him or her: if only for a moment, we can see ourselves as that person, we can provisionally assign ourselves that status. In our imagination, we can play at being the killer. (This identification, of course, serves as the basis for much of what we call 'literature', from *Œdipus Rex* to *Pulp Fiction*.) But at the same time, we should recall that there is no room for play or simulation in execution: execution is for real. That is precisely its appeal.

Here we might turn to the classic work by Frank Kermode, *The Sense of an Ending*. Kermode distinguishes between provisional endings, which are those of what he calls fiction and definitive ones, which are associated with myth. Fictional endings give us pleasure, and they enable us to think about different versions or models of experience: we can try them on, so to speak, knowing that they can just as easily be taken off and discarded. We identify with them, but only through supposition, play, simulation. Mythical ends are the ends of ritual and religion: we accept them as the truth, and that is it. Kermode writes:

> Myth operates within the diagrams of ritual, which presupposes total and adequate explanations of things as they are and were; it is a sequence of radically unchangeable gestures. Fictions are for finding things out, and they change as the needs of sense-making change. Myths are the agents of stability, fictions are the agents of change. Myths call for absolute, fictions for conditional assent.[28]

Kermode mentions the Nazis as an example of individuals who, out of purely cynical motives, elevate to the status of myth a fiction about which they themselves are sceptical or indifferent.

The tension in the death penalty is the pull exerted between fictional and mythical ends. On the side of fiction, we have the fundamental ambiguity between victim's family and victimizer – the fact that the family of the victim wants an end to a story means that, like it or not, it will end up accepting all the ambiguities inherent in story-telling; the fact that narrative pleasure is inherently fluid, that even the grimmest narrative can lead, through its end, to satisfaction, even *jouissance*, on the part of the reader (or consumer); and the fact too that death itself is a function of identification, of role reversal – that death can shift places between story and reader, victim and victimizer, thereby putting in question the absolute quality of any distinction between terms such as these. And no matter how certain the victim's family might be, it can never fully withdraw its provisional identification with the murderer, if only because doing so would mean losing all interest in seeing the murderer executed. The murderer can only become non-human – dead – if he or she is in some fundamental sense like us, human. A complicity, then, is inherent in the provisional status of identification: we too take pleasure from the event (just as we imagine the murderer taking pleasure from the crime); we too see ourselves as the killer, as the executed, as the dead. That is the only way the story of crime and retribution can mean anything for us. The death of execution is therefore a free-floating term, undermining our monosemic grief, our hatred and pain, our distance from – and our straightforward exchange of death with – the condemned. At any moment hatred can become desire, grief pleasure, distance intimacy or even identity. The end as simple end can become the rush of catharsis.

On the other hand capital punishment retains elements of what Kermode calls the mythic. It means only one thing: retribution – your death for mine, or that of my relatives. There is no ambiguity: the murderer does not get away with his crime, growing fat in prison. He or (rarely) she pays the full price. Nothing could be less fictional. There is one meaning only: you die. Finally – thinks the family of the victim – something is happening beyond mere words, mere appeals and delays. Death (as Hegel would say), is the absolute lord and master.

Execution, at least as it is carried out today, would seem to involve a confusion between fictional and mythical ending. We would all like a mythical ending to a crime – to all crime – and death seems to provide this: for what is less fictional than death? What is more real? But the provisional identification and play of story-telling – not just what is represented *in* the story but the roles of reader and story as well as the shifting pleasures of reading – would seem to preclude any certainty concerning death: who exactly it is that dies, the meaning of that death, the grim satisfaction that is a function of that death.

Execution does not necessarily *close* a story but rather opens it out to endless permutations. The story whose basis lies in fiction, but which is taken to be mythical (to use, again, Kermode's terms), will find itself caught in an indefinite effort to end, using the only device at its disposal: the most definitive, the most mythical, death. But death will prove the most slippery, the most ambiguous; to end definitively with execution – to execute – will also be to generate more death, more stories. We can find an instance of this in the section on capital punishment in *On Crimes and Punishments*, the work of the great eighteenth-century reformer Cesare Beccaria. I want to consider Beccaria's position on capital punishment not so much as a founding moment in the tradition of arguments against it (which of course it is) but rather as a demonstration, if you will, of the impossibility of using execution, of putting it to work to end a story in a satisfactory manner.

The problem with capital punishment, from Beccaria's perspective, is that it does not make enough of an impression. Life in prison is the punishment that keeps on giving, so to speak; the crime is avenged indefinitely, so that from one lowly criminal one can derive a lifetime of moral lessons. The observer will tend to forget an execution and the crime that led up to it; the continued presence of the perpetrator, however, and the harshness of a lifetime of suffering ('even more cruel that death', according to Beccaria) guarantee that its lesson will not be forgotten and that it will even 'inspir[e] terror in the spectator more than in the sufferer'.[29] Indeed the death penalty would seem to furnish a quick end to the punishment; death as end therefore contradicts the most basic premise of punishment, which is that it is a function of time. Only temporalized punishment – life in prison in the most extreme case – allows an end to become a story, the terrifying and edifying narrative of suffering undergone by the criminal. Punishment becomes inseparable from education. And education will stop the cycle of violence, thereby truly effecting an exchange between the victim's family and the criminal (the criminal will be eliminated, through punishment as education, not as a person but as a species). Beccaria writes:

> Our spirit resists violence and extreme but momentary pains more easily than it does time and incessant weariness, for it can, so to speak, collect itself for a moment to repel the first, but the vigor of its elasticity does not suffice to resist the long and repeated action of the second.[30]

Death as end in itself is eminently forgettable; lifelong suffering, on the other hand, is remembered for a lifetime. Lesson and punishment are therefore analogous in their temporality, or lack of temporality. As simple death, execution cannot lead outside itself and is therefore not so much satisfying or definitive as it is simply worthless for any spectator.

A dissonant note in Beccaria's essay emerges when he quotes an imaginary miscreant contemplating the death penalty. In this passage, Beccaria seems to justify, for a moment, crime on the part of the poor. Writing from the viewpoint of the criminal, he states:

> What are these laws that I am supposed to respect, that place such a great distance between me and the rich man? He refuses me the penny I ask of him, and, as an excuse, tells me to sweat at work that he knows nothing about. Who made these laws? ... Let me break these bonds, fatal to the majority and only useful to a few indolent tyrants; let us attack the injustice at its source. I will return to my natural state of independence; I shall at least for a little time live free and happy with the fruits of my courage and industry. The day will perhaps come for my sorrow and repentance, but it will be brief, and for a single day of suffering I shall have many years of liberty and pleasures. As king over a few, I will correct the mistakes of fortune and will see these tyrants grow pale and tremble.[31]

Beccaria creates this entirely sympathetic criminal persona only to demonstrate that the best way to foil him (or her) is to eliminate capital punishment. Execution generates, it seems, the phantasm, on the part of the criminal, of the righting of profound social wrongs: one is not afraid of an eminently justifiable criminal career if the only punishment is death. Death is but a moment – a nothing – that justifies, that generates, a whole lifetime of crime.

The strange ambivalence of Beccaria on punishment – here he seems to argue for the maximum cruelty of imprisonment, elsewhere he affirms its humanity as opposed to the 'barbarity' of execution[32] – is mirrored by his simultaneous justification and condemnation of crime. We sympathize with it, and yet (evidently) we want to see it repressed. Death itself is thus doubly coded: if we wish to see crime punished we will oppose death, but if we identify with the criminal – and Beccaria's rhetoric here gives us every reason to do so – then we will actually favour it! But in that case what exactly will we be affirming? Here we see the strange status of death not as the simple end but as the very generating principle of stories. Beccaria's imagined criminal – so articulate and certain – can only produce the story of his life out of the 'finality' of death. Knowing that a quick death is certain creates the freedom to commit any crime. Life is posthumous: the criminal is already dead, death is assumed and affirmed. Death is the opening-out of the possibility of a life story – indeed, such a story would seem the only one worth living. In fact that story – retribution (revenge against the rich) – is the very paradigm of punishment itself. The most effective fiction of retribution, and thus punishment, is the after-effect of the imposition of the death penalty. That penalty, in other words, does not end the story of the criminal but rather makes criminality as fiction possible, if the criminal is seen as one bent on revenge, on settling scores and on ending the story of the other (the rich person). The criminal, operating under the sign of death, will be free to improvise ever more outrageous stratagems, to create even more illicit meanings. Conversely, the degradation of life imprisonment is the real 'end' because it incessantly affirms a continuing life as ended: life is much more of an end than death; the endlessness of the end is more an end than the end.

Interestingly enough, death also makes a kind of Rousseauistic natural state possible. Beccaria's imaginary criminal says: 'I will return to my natural state of independence.' Death, with its always-already status, in other words, makes possible a return to a prelapsarian fiction of plenitude.

The larger problem in all this would seem to be indicated here by the slipperiness of Beccaria's identification with the criminal. If the death penalty is to be an example, not only does it not end anything, it seems to open an infinity of possible interpretations, of lives. At the most profound level, as we see with Beccaria's hoodlum, the death penalty is simple mortality itself, a kind of universal negation that hangs over everything, cancels everything and therefore grants a complete freedom to each individual to generate anything and everything – the freedom, in effect, to write one's own life story. Execution becomes a revelation not of the death of (a) man or woman but of the death of God: from here on all is permitted, starting, of course, with retribution: the rich will be punished, perhaps even put to death. And so the logic continues to circulate: there will always be more retribution, more exchange of death: this exchange will be called life.

How ironic it is, then, that execution traditionally has been seen as uniquely grave, uniquely terrifying – bearing, in other words, a single meaning rather than releasing a burst of provisional, open-ended meanings. In the case of Beccaria, we see the death penalty generating more criminality – generating the criminal, so to speak. Rather than ending anything, the 'end' – the mythical end which is finally a fictional end – always generates, as do fictional ends in general, *more*.[33] More stories, more ends.

If for Beccaria the death penalty generates always more life as criminality – instead of eliminating it – for Jean Genet it produces more life as victimhood. Again, in the logic of the 'myth' of execution, we could assume that execution would end not only the criminal but the victim as well: after the guilty one has been executed, after the violence has been exchanged, the victim's family ceases to exist. It is not that they die – on the contrary – but rather that once death has been returned, they are no longer victims. A unique brand of restitution has taken place, and, in principle at least, they have returned to what they were. 'Closure' has been attained. Beccaria shatters this logic, however, by showing how the imposition of execution generates always more life as crime, more victims and hence more execution.

Now in Genet something else takes place. Beccaria largely ignores the victim; he is concerned instead with how the capital crime itself is produced through execution. Genet shows us, instead, the victim, who, in this author's personal mythology, is always a petty criminal – not one worthy of being executed. But much of Genet's fiction is characterized by a cult of execution, in which the highest, noblest and sexiest beings are those slated for execution, or already executed. It is in this relation between the condemned (and/or executed criminal) and the petty criminal who is his worshipper and victim, that we see a new and more powerful version of execution's power to generate itself.

Genet's first novel, *Our Lady of the Flowers*,[34] opens with a dedication to Maurice Pilorge, a man executed, we are told (in 'L'homme condamné à mort') at the age of twenty, for the murder of his (male) lover.[35] The opening paragraph of the novel describes a newspaper photograph of the murderer Weidmann, his head swathed in bandages, taken after his arrest. Indeed this photograph was a kind of icon for Genet.[36] Clearly the executed murderer becomes a sacred figure: 'Beneath his picture burst the dawn of his crimes: murder one, murder two, murder three, up to six, bespeaking his secret glory and preparing his future glory'.[37]

What is the nature of this glory? Clearly it involves haunting 'mirthless bourgeois', who will perhaps be terrified in their sleep by Weidmann and his ilk. The narrator of the novel – whom I will call 'Genet' – decorates the walls of his cell with a number of photographs of (preferably executed) killers like Weidmann: he cuts those 'vacant-eyed heads out of magazines'.[38] This vacancy or emptiness seems to be quite important, because it is profoundly related both to Genet's status as victim of these fantasy-men, and to his act of writing or confessing. He states:

> I say empty, but if they [the executed men] become more disturbing to me than are huge prisons to the nubile maiden who passes by the high barred windows, prisons behind which sleeps, dreams, swears, and spits a race of murderers, which makes of each cell the hissing nest of a tangle of snakes, but also a kind of confessional with a curtain of dusty serge.[39]

Whereas the narrator not so subtly compares himself to a 'nubile maiden', the fantasy prisoners – the already executed – are extremely dangerous, like the hair of Medusa. But, strangely, at the same time these vicious killers are like priests, in that their lair is a confessional.

There is a nexus here that links, on one side, murder, execution, petrifaction (the seeing of the snakes) and violation of the innocent and, on the other side, the confession (and desire for confession) by that innocent one of his (or 'her') sins – probably the very sin of desiring the killer and wanting to be violated. The confession, in turn, alone makes the violation possible, since the prisoner-victim is alone in his cell: his violation can only 'take place', through the act of telling his story by writing it down.

Surrounded by crumpled pictures torn from tattered magazines, the prisoner-narrator finds his pleasure in being violated by
the 'empty' gaze of the executed: they are his society.

> Smiles and sneers, alike inexorable, enter me by all the holes I
> offer, their vigor penetrates me and erects me. I live among
> these pits. They watch over my little routines, which, along with
> them, are all the family I have and my only friends.[40]

What is more, in a kind of terrifying reversal the narrator is possessed to such an extent that he ceases to exist – he becomes the
vacant murderers he gazes at, who gaze at him, and to whom he
writes. 'Entering me until there was no room left for myself, so
that now I am one with gangsters, burglars, and pimps, and the
police arrest me by mistake'.[41]

The executed and their spawn now *are* the victim; through his
writing, he becomes the vacancy of the absent and the dead. But
in their very vacancy the worst criminals are the most present:
not only are they the narrator, they are his writing, his story (he
can only write his story because there is no one to tell it to – there
are only the pictures). He is lost, brutally violated, in the snakepit
of his confession.

The (auto-)eroticism of this eclipse – which is also an infinite
self-aggrandizement – is inseparable from execution. Under his
sheets, on his filthy mat, he masturbates until his wrist is sore,[42]
but that gesture is also the one by which he, as imaginary rape
victim, becomes imaginary murderer, execution victim and finally
even executioner. He writes:

> I wanted to swallow myself by opening my mouth very wide and
> turning it over my head so that it would take in my whole body,
> and then the Universe, until all that would remain of me would
> be a ball of eaten thing which little by little would be annihilated
> [*s'anéantirait* – literally, would annihilate itself]: that is how I see
> the end of the world.[43]

The narrator/prisoner/victim now generates his own executioner;
the crime is his own murder, which he both commits and expi-
ates. He is his execution: all that remains is the severed head,
turned inside out, devouring itself, as a hole filling itself with
itself, and then decomposing, 'annihilating itself'. The self-severed

head – it does not even need a guillotine – rolls like a dead planet in a void, since its eatenness is also the end of the world. The perfect solipsism of the victim (his end is the end of everything) is also the omnipresence of execution, the plenitude of all that is not him: he is filled with himself, but that very filling is a severing, a self-separation and annihilation.

In Beccaria, we saw that the execution of the criminal generated only more crime, more execution. In Genet, something larger and more sinister, more troubling, is taking place. The death of the victim now generates not only more crime, more execution – in a circular, infinite repetition (of self-devouring) – but the universe as well. That self-devoured head/globe not only executes itself – it exists through that execution, since it is the rotting world, annihilating itself but in its very annihilation always again existing.

The victims live the end through their production of the executed. And they are eliminated through the omnipresence of the executed whom they create. The execution of the criminal generates not freedom for the victim – the freedom from the crime, which we see in the commonly held idea of execution as an exchange through which the death borne by the victim, or by his or her family, is taken on exclusively by the killer – but the violation and elimination/execution of the victim as well as the guilty. And the entire earth, the universe itself, is now the victim. The victim is always already guilty as a kind of transfer takes place – another exchange, going in the opposite direction from that which 'victim's rights' advocates might hope for – between criminal and victim (criminal as victim, victim as criminal), and this produces always more guilt, more guilty pleasure, more desire for guilt, in the victim, in the ex-victim, now criminal (and there can be no difference). Crime is the death of the victim, expiated through the death of the victim as criminal; expiation itself is an eroticized devouring that can only be more guilty, more forbidden, more liable to cause the repetition of execution. It in turn is confessed in a story that is this devouring and that can only repeat it, and end itself, indefinitely, as the end.

But what of the observer in all this? Genet's account collapses everything into a house of mirrors, in which one victim-criminal-executioner is reflected to infinity. No doubt this is a valid representation of one version of the execution story, of execution as story. But there is more, because there are always witnesses. The victim, or the victim's family, is always supplemented by the thousands who watch the head fall off, by the millions who read of it approvingly in the newspapers or who silently cheer on, in the security of their living rooms, staring at the television set, the pro-death protesters clamouring in front of a prison on the night of an electrocution.

What will the observer gain from this witnessing? Execution is in a sense carried out in order to be observed – even when it takes place behind closed doors. It is done for the edification of the public; they will witness it at least in their own imaginations. They will each be a miniature Genet, carrying in themselves the image of the condemned man, the moment of his death, and, deriving from that, presumably, the one lesson to be had, the one pedagogically correct story.

In the case of Genet we go so far into his head that we end up with nothing more than an opaque, decomposing ball. But there is another way to go as well: in the direction of the multiplicity. Is it any less opaque? Can the story be ended in a more satisfying way, once and for all, in the heads of the multitude of observers?

Execution traditionally has been portrayed (by politicians, for example) as uniquely grave, uniquely terrifying – bearing, in other words, a single meaning rather than releasing a burst of possible, open-ended meanings. Paradoxically, however, this monosemic aspect of the story of legally imposed death is nevertheless tied to the perceptions of enormous numbers of observers – we are all, in a sense, witnesses to the executions that take place nearly every day. How can anyone expect to control the meaning of the stories told, and ended, in and through the moment of death? If it were only a question of the victim's family, we might imagine it – but the family is doubled, reflected to near-infinity, by all of society, which is aware of the carrying out of the death penalty. It is not just the end of the story of the death of the victim, accomplished through the death of the guilty one, carried out for the family: we are all, by proxy, members of that family, and the act is carried out for our benefit. But will we react the same way as (supposedly, at least) the victim's family?

The disparity between the illusory single (grave) meaning and the inevitably disappointing multiple meanings and stories of execution as it witnessed by others, is itself the topic of an account – a story, perhaps a fiction – by Ivan Turgenev, 'The Execution of Troppmann'.[44]

Turgenev's reportage, which dates from 1870, is the account of an observer witnessing the last hours of a condemned man, Troppmann, a 'moral monster',[45] sentenced to death for the slaughter of the Kink family.[46] Turgenev arrives at the Roquette prison with his Parisian friend, the noted photographer and social historian Maxime du Camp. From there he is introduced to the prison warden, M. Claude, and led to a room where he will wait for the procession to the guillotine. Troppmann is still sleeping; he is not to be awakened until 6.30 am; execution is set for 7.00 am.

While Troppmann and the other reporters and official witnesses are waiting in 'irksome and tedious – yes tedious – discomfort',[47] the unofficial witnesses – the crowd around the prison – is behaving quite differently.

> Up ahead, from behind the mass of the stirring, shoving crowd, one could hear exclamations like '*Ohé, Troppmann! Ohé Lambert! Fallait pas qu'y aille!*' There were shouts and shrill whistles. One could clearly make out a noisy argument going on someplace: a fragment of some cynical song came creeping along like a snake – and there was a sudden burst of loud laughter that was instantly taken up by the crowd, ending with a roar of coarse guffaws.[48]

Although the 'invited' witnesses in Turgenev's account are for the most part not named, they are individuals – bored, sleepy, feeling discomfort – who are there for a reason and who are reacting in a comprehensible way to the terrible events of the morning. The crowd, on the other hand, is strangely depersonalized; it is the mere conduit for vulgar noises and songs which alone have a discernible form – the cynical song 'moves like a snake'. 'Their shouting was elemental, that is, senseless'.[49] Turgenev cites the case of a young working man whose behaviour is completely incomprehensible:

he stood there grinning, with his eyes trained on the ground ...
then he would suddenly throw back his head, open his mouth
wide, and begin to shout in a drawn-out voice, without words ...
What was going on inside that man?[50]

The sound of the crowd is utterly inhuman: it resembles the distant roar of the sea.[51]

If the crowd has lost its human attributes, so too has Troppmann. But Troppmann, like his name, is somehow too human; he
is the very picture of health and composure. '[N]othing in him
disclosed – I won't say fear, but even agitation or anxiety.
We were all much paler and more agitated than he, I am sure'.[52]
Troppmann's perfect calmness – he neither faints nor 'brazens it
out' – indicates that somehow he has eluded all possible categories of human experience; at the very least he was not 'in his
right mind'.[53]

As Troppmann bends his head so that his hair may be shorn in
preparation for the guillotine blade, Turgenev 'cannot help asking
[him]self what that ever-so-obediently bent head [is] thinking
about'.[54] This indeed is the great problem: not only is Troppmann's head a mystery but so too are those of the spectators, the
vast majority of whom are not even in a position to see the execution. They are elemental, with the incomprehensible force of
natural forces, and hardly human.

The noise and spectacle of the crowd, the seemingly endless
struggle to clip Troppmann's hair, remove the collar of his shirt,
modify the leather straps that will bind his body (so that they can
hold someone of such a slight girth) – all of these delays, noises,
visions serve only to nauseate Turgenev and the other official and
semi-official witnesses. What is most striking, finally, is the utter
incongruity between the implied – but never completely presented – 'reason' for the execution, and its actual effect – on the
witnesses, and on the condemned man. Turgenev has this to say
about the condition of the journalists who accompanied Troppmann through the prison to the scaffold:

I felt very tired – and I was not the only one to feel like that.
... *[N]ot one of us, absolutely no one, looked like a man who*

realized that he had been present at the performance of an act of
social justice. Everyone tried to turn away in spirit and, as it
were, shake off the responsibility for this murder.[55]

The official reasons for this execution – to teach a lesson to the
crowd, to dispense social justice, to carry out retribution – are
beside the point. No one reacts as they are supposed to: the people in the crowd are transformed into zombies; Troppmann himself is demented yet splendidly healthy, almost a wild animal; the
authorities and intellectuals are disgusted and alienated, on the
verge of physical illness. The act that was to end in repentance
and retribution, in a solemn lesson and in the august certainty of
the authorities, lurches out of interpretive control. Rather than
ending anything, it only generates confusion, hooliganism and
intellectual dissension. What cannot be known – the crowd's
motives, Troppmann's motives – gives rise only to more speculation, endless speculation now, in fact, since execution does away
with the condemned man, leaving the field open not to systematic
study but to vulgar story-telling. In the end the fundamental inap-
propriateness of execution – its incongruity – generates of necessity one final text. Turgenev closes his account with these words:

> I will be content and excuse my misplaced curiosity [concerning
> the execution] if my account supplies a few arguments to those
> who are in favor of the abolition of capital punishment or, at
> least, the abolition of public execution.[56]

Once again we see demonstrated in the most dramatic way the
extent to which the truth of capital punishment, its myth in and as
unitary meaning, gives way to the multiplicity of fiction. For the
end of execution is not simple: it is certainly definitive, but exactly
to the extent that it is total, it is nothing – or, rather, it is the blank
screen on which is projected all the frustrations and desires of
those who witness it. In the case of Troppmann's death, the
authorities would authorize one meaning, and indeed they
depend on the emergence of that meaning; but sense is not universal, it is precisely not absolute, like death. People respond as
they will: they trivialize death – and trivialize, brutalize, themselves – or they are sickened as they realize the gap between the
definitive nature of the event and the inevitable (comparative)

triviality of the events and interpretations with which that death is confronted. Rather than the shocked silence of those who come to see affirmed somehow, in execution, the sacredness of life, the hooting crowd recognizes only the worthlessness of life and the universal dishonour of anyone who would question the honour of the authorities – i.e., themselves. If they are always already dishonoured – through their identification with the criminal, through their presence at such a disgusting spectacle – there will be no reason for them to refrain from crime; indeed the execution is their justification for a life of crime. The State that executes is just one more criminal. The impossibility of execution as myth opens the way for execution as fiction: uncontrolled, uncontrolling meaning that generates the very things execution would 'oppose': murder and more execution.

Execution, whose meaning should be absolute and incontrovertible, falls into place as just another fiction – a hypothetical model of events, with an end – but it is a fictional scenario that cannot be controlled, and it is never universal. In fact, as we see here, a call for the abolition of execution is one of the after-effects of the imposition of a seemingly all-silencing death. The residue of death is more crime, as well as (on the part of Turgenev, for example) questioning, further hypothesis and the re-attribution of dishonour to execution itself; it is not some grimly satisfying and edifying end. Instead, it is end as the indefinite repetition of endings. The unitary is inseparable from the return of an indefinite number of crimes, some legal, some illegal.

Execution is a variety of fiction, but it confuses definitive and provisional ending, just as the victim's family may confuse a certain *jouissance* with 'grim satisfaction'. This very confusion, and the bad faith it implies, serves as the impetus for ever more execution. One is never sure of the efficacy of execution; one doubts it; it can never be imposed often enough. Clearly if it were truly efficacious, if it really did deter, if it really did end the story with a return of death to the perpetrator's camp, it would only have to be carried out once. Death, being for good, the 'absolute lord and master', would have to be exchanged only once in history. But there is always a glimmer of doubt – Did he do it? Is it the correct penalty? Why? Maybe it's not – to which the answer is: Yes, by

God, and to show him he can't squirm out of it, we'll shoot him, gas him, inject him, etc. The continued imposition of death is a response to a radical doubt – Which end for the guilty is appropriate? What is enough punishment? Which end will really do it? – to which the answer is: enough is death – the simple end. Execution is a response to the confusion between provisional and definitive ends: it is a way of attempting to end that confusion, to silence it. It is the end of the debate about ending. But it can never end it, so it goes on, endlessly ending. Execution can end a life, but it cannot, obviously, end doubt, questioning or the repetitious guilty pleasures of the story. Fiction triumphs in and through myth.

Notes

1 H. A. Bedau, 'American Populism and the Death Penalty: Witnesses at an Execution', in *The Howard Journal of Criminal Justice*, 33:4, November 1994, 289–303.
2 'California Execution Nears, Stirring Debate on Issue', *New York Times*, 3 August 1997, p. 12.
3 As noted by Bedau in 'American Populism and the Death Penalty', p. 292.
4 Bedau, 'American Populism and the Death Penalty', p. 292.
5 *Ibid.*
6 Bedau, 'American Populism and the Death Penalty', p. 301.
7 This is the logic of Durkheim's work on punishment; see Emile Durkheim, 'The Evolution of Punishment', in *Durkheim and the Law*, ed. S. Lukes and A. Scull (Oxford: Basil Blackwell, 1983), pp. 102–32.
8 See W. M. Evers's position paper, *Victims' Rights, Restitution, and Retribution* (Oakland, CA: The Independent Institute, 1996).
9 Evers, *Victims' Rights, Restitution, and Retribution*, p. 6.
10 Evers, *Victims' Rights, Restitution, and Retribution*, p. 7.
11 Evers, *Victims' Rights, Restitution, and Retribution*, p. 2.
12 Evers, *Victims' Rights, Restitution, and Retribution*, p. 5.
13 In fact, a number of victim's rights groups are firmly committed to the death penalty. For them, executing the criminal amounts to affirming the rights of the victim. See, for example, the website 'Justice against Crime Talking' (http:users.deltanet.com/users/ghc).

14 Although recently, in the absence of a condemnation and suitable sentencing, victims' families have proved willing to accept monetary compensation, but more as a symbolic gesture than for any real recompense. Most notably, Ron Goldman's family was awarded a large monetary settlement from O. J. Simpson, who was found liable for Goldman's death. In this case, quite clearly, the very large sum, Simpson's entire net worth, was only a substitute for what the family really would have liked – life imprisonment or death. The family made it clear that they were interested in punishment, not money.

15 D. van Drehle, *Among the Lowest of the Dead: The Culture of Death Row* (New York: Times Books, 1995), p. 366.

16 van Drehle, *Among the Lowest of the Dead*, p. 370.

17 On the scapegoat, see above all René Girard; for example, *The Scapegoat*, trans. Y. Freccero (Baltimore: Johns Hopkins University Press, 1986).

18 Sr H. Préjean, *Dead Man Walking* (New York: Random House, 1993), p. 214.

19 Préjean, *Dead Man Walking*, p. 226.

20 S. Freud, *Beyond the Pleasure Principle*, trans. J. Strachey (New York: W. W. Norton, 1961), p. 30 (Freud's italics).

21 Freud, *Beyond the Pleasure Principle*, p. 33.

22 See G. Bataille, 'The Use Value of D. A. F. de Sade', in *Visions of Excess: Selected Writings, 1927–39*, ed. and trans. A. Stoekl (Minneapolis: University of Minnesota Press, 1985), p. 99.

23 P. Brooks, *Reading for the Plot: Design and Intention in Narrative* (New York: Vintage Books, 1984).

24 Brooks, *Reading for the Plot*, pp. 101–2.

25 Brooks, *Reading for the Plot*, pp. 107–8.

26 Brooks, *Reading for the Plot*, p. 108.

27 The Oxford English Dictionary, for example, notes that the word 'execution' indicates, along with the 'infliction of capital punishment', the 'effecting or carrying out (a prescribed or designated operation or movement); the production (or a work of art or skill); the vocal or instrumental rendering (of a musical composition), etc.'

28 F. Kermode, *The Sense of an Ending: Studies in the Theory of Fiction* (Oxford: Oxford University Press, 1967), p. 39.

29 C. Beccaria, *On Crimes and Punishments*, trans. H. Paolucci (Indianapolis: The Library of Liberal Arts, Bobbs-Merrill, 1963), p. 48.

30 *Ibid.*

31 Beccaria, *On Crimes and Punishments,* p. 49.

32 Beccaria, *On Crimes and Punishments,* p. 50.

33 Indeed Peter Brooks, in *Reading for the Plot,* has this to say: 'It may finally be in the logic of our argument that repetition speaks in the text of a return which ultimately subverts the very notion of beginning and end, suggesting that the idea of beginning presupposes the end, that the end is a time before the beginning, and hence that the interminable never can be finally bound in a plot' (p. 109).

34 All quotes are from J. Genet, *Our Lady of the Flowers,* trans. B. Frechtman (New York: Bantam Books, 1968).

35 E. White notes in *Genet, A Biography* (New York: Knopf, 1993), that Pilorge was not twenty at his death (he was twenty-five) and that his victim was certainly not his lover (pp. 178–80).

36 Edmund White provides a photograph of this icon, as well as a brief description of Weidmann's crimes. Weidmann was, in fact, the last man executed publicly in France; his guillotining was a national scandal, with members of the public fighting to get close enough to dip their handkerchiefs in the blood. No doubt the scandal of this execution story appealed to Genet and served as further incentive for his idolization of Weidmann.

37 Genet, *Our Lady of the Flowers,* p. 51.

38 Genet, *Our Lady of the Flowers,* p. 52

39 Genet, *Our Lady of the Flowers,* p. 53.

40 Genet, *Our Lady of the Flowers,* p. 54.

41 Genet, *Our Lady of the Flowers,* p. 60.

42 Genet, *Our Lady of the Flowers,* p. 77.

43 Genet, *Our Lady of the Flowers,* p. 75.

44 'The Execution of Troppmann', in *The Essential Turgenev,* ed. E. C. Allen (Evanston, IL: Northwestern University Press, 1994), pp. 791–811.

45 Allen (ed.), *The Essential Turgenev,* p. 811.

46 For a short biography of Troppmann and an account of his crime, see W. Bolitho, *Murder for Profit* (New York: Time, 1964 [1926]).

47 Allen (ed.), *The Essential Turgenev,* p. 794.

48 Allen (ed.), *The Essential Turgenev,* p. 796.

49 Allen (ed.), *The Essential Turgenev,* p. 799.

50 *Ibid.*

51 Allen (ed.), *The Essential Turgenev*, p. 798.
52 Allen (ed.), *The Essential Turgenev*, p. 803.
53 Allen (ed.), *The Essential Turgenev*, p. 804.
54 Allen (ed.), *The Essential Turgenev*, p. 807.
55 Allen (ed.), *The Essential Turgenev*, p. 810 (my emphasis).
56 Allen (ed.), *The Essential Turgenev*, p. 811.

10

Of ghostwriting and possession: translating 'my father', or *s'expliquer avec la mort*[1]

DAVE BOOTHROYD

... At Half-Mast.[1]

If a person very close to us is dying, there is something in the months to come that we dimly apprehend – much as we should have liked to share it with him – could only happen through his absence. We greet him at the last in a language that he no longer understands.

Walter Benjamin, One Way Street

In the first place; in lieu of the first person ...
This text comes in-between you and me; it is a product of our irreducible heterogeneity, and I begin with reference to its nature as such an interstitial event, as belonging from the outset to the order of what is discussed here under the name of the *spectral.*

It was summoned into the region of spectral events, in response to two invitations to appear at conferences, the first entitled 'Death and Its Concepts', organized by the editors of this volume, and the second entitled 'Phantom f(x)', an event at Stirling University, for which no particular theme or title, other than 'the spectral', was specified; a theme to be entirely, freely interpreted by the speakers. As a philosopher, I found that the opportunity to work between 'death' and 'spectral return' appealed to my academic interests in Heidegger, Levinas and Derrida on these subjects. Shortly after I accepted both invitations and commitments to appear in person, events of a different nature – personal circumstances, to be precise – intervened in a way that was eventually to make my appearance at either conference impossible. Caring for a terminally sick father with, at that time, an uncertain prognosis necessitated my immediate withdrawal from 'Death' (the irony of which was not to be lost on me), but before long the second deadline was clearly a date which, it seemed in all likelihood, would arrive quite some time after his anticipated death, so I was, at the time, able to accept the second invitation. As time passed, events were to overtake my work in more senses than one. My decision to appear/not to appear at 'Phantom f(x)' was consequently postponed and was only finalized at the last minute, as my father's dying took longer than I had originally been given to think could possibly be the case. It gradually became clear that the deadline of the date set for my appearance, with a text, and my father's deadline for his disappearance were accelerating towards a point of convergence. As a consequence, the scene of my vigil in those last days of his life became the scene of this text's writing. I tell all this in advance, because time really is out of joint here for *this* textual event: expression in print has a temporality all of its own, and I wish to note here that the text below was originally intended not so much for publication as presentation. It was a presentation to be given, which in an unpredictable manner – and, it seemed to me, with a certain necessity – would also be a bearing witness to an experience that, at that time, was still in the future. I was bound in some sense to plan my intellectual incorporation of the death of an other (a particular other) into a 'future thinking' that was yet to be undertaken (during 'the "not yet" that bends us toward death').[2] This was clearly as much a matter of temporal logics as one of the unpredictable intensity which, I assumed (quite rightly), would stir my watery reflections on death, spectrality and ghosts.[3]

The time of this text and the temporality of writing in general – as I intend to show – is determined by the *death of the other*. This is not so much an idea based on my particular experience at the scene of this writing, or to do with the nature of what was, literally, my experience, but to do with the nature of writing in general. And therein lies the rub: the onus of any 'demonstration' is that it operate at the level of the text rather than with respect to (what are ordinarily regarded as *outside* the text) life and death *themselves*. (The instability of this distinction imposes itself throughout here, rather than being taken as a theme.) The reflections presented here on the theme of 'spectrality', explored in relation to death, ghosts, the border, repetition and 'the father', proceed *above all* by way of readings of several recent texts by Derrida – texts that are the occasion, among other things, of his revisiting yet other texts on death, by Levinas and Heidegger. So, it is only a coincidence for this author to have been so entrenched in the quotidian aspects of death, ghosts and the thought of 'the father' at the same time as trying to research these themes in various philosophical texts. For this reason, I have chosen not to change the text that, finally, as I shall explain, nonetheless made its own 'spectral appearance' without 'me' at the conference at Stirling University. The temporality of the coincidence spoken of just now – of the death of the loved one and philosophizing on death – is here being remarked throughout.

This text is in fact a transcript of a video 'presentation' which was shown in lieu of my personal appearance at 'Phantom f(x)'. A spectral technology allowed me to 'be' in two places at once. It also allowed me, by chance, to instantiate a 'phantom effect' while raising the question of the relationship between the spectral and appearance as such – something that is intrinsic rather than extrinsic to *writing* or *the text*, as this is generally understood on the basis of deconstructive thinking. However, what is more significant than the fact that the spectral might be staged in this manner framing (quite literally) my 'appearance' is the fact that its occasion had been necessitated by the attendance (elsewhere) to the death of another: my 'thesis' was in some sense a structural repetition of events. It is, emphatically, quite independently of those personal circumstances in the strictest sense, of what was happening to me (and him) *at that time*, that the following is presented 'here and now', and on the ground that it might be of a *general* interest with respect to 'the spectral'. It is the necessary and indefinite postponement of a text's 'ending' (of a dying which was forever *not yet*) in a reading, which renders *any* text epithetic in the general, broader sense, which this text attempts to investigate.

I begin (again) …

White noise, title, talking-head
It will have been my aim to be in keeping with the spirit of 'Phantom f(x)', which invites the unexpected, the defiance of expertise and risk-taking and, therefore, as always in these situations, the exposure of oneself to the possibility of death: of dying, as comedians say, here on stage, in the very act of acting something out, staging a kind of performance – one for which, I must apologize, I am not in a position, today, to answer for. An invitation to participate in an event always comes from the future and anticipates that between the asking and the appearance, death will not intervene. My spectral appearance here today on video (or in print) has not been compromised by my own death as such – and my 'absence' does not bear that excuse. However, that is not to say that this text, and perhaps every text, is not overshadowed by death and the ways of thinking about death that are available to us.

It would be pointless to become ensnared in a discussion of what the spectral *is* as such, but I shall, nonetheless, attempt to indicate at the outset what I have in mind here. The spectral, and its foregrounding in Derrida's recent writings, is not itself surprising, given the figuring and the play of presence/absence that has always been central to the articulations and work of deconstruction, undertaken over many years. I do not claim to be one who sees spectres *coming*, as such, as spectral – I am not a medium – but spectrality and the work of spectralizing deconstruction, when it arrived or announced itself, *unsurprisingly* emerged on the scene as if out of a blind spot, as if it had always been around but peripheral, a kind of real but unnoticed thing, transparent, as one might expect of all things spectral. Once recognized, it seems hard to imagine that it had not been foregrounded as such, long ago. True to the concept of the ghost, it surprises *and* returns in the same moment: 'reapparition of the spectre is apparition *for the first time*'.[4]

The medium of the spectral
What is the proper medium for the discourse of the spectral and of ghosts if not that of deconstruction, the *writing* (*écriture*) in which the ghost *qua* ghost comes through (*advient*) and can

be heard, *in absentia*; as 'voices off'; heard as if by means of an act of ventriloquism; the animation of the one by the other, almost as in occult 'possessions', in which one acts out an other? This is a necessarily imperfect act, in which we find ourselves doing the talking, making sense to ourselves; hearing ourselves speak, but also hearing in those words a voice that is never wholly our own: an articulation of language in which we suppose we hear, and are able to trace, an alterity. What kind of an audience – or a *scéance* – are we, here gathered to address the spectral? And what is it that we are attending to – right now, even? In the decision of this matter, we have an inkling that everything is at stake:[5] in making it, we decide between, for example, monotheistic mysticism, modern science, psychoanalysis, phenomenology, and so on, as our way of thought or truth (and also concerning everything we do not know). It is equally so, even if we decide, if it can be put this way, for the *between itself* of deconstruction: the relational re-location; the interstitial; the aporetic *in-lieu* of (any) position: which is *not* to decide, *not* to reduce to a meaning, *not* to translate. That is the game, the unmasterable game, the game without end, in which the only aim is to be in the wake (also in the sense of a mourning or remembrance) of the other.[6] This is acted out, for example, in Derrida's analysis of the expression '*tout autre est tout autre*' (every other one is wholly other): in the play of words 'which seems to contain the very possibility of a secret that hides and reveals itself at the same time within a single sentence ... and within a single language (and) linking alterity to singularity'.[7]

These thoughts aim, then, at the conjunction of a discourse on the alterity of death with the *spirit* of writing: they link the question as to whether I can die in the place of the other (the question of ethics) with the question of whether I can write in the place, in lieu, of the other (the question of the text). Or, with the question of 'the father'; paternity; the blood line; the tradition: the grand question of the limits of tradition and the beyond; the relation of the question of how I should live with the question of how I should write. These matters subtend the relationship between 'life' and 'writing'; my inscription in the world and the ethical relation to the other.

'Of ghost-writing: translating "my father", or *s'expliquer avec la mort*'

Supplying a title is inevitably a bid at deciding how a text may be recalled or remembered, made sense of, located, or archived, for instance in the event of death. But, as Derrida's English translator says in his note to *Archive Fever:* 'At some point one simply has to give up'[8] – on translation, at least. In this case the 'translation' of this text into a readable title, one which might head these words, entombing them, meaningfully, at least for the duration of their delivery.

I have to confess a troubled stomach, adrenalized by this occasion of my own spectral projection towards an event in the near future, perhaps, but also in psychosomatic sympathy with another, in some other place today, dying, and with stomach pains of another order. What do I want to contribute to a discussion of phantom effects and the spectral, in the proximity of a dying father? The spectral may be current as a theme, but it is something that has always belonged in some as yet undecided manner to the diet of Western philosophy on which I was raised, always wondering who or what *I am*, or what 'I am' means, on the basis of this alimentation, in which the other becomes always, in *being thought*, a part of the same 'me', and which, at times, afflicts me with an indigestion (because what is given to me never simply becomes me or my own but remains, partly, a foreign body) assuaged only by regular episodes of regurgitation or excretion.

My power over the spectral voices echoing here, in terms such as these, in titles, and loaded terms, is limited. Is the risk I accept in the form of an invitation *to appear* (to which *this* is my response) the risk of a mess (that I will perform a subjective televised rant) – this death of all deaths being, in this moment, upon me – a mess that will have been all of my own making and from which I am even planning, in advance, to be absent; in lieu of myself, staging my own disappearance into my text? (No one else has told me I must speak to this theme, right now. But when else would be more appropriate?) I am wondering already, and shall return to this theme: *what are the limits of my responsibility* in all of this? Both with respect to a 'phantom event' such as this, involving *the presentation of a thesis*, and with respect to my responsibility for the other human being, typical of everyday life itself, and above all in relation to (this) death. Why *must* the everyday be philosophized about at all?

Intimate interruptions and 'the privileging of death'

During my father's terminal illness, he seems to be concerned most directly not with the imminent 'nothingness' approaching but rather with 'not making a mess'; with the increasing ambiguity of responsibility for the body over which he is losing control. I intend no pathos in mentioning here (once again) the circumstances of the production of this text. I am not present today, not facing you in the person of my own corpus, because of my attendance to his. (Quite independently of the possible 'mess', I seek here to abdicate my sovereignty in this matter: I am no longer able to *judge* this situation and this writing. For, indeed, in every case perhaps, the death of another trumps the burden of self-judgement.)

To what end I weave in this 'intimacy' here, will become clearer as I proceed. I wish to speak here of a conjunction between philosophy and the ethical as non-philosophy; of the difference between a life made thinkable on the basis of philosophy and a relation to death which opens the 'possibility of impossibility' or the *beyond death*, expressed, for example, in the idea of the spectral, whose ethical significance is at issue here. The way to do this is to consider in more detail the manner in which the spectral deconstructs the 'privilege of death'.

The 'privileging of death' is at issue here in more ways than one, and it is a privileging that is challenged, as well as confirmed, in what imposes itself upon us, in the form of the spectral. Derrida's way of reading death – for example in Heidegger, Levinas, Freud, Kierkegaard and others – in such texts as *Aporias*, *Gift of Death*, and *Archive Fever*, employs the characteristic deconstructive strategy of setting different voices against each other, 'speaking in the name of' those texts under scrutiny; combining a fidelity to ideas with the exposure of the text to its own limits, and so on. In his wanderings in the neighbourhood of death, Derrida's engagements with the spectral – the *arrivant*, the *revenant*, the *advient*, the ghost and other 'hauntings' – disturb the foreclosure of any discussion of death, responsibility, alterity, singularity and the universal: the discussion, or reading, that would otherwise *seek death in the form of the finality of an interpretation.* In all of these writings, and perhaps throughout the entire Derridean corpus, Derrida's thinking could be said to interrupt death: death as 'meaning something' never takes place. Derrida's readings, characteristically, do not lay to rest any of the texts they deal with; they do not bury them or entomb them in the finality of an interpretation as such. To do so, even when lovingly, would be to confuse fidelity (this desire to be true to the original) with necrophilia; a perverse attempt at consummation – a consummation which death itself interrupts and forestalls and which is thus predisposed to 'failure', as one cannot 'find oneself' in the death of the other.

At this point I shall limit my focus, turning now to the privileging of death in Heidegger and Levinas and to how Derrida's reading between the two, spectralizes death. To help make clear what it is that I am making an issue here, I shall first sketch these parameters.

Heidegger

Heidegger thinks death as *Dasein*'s very mode of being-ahead-of-itself (*sich-vorweg-sein*) and as that which gives rise to the very possibility of thinking (at all) as a thinking which is *mine* or the very event of 'mineness' (*Jemeinigkeit*). *Dasein* is privileged as the possibility of possibility in general, because in the ontological difference between Being and There-Being (*Da-Sein*) it projects (itself) in anticipation of death, which is first and foremost 'mine'. In Heidegger, the possibility of possibility in general is thinkable as such on the basis of the possibility of impossibility, or, in other words, death is the ground for all possibility: to be *Dasein* is to be able to die. For example, the possibility of this text as a symbol of 'me', of a thinking which is mine (no matter how plagiarized it might be finally judged to be!) becomes what it is in the time between now and an anticipated time limit – namely, the time of my death, (– or, about forty-five minutes, the time allotted for this spectral presentation, and whichever comes first.) Either way, the *possibility* of (any) presentation, as such, arises in the temporal 'ecstasis' of *Dasein* as a projected being-towards-death (*Sein-zum-Tode*). In other words: the being-there of anything as a possibility is tied to my *possibility of impossibility* – the only certain possibility, which is my death.[9]

Levinas

Despite acknowledging the philosophical significance and radicality of Heidegger's attempt to think time in relation to death, which displaces the thinking of time in any number of anthropocentric determinations – for example, as eternity in religion or as atomic decay in physics – and despite the necessity of this philosophical passage through Heidegger, Levinas incessantly attempts to articulate the ethical shortcomings of the philosophy of existence which claims its origin in the 'fundamental anxiety' over *my own* death. Against this, he proposes a reversal that amounts to thinking death from the perspective of time.[10] In Levinas, the 'first death' (the thematically privileged death) is the death of the other. This could be summarized in the following proposition: time *comes* to me; it becomes mine, *starting* from the other. This does not throw me back on the contingency of my longevity in comparison to the lives of the others, reasoning that I, therefore, naturally always still have time for her or him. For with this, the thinking of time would simply collapse back into a form of chronological calculation. It is rather to propose that the being of the 'I' in its singular existence is given to it in its *attending to the death of the other*, whose death articulates its very existence as a kind of waiting-on, attendance or witness, to the death of the other. Responsibility, for example, manifests itself in the fundamental form of my being-for-the-other – an event in which, Levinas would say, I am a *hostage* to (my) responsibility, which is something I have not freely taken on but which obliges me.[11]

Derrida

Derrida's reading of these thinkers (and others) on death is of course subtle, complex and, throughout, in a very qualified way, *undecided*. However, I think that it is useful here to summarize it by saying that, notwithstanding everything which Derrida can say on the basis of, or 'in the name of', Heidegger and Levinas, and often speaking against one in the name of the other, in several of his recent writings he summons both on the charge that they each fail to take account of the *spectrality* implicit to death.[12]

On the one hand, in the case of Heidegger, this is a consequence of the refusal of any ontological significance for the everyday experience of the death of a loved one; the death of the *unique* other. Derrida makes this point 'in the name of Levinas'. Indeed, the everydayness of death is set up as that which must be overcome in the existential analysis which aims to relegate all hitherto unexamined thanato-anthropocentrisms to the 'sub-philosophical'; to the ontic.[13]

On the other hand, in view of Levinas's insistence on how my relation to the other person enacts the relation to the 'wholly other' (*tout autre*) beyond the finitude marked by my death, and for which, or *for whom*, my responsibility, Levinas says, is infinite, and that 'it is for the death of the other that I am responsible, to the point of including myself in death', Derrida chooses to recall a moment in which Levinas simplifies his position in a telling fashion, offering the more acceptable proposition: 'I am responsible for the other in so far as he is "mortal".'[14] With respect to this, Derrida will then say 'in the name of Heidegger', that Levinas's thinking is itself susceptible to the Heideggerian account of inauthenticity.[15]

So, on the one hand, we have Heidegger's analytic of *Dasein*, which lays open for analysis the historical contingency of mortal life conceived as subjective individuality and the inauthentic everyday thinking of death that goes along with it. In view of this we have, on the other hand, an argument that Levinas's attempts to account for how my infinite responsibility comes to me always in the form of my *personal* responsibility for the other individual fall foul of the thinking of the ontological difference by remaining in the order of the ontic, (thereby confirming the Heideggerian account of the co-originality of being-with-(the other) (*Mitsein/ Miteinandersein*) and being-towards-death.) Derrida argues, moreover, that this is a co-originality which 'does not contradict, but on the contrary, presupposes a mineness of dying or of being-toward-death, a mineness (even if) not that of the ego or of an egological sameness'.[16]

It is at this point that Derrida indicates that this philosophical problematic of death could be supplemented with a consideration of what he calls 'originary mourning'. What such a 'mourning' signifies for the thinking of death, I shall consider later. (I will say immediately, however, that what Derrida means by this is that the whole of Writing is, in a sense (always 'in a sense'), *the being of the oneself in mourning for the other*, something which, in a moment, I shall consider as the form of *s'expliquer avec la mort*.)

This entire analysis unfolds, then, between the certain possibility of my death and the haunting possibility, the possibility of the spectral; the *possibility of the impossibility* of the death of the other. This impossibility is 'experienced' in the postponement of the death of the other, which Levinas expresses in his contra-Heideggerian text 'La mort et le temps'[17] when he says, 'death does not seem to us to amount to annihilation'.[18] Derrida's thinking here wanders between Heidegger and Levinas on death; travelling along a path (*Holzweg*) cut by Heidegger and signposted 'existential analysis of being-towards-death as the fundamental mode of *Dasein*'. But, according to Levinas, this is a path which leads, ultimately, not to the clearing (*Lichtung*) of thought but to the death camp and the *trauma* of death by murder, which is not simply 'annihilation' but also 'survival' or 'witnessing'; the living-on (of the possibility of impossibility) which haunts death (that is, the thinking of death as the impossibility of possibility).

In a return to the theme of the economy of violence, discussed in *Violence and Metaphysics* (1964/67) and again in *Archive Fever* (1995) Derrida examines the idea that:

> As soon as there is one there is murder, wounding, traumatism. *L'un se garde de l'autre*. The one guards against/keeps some of the other. It protects itself from the other, but in the movement of this jealous violence, it compromises in itself, thus guarding it, the self-otherness or self-difference (the difference from within oneself) which makes it one. The One 'differing or deferring from itself'. The One as the Other. At once, at the same time, but in a same time that is out of joint, the One forgets to remember itself to itself, it keeps and erases the archive of the injustice that it is.[19]

Heidegger's analysis refuses to attend to the possibility of murder as 'impossibility' (or, 'impossibility of murder'); to attend to, as Levinas calls it in 'La mort et le temps', 'the culpability of surviving the death of the other', which is what 'opens' the possibility of murder, as such, *as* the possibility of murder, in the first place. It is 'in the culpability of surviving the death of the other, (that) the death of the other is my affair'.[20] This triumph over death, marked by survival, witness, and so on, is not, says Levinas, 'a new possibility' – for a subject or an 'I' – 'offered after the end of every possibility' (the Lazarus syndrome), but a resurrection 'in the son in whom the rupture of death is embodied'.[21]

Death as aporia

Although it may be Derrida's most explicit teaching that the aporetic does not belong exclusively to any particular context, or 'genre' of writing *about* aporia *qua* aporia, in *Aporias*, death is, nonetheless, aporia *par excellence*: where there is aporia, death is never far away; death not only 'instantiates' aporia but is also the condition of aporia in general. And when Derrida raises the question of aporia *qua* aporia we can, I propose, substitute unproblematically, 'death' for 'aporia'. To demonstrate this, in the following citation I make this substitution:

> [W]hat takes place, what comes to pass with the death? Is it possible to undergo or to experience the death, the death *as such*? Is it then a question of the death *as such*? Of a scandal arising to suspend a certain viability? Does one then pass through this death as such? Or is one immobilized before the threshold, to the point of having to turn around and seek another way without a method or an outlet of a *Holzweg* or a turning (*Kehre*).[22]

Thinking through the aporetic, we must 'go with death', for death is the name of our mortality itself, and that which opens the scene of philosophizing in general. In fact this discussion of aporia has already been framed by the question of death and its borders at the outset, when Derrida poses the question: 'What about borders with respect to death? About borders of truth and borders of properties?'[23]

I am here in the company of ghosts, three of them (at least), all of whom are, indisputably, deconstructing angels of death and the life/death dichotomy. They are ghosts whom I would not claim to know well or fully comprehend but with whom I am so intimate that they drop in and out of my vigil, *in this moment,* over my father's death; my attendance to the death of this other one, giving rise to a kind of atheological convocation; a trinity of father, son and ghosts. And with this thought, I skid once again towards the thought of the end that keeps returning to my text. Some possible last words come to mind: an imagined dialogue at the scene of the death which is so close.

Dying father to son: 'Be a man'.

Son to dying father: 'Be a Ghost'.

Death is not visible, not even to the dying, who must *back* into death, like Benjamin's angel of history, still looking forward through the eyes (even though they are almost always closed now), in any case through vision, back into life and to the possibility which still remains, namely *to be,* just a little bit more, even in a state of almost total ruination and suffering; in the death agony of 'the impossibility of ceasing'.[24] Hence, the imperative, or instruction, 'be', always refers us *back* to such a possibility (of impossibility). But the 'be' in the expression 'be a ghost' is, from the first, paralogized by the spectral nature of its object and despite its still being a part of life. Any ontological imperative is already thus haunted by impossibility, and any border between 'continuance' and 'end' must be founded on such a *hauntology* rather than an ontology,[25] the fundamental orientation of which is a pointing beyond the life of anyone; beyond any singularity. In fact, rather than 'be a ghost' being an imperative or an instruction, it can only be *thought,* as such, as an expression of pathos; a hopeless hope of continuance *in being*, an idea expressible only in the language of being.

S'expliquer avec la mort: epithet from the edge

At the end (of this text) I will have wanted to speak to my title; to the pressing conjunction of 'my father' and 'explaining myself' with respect to (his) dying. But it occurs to me that, all along, it could have been anything, even 'X', because the text is 'parasited, harbouring and haunted by the possibility of being repeated *in all kinds of ways*'.[26] Whatever else this ghostly presentation will have been at 'Phantom f(x)' – a live event – then it will have been at the same time (or in another time), *at the same time out of joint*, a coming to terms with death. *S'expliquer avec la mort* is a matter neither wholly intimate and private nor wholly public, despite the occasion, something neither held entirely in reserve nor fully expended, but between life and death.

S'expliquer avec la mort: To 'explain oneself with …', to come to terms with, death, Derrida notes in the 'Exordium' of *Spectres of Marx*, is the condition for 'learning to live'. 'Learning to live' has an epicurean ring to it, indeed for Epicurus the secret of this also lay in death, of which he famously says: 'If you are it is not; if it is you are not.'[27] A suitable epithet on his tombstone might have been: 'Here lies Epicurus, only his epithet, "if you are it is not; if it is you are not" survives him.' The epithet within the epithet; the familiar *abyssal* condition – for the return of 'ghostwriting'. Writing is the technology of haunting *par excellence*, and Levinas, writing in 1947, was far ahead of his time, and certainly not yet dead, when he wrote of this Epicurean remark on death that:

> it misunderstands the entire paradox of death, for it effaces our relationship with death, which is a unique relationship with the future. But at least the adage insists on the eternal futurity of death. The fact that it deserts every present is not due to our evasion of death and to an unpardonable diversion at the supreme hour but to the fact that death is *ungraspable*.[28]

Slipping seamlessly back to Derrida and to the 'Exordium' of *Spectres of Marx*, which is haunted more by the spectre of Levinas than Marx (ghosts obeying no law, or order, of appearance), we find him possessed of this same thought, which he completes, or repeats, by saying:

> To learn to live, to learn it *from oneself and by oneself*, all alone, to teach *oneself* to live, is that not impossible for a living being? Is it not what logic forbids? To live, by definition, is not something one learns. Not from oneself, it is not learned from life. Only from the other and by death. In any case from the *other at the edge of life*. At the internal border or the external border, it is a heterodidactics between life and death.[29]

As I write at the edge – the edge of my father's bed, right at the edge – I think about the edge of life. Always the edge: this is Derridean territory; the thinking of the edge, always writing on the edge – of the *pas au-delà* and the 'no step beyond without also remaining this side'. This is an 'idea', which, *to think it*, can crush you. It marks Derrida's incorporation of the Nietzschean eternal return – from the edge.[30] Ghosts return, not from nothingness but from the edge, or border, of life. For Heidegger, the 'first death', the *decisive* death, is mine. For Levinas, the 'first death' is the death of the other (person). For Derrida, death is neither first nor last but *of the edge*, between the 'I' (*le moi*) and the other. Death is encountered in the coming back from the edge as an ego-less alterity – the only 'true' form of which, as Derrida has given us to think over so many years and in so many texts, is *Writing* (*écriture*).

Coming to terms with death (philosophically or *of another*) has the structure of an 'asymmetrical address', despite the fact that the learning is always both the meditation of a *oneself* and the address of one to an other (spectral or human). This address might, for example, occur in the form of conversation[31] between a son and dying father, or between any one and any other one, for example, between a mother and a son, as is the case with Derrida himself, writing on the dying of his mother in *Circumfession*. Just before this return to intimacy, back again to the 'Exordium' (*Spectres of Marx*): 'What happens between two, between all the "two's" one likes, such as between life and death, can only *maintain* itself with some ghost, can only talk *with or about* some ghost.'[32]

Again the familiar aporia of the communication of the incommunicable: we can talk, in life, in our finitude, about the alterity of the ghost, in whatever form, context or way it comes to us, but the condition of possibility for this dialogue, this 'heterodidactics', as Derrida calls it, is that it is also, inescapably, a coming to terms with death, 'mine as (well as) that of the other'.[33]

On intimacy
Another of the 'twos' that these texts of Derrida work through is the public/private, and I want to turn to this aspect of 'coming to terms with death' now, as this is, in *this* text, neither simply a

theoretical nor simply a practical matter. Consider the insepara-
bility of living and philosophizing in general: if this unity proceeds
from or as a 'coming to terms with death', giving rise to anxiety
over death, then what is at issue in the difference between thinking this anxiety as the anxiety I experience before my own death
(as for Heidegger) or as the anxiety over the necessity of (my)
betrayal of the other? There is nothing simple, obvious or deci-
dable about this betrayal. On the one hand, in coming to terms
with death in public, I stand to betray the intimacy of the relation
to the other person in death. On the other, to pretend, to deny or
even to insist (as does Heidegger) that any thematic discussion of
death can proceed without also being a coming to terms with
death – which is *always* of a *singular* other – betrays, or devalues,
the uniqueness of the teaching which comes to me in my attendance to the death of the Other *qua* other person. In other words,
must we not conclude that to speak of death, without also
accounting for my responsibility for the other's death, is impossible? Surely, death is never simply a theme for philosophy, and
philosophy is never simply a theoretico-objective consideration
of its objects of inquiry (for example, 'death'). The only choice is
between betrayal or silence, which is not an alternative at all, as
silence itself would be but a betrayal *by* silence.

Of all of Derrida's reflections on the relationship between the
public and the private, I find none more poignant and apposite to
my theme than a line of thought in *Circumfession*, marked by this
passage:

> [F]rom among [the] remorse with respect to my mother, [I] feel
> really guilty for publishing her end, in exhibiting her last
> breaths and, still worse, for purposes that some might judge to
> be literary, at risk of adding a dubious exercise to the 'writer
> and his mother' series, subseries 'the mother's death', and what
> is there to be done, would I not feel as guilty, and would I not in
> truth *be* as guilty if I wrote here about myself without retaining
> the least trace of her, letting her die in depth of *another time*[34]

This opens the question of the temporality of ghosts, the time
of death and what Derrida gives to us in the form of the expression *donner la mort*, the gift of death. The principal direction of

this chapter, which is also *with or about* Derrida, will have been to explore the logic of *giving* it proposes, and the possible response which I, or 'the I', make/s in the attempt to be responsible in death. In the remainder, albeit all too briefly, I shall consider the manner in which death and responsibility touch upon the question of our relations to ghosts, phantom-effects, the spectral and thinking in general and how the attempt (and experiment) of thinking/philosophizing/writing is an ethical matter whose ethicality is *given* (to it) by 'life' being redefined as responding to (the death of) the other. This could be called the 'haunted life' or 'the spectre of the other within the same'.

Who 'gives death' and to whom? And, who is responsible for whom in all this? Or, who dies? If we conclude, as we are inclined to, after Derrida, that such questions 'haunt' us and come to us by way of ghosts, then it may be objected that this 'haunting' is merely an imprecise, unphilosophical figure that substitutes for what could be more straightforwardly expressed in terms of an intellectual and cultural inheritance and in relation to their 'effects' on my experience of death – for example, in terms of religion, or the history of ideas and concepts, *given to me* as the parameters of my thinking of death in terms of the presently thinkable. Alternatively, it may be objected that the haunting (concept) is a sign of, or is founded on, universality, or a universal law, and that the disjunction between the law and the affairs of humanity will always unsettle, disturb and manifest itself in forms such as conscience, guilt or hallucinations, or simply in the form of the natural or 'animal' fear for oneself and one's loved ones. But to conclude thus would render the communication with ghosts (a figure of the 'impossible possibility' mentioned above) merely a 'personal' affair and a psychological disturbance. It would neither enable us, nor hold the promise of our being able to rise, to the question of justice: it would, rather, make of the relation to the ghost a matter of calculation, and the relation to the other in death (and to 'death' in general) a matter of settling accounts and the payment, or writing-off, of debts and the assuaging of guilt. Mourning the dead would not be necessary and, *by the same logic,* nor would writing.

But, in death, who owes a debt to whom, what constitutes

payment, who or what decides the mechanics of its incurrence, interest, repayment and so on? In *Circumfession* Derrida is unclear – that is, in a state of uncertainty – with respect to his guilt of betrayal, incurred in the publication of his mother's 'end', which is, as for everyone, also a matter of intimacy between the two of them. In the same text, Derrida is also obliged to deliver on a promise to Geoff Bennington, his 'co-author', to produce a 'surprising' text, one that will breach the systematic account of Derrida's thinking which Geoff Bennington is writing as a 'conterminal gift', if I may put it that way, to all readers of 'Derrida'. The two *matrices* (of 'editorial requirement' and Derrida's mother) and the identity of the signature 'Derrida' are in play at once here: it is only by writing such a text, namely one in which the reader is included in the structure of this predicament, that Derrida might recover ownership of his signature. The project of Bennington's *Derridabase* in one sense threatens to rob Derrida of his singular ability to surprise by implicitly anticipating his text (and any future text he might write), but it also, in another sense, recognizes and acknowledges his identity: that is, as 'Derrida' and, precisely, as if *he* (Jacques) were dead. We learn something here about the structure of the indebtedness of the one in relation to the other, and I shall draw to a close now not with a signature but with a few remarks on the *counter*signature and the idea of fidelity associated with it and on how death is always also the end of fidelity.

Towards the end; the countersignature of fidelity
Despite the feebleness of his grasp on life as well as of his own hand, my father was upset, just now, that in the midst of the family affairs I am trying to sort out, I had, in order to save him the trouble, forged his signature. In fact, I can now quite easily write his signature more convincingly than he can. At the time, I figured that as ever, the law-abiding father is, to the last, still angered by the flippant son's casual disrespect of every law and the dogma of lawfulness itself. It strikes me now, after days of sitting on the edge, that it is in the nature of 'the father' always to reject fidelity in the form of the countersignature of the son, as it announces, always still too soon, the inevitable death of the father. How

should I respond to this and at the same time speak to you? What Geoff Bennington refers to as the 'pedagogical project' of *Derrida-base*, the communication of 'Derrida' to his readers, as he himself is fully aware and wary of, involves writing about Derrida as if he were dead and unable to surprise us again; unable to repeat by *surprising again*.

What would be the response of true fidelity to 'the father', in either of these, or any other, senses; to the traditional discursive activity of representing in themes by means of excluding the quotidian origins of all concepts and tropes, in life and death *themselves*? Is there a proper way to 'possess death' other than by dying? Should one write as if one were one's 'father'? Clearly not, for this would be the ultimate betrayal and unfaithful to the understanding of 'Derrida's' relationship to his textual offspring, but mostly because the notion of writing as 'ghostwriting' is given heterodidactically; namely, because ghostwriting is *a writing in the wake (or 'trace') of the other*. What might be called deconstructive ghostwriting is a ghostwriting of the unassailable *tout autre est tout autre*: a writing *this side*, which emerges out of the interface, or edge, between mortals, and through which the relationship to *the other comes* (to pass). Only the writing which is such an originary mourning of the passing of the other is ghostwriting in the sense given to it here. As such, ghostwriting can serve the ethical purpose of allowing the other to die well, in acceptance of his gift (of death); of *everything* which is happening here and now, in this unending 'interval of discretion'.[35]

Notes

1 This is an expression used by Derrida in the 'Exordium' to *Spectres of Marx*, to which the English translator, Peggy Kamuf, appends the following note: 'literally, to explain oneself with death. But, the idiomatic French sense here is close to the German expression *auseinander-setzen*, to have it out with someone, to argue with someone, to come to grips with a problem'. J. Derrida, *Spectres of Marx*, trans. P. Kamuf (London: Routledge, 1994), p. 177, n. 1.

2 J. Derrida, *Aporias: Dying – Awaiting (One Another at) the 'Limits of*

Truth', trans. T. Dutoit (Stanford: Stanford University Press, 1993), p. 69.

3 This temporal disruption at *the 'place' where death touches writing*, a primary concern here, is remarked by Derrida at the scene of his mother's death (referred to below) 'knowing in advance the non-knowledge into which the imminent but unpredictable coming of an event, the death of my mother, Sultana Esther Georgette Safar Derrida, would come to sculpt the writing from the outside, give it its form of incalculable interruption'. J. Derrida, *Circumfession*, trans. G. Bennington, in *Jacques Derrida* (Chicago: Chicago University Press, 1993), pp. 206–7.

4 Derrida, *Spectres of Marx*, p. 4. Later, I shall return to this idea of familiarity, the unsurprising surprise, or, predictability, in so far as this is implicated in the systematic representation of a body of thought, such as Derrida's, for example in a work such as Geoff Bennington's *Derridabase* (Chicago: Chicago University Press, 1993). This is a work that, on one level, sets out to entomb Derrida in a systematic representation of his thought, and is, so to speak, a 'ghostwritten' philosophical biography of Derrida, but which is also part of a project which poses a challenge to Derrida: to *surprise*, yet again, in *defiance* of the death it imposes upon him by its very nature. (Derrida, *Circumfession*, p. 16.) Later I shall speak of a project of this kind as an act of fidelity.

5 The theme of 'everything' being related to the 'decision of literature', the decision of the meaning and identity of the literary, as a 'standing on the edge of everything', is referred to in 'This Strange Institution Called Literature: An Interview', in D. Attridge (ed.), *Acts of Literature* (London: Routledge, 1992).

6 'It is impossible to over-emphasise the importance of what is *being decided*, so authoritatively and so decisively, at the very moment when what is in question is to decide on what *must remain undecided.*' Derrida, *Aporias*, p. 54.

7 J. Derrida, *Gift of Death*, trans. D. Wills (Chicago: Chicago University Press, 1995), p. 87.

8 J. Derrida, *Archive Fever*, trans. E. Prenowitz (Chicago: Chicago University Press, 1996), p. 106.

9 Derrida, *Aporias*, pp. 23ff, on Heidegger, *Being and Time*, Section 50.

10 At this point, my brief summary of this thread in Levinas's 'La mort et

le temps', takes its guidance from a text (to my knowledge, as yet unpublished) by T. Chanter, 'Traumatic Response: Levinas's Legacy', for which I express my gratitude here.

11 In *Aporias*, p. 60, Derrida explicitly proposes the nature of the connection between the Levinasian trope of the 'hostage' and the 'ghost' (as members of the same series: 'This is the series constituted by hostage, host, guest, ghost, holy ghost and *Geist*.'

12 Derrida, *Gift of Death*, pp. 47ff.

13 Derrida, *Aporias*, p. 60.

14 See, for example, Derrida, *Aporias*, p. 39.

15 Derrida, *Aporias*, pp. 68–78.

16 Derrida, *Aporias*, p. 39.

17 E. Levinas, 'La mort et le temps', in *Cours de 1975–76* in *L'Herne 60* (Paris: Editions de L'Herne, 1991). Also in *Dieu, la mort et le temps* (Paris: Grasset, 1993), which has different pagination from L'Herne.

18 Levinas, 'La mort et le temps', p. 37; Chanter, 'Traumatic Response', p. 13.

19 Derrida, *Archive Fever*, p. 78.

20 Levinas, 'La mort et le temps', p. 44; Chanter, 'Traumatic Response', p. 18.

21 E. Levinas, *Totality and Infinity*, trans. A. Lingis (Pittsburgh: Duquesne University Press, 1969 [1961]), pp. 56–7. The text continues (p. 57): 'Death – suffocation in the impossibility of the possible – opens the passage toward descent. Fecundity is yet a personal relation, though it not be given to the 'I' as a possibility.' Space does not permit a digression at this point into Levinas's account of this rupture of the time of 'the subject' in the form of the 'fecundity' of the child. However, it must be noted that this is central to his 'thesis' that 'death is not the end'. Nor, regrettably, is there space to consider the important critique of Levinas's account of 'fecundity' undertaken by Irigaray, on the basis of which a 'sexing' of the relation to death may be possible (cf. L. Irigaray, 'The Fecundity of the Caress', in *An Ethics of Sexual Difference*, trans. C. Burke and G. C. Gill (London: Athlone, 1993), pp. 185–227).

22 Derrida, *Aporias*, p. 33.

23 Derrida, *Aporias*, p. 3.

24 Levinas, *Totality and Infinity*, pp. 56–60.

25 Derrida, *Spectres of Marx*, p. 10.

26 Jacques Derrida, 'Limited Inc. abc ...', in *Limited Inc*, trans. S. Weber and J. Mehlman (Evanston: Northwestern University Press, 1988), p. 90. This is just one of Derrida's formulae for the figure of haunting and the spectral in his reading of Levinas's account in *Totality and Infinity* of the relation to the infinite thought from within the finite: of how the face-to-face between mortals and the relation to an Infinity 'beyond the face' are connected. Spectrality here serves to re-articulate Derrida's longstanding rejection of the idea that my relation to the other person can *at the same time* be said to be a relation to the infinite: to the idea that, as Levinas puts it in his 1976 lectures, 'the relation with infinity is nothing but the responsibility of one mortal for another'. (Levinas, 'La mort et le temps', p. 35; Chanter, 'Traumatic Response', p. 22.)

27 E. Levinas, *Time and the Other*, trans. R. A. Cohen (Pittsburgh: Duquesne University Press, 1987 [1947]), p. 71.

28 Levinas, *Time and the Other*, p. 71.

29 Derrida, *Spectres of Marx*, p. xvii (my emphasis).

30 This is, surely, a Derridean teaching *par excellence*: 'This edge would itself be the place of the first problematic of closure, of a domain of questioning or of absolutely preliminary research.' (*Aporias*, p. 42). 'Literature' as much as 'death' is of this edge (c.f. 'This Strange Institution Called Literature: An Interview', in *Acts of Literature*).

31 In *Totality and Infinity*, Levinas understands language (the language of the 'ethical relation' or 'face to face'), 'primarily' as *conversation*.

32 Derrida, *Spectres of Marx*, p. xviii.

33 *Ibid.*

34 Derrida, *Circumfession*, p. 37 (my emphasis).

35 Levinas, *Totality and Infinity*, p. 58.

11

Deadly tales

GRISELDA POLLOCK

Prologue
I offer you a self-portrait of a feminist intellectual haunted by death. It is an installation – with a hard, metallic body, a memory cabinet, trying to keep things in order, classified in separate compartments. The video monitor, its transparent head, offers a glimpse into the space of thought, imagination and fantasy that screen a trauma. The images that track across these spaces are silent. You, the witness, must hear the words that struggle with and against the loaded image. You must hear them in your own body and space, a chair placed at the other side of the room. Now, encountering the trace of this performance in a book, you must read what once would have echoed in your head through head phones, what once my body spoke, what now I publicly reclaim and own.

The performance falls into seven parts, moving in, frame by frame, from cultural texts (a painting and a play) to two Jewish theorists of modernity haunted by fascism (Walter Benjamin and Sigmund Freud) to two men mourning their parents (Paul Bryant and Roland Barthes). At the centre, there is the 'dark core' of my dead mother circled by my bereaved motherhood.

First deadly tale – 1636
In 1635–36, the English painter John Souch painted *Sir Thomas Aston at the Deathbed of his Wife*.

Set in an imaginary bed-chamber, the painting divides into distinct compartments. These generate a web of meaning.

Magdalene Aston died in childbirth on 2 June 1635, leaving her husband, Thomas, and young son, Thomas, who would himself die but two years later.

The draped cradle surmounted with a skull signifies another recently deceased child.

Its sombre darkness – creating a central void in the painting – contrasts dramatically with the pallor of the laid out mother who has died in childbirth.

It is perhaps a little unnerving, if inexplicable, to find this same Magdalene Aston represented a second time in the painting, appearing to be alive, elegantly seated in the classic posture of melancholy at the foot of her own death-bed. This curious doubling is a feature of the sixteenth-century theory of 'two bodies': the natural, which dies and decays, and the social, which should be preserved in an elevating representation as 'an element in collective memory'.[1]

The painting can also be read in relation to the historical concepts of the family.

The body of the woman is positioned iconically as the instrument not merely of procreation but of dynasty.

Magdalene Aston's body is the point of passage between Sir Thomas Aston and his offspring, a prospective Sir Thomas Aston.

Different bodies, same names, they would by succession keep the social body of the Aston family in a continuous present.

The painting exposes Magdalene Aston's failure to repeat and thus secure this patriarchal lineage. The draped cradle *cum* catafalque occupies the centre of the painting as a sign linking femininity and death.

It serves as the dark hinge between the erect masculine, symbol-laden lineage of father and son and the languid, deadly, 'feminine' domain of life and natural death, with its secondary existence in representation, but only in the emblematic form of female melancholy.

Second deadly tale – 1940 (Walter Benjamin, 1892–1940)

In July 1992, I attended a conference held to celebrate the work of Walter Benjamin, which coincided, more or less, with the anniversary of the date of his birth in 1892. A few weeks later, I was discussing this event with a friend who had found himself, by chance, on the very day of that anniversary, in Port Bou, the Spanish village in the Pyrenees where Walter Benjamin had committed suicide on 26 or 27 September 1940.

I found myself wondering, belatedly and yet for the first time, about the details of what I had frequently taken simply as a symbolic caesura in the history of critical theory rather than a concrete event enacted on and by a real body.

How did Walter Benjamin die?

At what time of day?

Did he suffer?

What happened to his body?

I turned to Gershom Scholem's story of his friendship with Walter Benjamin. He writes that he learned of his friend's death (which took place on the night of 26–27 September 1940) only on 8 November, from Hannah Arendt, who had visited Port Bou but had found no trace of a grave. Scholem reproduces a letter that provides the only firm information about Benjamin's self-administered overdose of morphine and the disposal of his body in a grave bought by Frau Gurland for five years. No trace of the grave that Hannah Arendt went to seek has ever been found. Scholem concludes his book with the following paragraph:

> Many years later, in the cemetery that Hannah Arendt had seen, a grave with Benjamin's name scrawled on the wooden enclosure was being shown to visitors. The photographs before me clearly indicate that this grave, which is completely isolated and utterly separate from the actual burial places, is an invention of cemetery attendants, who in consideration of the number of inquiries wanted to assure themselves of a tip.[2]

Benjamin's death and his apocryphal grave are part of a much larger, more terrifying and indeed almost unimaginable collective experience of death murderously inflicted on over six million Jewish people in what is known as 'The Event', 'That which Happened', and simply 'The Destruction: *Ha-Shoah*'. This administrative, industrial death was inflicted on the natural body, but it finds no social body to traverse that terrible darkness that opens up between the dead and their memory.

Third deadly tale – 1992 (Pavel Blumenzweig, 1913–92)
In May 1992, my father-in-law, Pavel Blumenzweig, known after 1940 as Paul Bryant, died in Leeds at the age of seventy-nine. He was born in Teplitz, in what is now the Czech Republic in 1913. Not a name curated by collective memory, he was, nonetheless, a historic figure – a figure of that history of those people who escaped the Nazi invasion of Czechoslovakia in 1939 and survived.

He survived.

I say, 'He survived'.

He was not untouched, however, for he was condemned to live with the experience of that monumental twentieth-century death.

He was sentenced to carry with him the knowledge that his own parents did not die of disease, of old age, of an accident, but had been callously destroyed.

These were old and trusting people, who could not believe what he told them about the threat against them because it surpassed the imagination, even in a world where anti-Semitism was an everyday part of the national culture.

They were imprisoned and starved, terrorized and then horribly put to death, poisoned and suffocated by gas. Their bodies were burnt. They have no grave. This manner of extinction changes the very ways we, who come after, forever contemplate that most singular of life-events, death.

Benjamin's associate Theodor Adorno, later wrote in 'After Auschwitz':

> The administrative murder of millions made of death a thing one had never yet to fear in just this fashion. There is no chance anymore for death to come into the individuals' empirical life as somehow conformable with the course of that life. The last, the poorest possession left to the individual is expropriated. That in the concentration camp it was no longer an individual who died, but a specimen – this is a fact bound to affect the dying of those who escaped the administrative measure.[3]

In the aftermath of my father-in-law's unexpected and sudden death, as part of the curation of his social body, the collating of his papers, we found a short letter in his files. It was from the

International Red Cross Tracing Agency, dated 1957, and bleakly informed Paul Bryant of Middlesex of the exact date and precise number of the transport that had carried his parents from the ghetto of Terezin, or Theresienstadt, to Oswieciem, better known by its German name, Auschwitz. They were probably part of one of the Nazis' calculated deceits. Several transports from Terezin were sent to Auschwitz in December 1943 and allowed to live there in what was called the Czech family camp. Families were together and they had better rations. They had to write back to Terezin with their positive reports. Then after three months they were abruptly gassed.

My father-in-law survived and he lived to be stolen from his family by an undiagnosed cancer.

Cancer is a thief.

It silently crept upon us and snatched him away in ten days.

On the last night, I sat by his hospital bed and saw death creeping over him.

Death seemed like a pillow slowly suffocating a struggling man. It was visible, this struggle, not against this or that disease but against the impossibility of the physical body fighting off its systemic failure. I suddenly saw a biochemical system being poisoned. His already weakened heart could not withstand the assault. After a last-minute attempt to save him by surgery, he died without recovering consciousness. They laid him out in intensive care. We took our leave of him. In death he looked like a great warrior on his funeral bier – for the poison had been swift in its devastation and the outer corporeal envelope betrayed no trace of the organic breakdown within.

Fourth deadly tale – 1964 (Kathleen Pollock, 1911–64)
This is the second time cancer has robbed me.

My mother died in 1964, when she was fifty-two, of cancer of the colon which had spread into her spine.

Undiagnosed by doctors, her symptoms were misattributed to menopause – to middle age and femininity.

Not unlike me in size and build, she weighed less than forty pounds at her death.

When not bemused by the heavy doses of painkilling morphine, she was both horrified and fascinated by what the deadly disease had done to her. Stick-like legs protruded below a distended belly, like some Oxfam poster showing a victim of famine – or an adolescent pregnancy.

Here was an outrageous morphology: the shape which promises life contained the ghastly growth that signalled imminent death. Something within that natural body was gnawing away at whatever the social body is meant to encase: humanity, personhood.

I have never come to terms with this death.

Its physicality was too outrageous.

The distortion of the maternal body was too grotesque to allow recovery and re-internalization of the beneficent image of the mother as either an imago of identification or a memory of plenitude and desire.

All other traces of her were traumatically cauterized by the final victory of the diseased natural body over all that in life makes the body a social being and the stuff of dreams.

The only moment of relief from terminal loss occurred when I was to become a mother myself.

Innocently, naively, I imagined that it would be an easy, complete antidote to death – fullness instead of emptiness, presence in place of absence.

I miscarried.

In that, my first pregnancy, I dreamed the transitivities of feminine identity. I oscillated between the mother and the infant, between recreating my own mother, reaching out to her again, and imagining the joys of being a child cradled lovingly in the safety of another's body.

I created an imaginary realm of comfort, which promised to bind a traumatized past to a healing future, offering restoration in an experience of maternal plenitude and power through the new life that was developing within the matrix of my own body – a singular space of doubling, oneness and otherness, where an I and a non-I co-exist harmoniously yet unknowing.

Pain exploded this dream. Instead of life inside this uterine matrix of companionship, I carried death internally that led to a parody of birth as the no-longer maternal body contracted to rid itself of dangerously decaying physical matter.

I did not know who was being mourned.

With pregnancy, I had once again become the child to be nurtured a second time round through the surrogacy of my own nurturing of my child.

I was also my mother.

I was also giving birth to her again.

I was being given, in the female child I was sure I was carrying, another chance to love her better so that she would not die through any act of omission on my part.

I failed again to defeat that history.

Doubling life gave way to redoubled grief.

Julia Kristeva asks: 'Who is the subject of gestation?'

I ask: ' Who is the subject of death?'

It happened, therefore I am not there. I cannot think it, yet it is happening.

For the dying and dead, death annihilates subjectivity.

Someone survives another's death to be its bearer.

The living are the subjects of death. The living bear the event that happens elsewhere to another to a natural body. The bereaved are its social body. This is why the philosophers never get it. They talk of death as human infinitude. But I talk of death as something that happened to me who is its living witness, the carrier of its memory.

Can death then be gendered?

Fifth deadly tale (Roland Barthes, 1915–80)

I offer this text as a feminist interruption of the prevailing discourse on the mother, the maternal body in particular, and on masculine death's deadly relation to both.

In 1992 I belatedly read with care the central sections of Barthes' *Camera Lucida* (*La Chambre claire*). While I was gazing helplessly at photographs of my own mother, hoping to pierce the utter fixity of the photographic image and reclaim some grain of recognition from its aesthetic freeze, I found Barthes had elegantly been there before me. Or had he?

> There I was, alone in the apartment where she had died, looking at these pictures of my mother, one by one, under the lamp,

gradually moving back in time with her, looking for the truth of the face I had loved. And I found it.[4]

He was writing about a photograph of his mother aged five, taken in 1898, in a conservatory or winter garden, and in this pre-figuration of her adult face Barthes found the image of his mother. This photograph – which he will not show – is the heart of the book, its navel, says Elisabeth Bronfen. His mother is kept safe from our eyes; she is kept safe for his only. Barthes tells us about the last period of this five-year-old child's later life, by which time she is his mother: she has no name, no being in this text except as 'my mother' – his Other.

> At the end of her life, shortly before the moment when I looked through her pictures and discovered the Winter Garden Photograph, my mother was weak, very weak. I lived in her weakness … During her illness, I nursed her, held the bowl of tea she liked because it was easier to drink from than from a cup; she had become my little girl, uniting for me with that essential child she was in her first photograph … Ultimately I experienced her, strong as she had been, my inner law, as my feminine child. Which was my way of resolving Death. If, as so many philosophers have said, Death is the harsh victory of the race, if the particular dies for the satisfaction of the universal, if after having been reproduced as other than himself, the individual dies, having thereby denied and transcended himself, I who had not procreated, I had, in her very illness, engendered my mother.[5]

Death seems, therefore, to stage the oscillations between mother and child trapping us into imaging once again a cor-respondence between life and death, or at least life-giving and death. No, this is not what is happening here, for this death is a radical rupture, in Barthes' case, from a dyad of mother and son to a curious unity of male mother and ancient daughter, a shift to the feminine significantly recouped by the use of the verb *engen-drer*. *Engendrer* means to beget – which has overtones of biblical narratives where a male genealogy is aligned down the genera-tions through much begetting of father and son. Does this bring us back to the left side of the Souch painting? – with Barthes strung out across its different spaces and registers, his mother occupying that empty cradle atopped by the skull.

He nursed her, feeding her as a mother would a child.

The mother became his *feminine* child – *enfant féminine* is the word used, so she is not merely, matter of factly his daughter, his offspring. That feminine child is also him, my child, the child within me, the desired space of being a woman child to a mother, rather than a childless son to a dying woman.

Sixth deadly tale (Œdipus–Smœdipus – so long as he loves his mother)

In psychoanalytic narratives – another mother-killing death narrative – a stake is important. Montrelay says women are the ruin of representation because they do not have a stake, something to mortgage to the symbolic and language. Their sexuality and fantasy life retain the stamp of that archaic, precocious femininity entangled in the maternal body. With the son's bereavement, and no child created through his passage into and beyond a woman's body, Barthes lost his: except in being an intellectual.

I think Freud was really writing not about Œdipus and the castration complex but about another legend concerning death and the generations: about Isaac and the father/son death complex. The founding contract of sociality and the submission to the paternal law is better told in the Bible story of Abraham, called by his God to sacrifice his by then only son – the belated first fruit of Sarah's aged womb. The human social contract is established when Abraham's one unnamable God lets Abraham off killing his (legitimate) son with a big knife, displacing the actual sacrifice of the child of Sarah's womb by substituting a *symbolic* act, the killing of a ram, which will stand as a metaphor for what God actually wanted from Abraham, namely his obedience to the law. In a sense, he wanted Abraham's being, which is what we concede to the symbolic, to language, finding ourselves reformed and displaced through its signifiers.

This biblical narrative concludes with no further discussion of Isaac – so named because he made his mother laugh – but with the death of Sarah, the mother. The maternal process of creating the child is overtaken by the divine act of threatening its life and restoring it but only in an exclusive lineage of father to son.[6] The Greek version of such mythic material, the Œdipus legend, within which Freud disguised and thus disfigured his profound understanding of the symbolic contract of the binding of Isaac, is much more overtly about sexual organs, and desire itself – and the mother is a major figure.

Instead of dying, out of sight, like Sarah, Jocasta acquires the characteristics of the Sphinx, the animal world over which the Greeks imagined man triumphed by his reason and self-recognition alone. Jocasta, the mother becomes the figure of Death who can equally never escape being the lure of masculine desire.

But what of Roland Barthes, the Protestant, not surrounded in childhood with that Greek and ever older, pre-Judaic image of the Mother and Child which has persisted in Western Catholicism? After recounting his begetting of his feminine self/child in the mortal image of his lost mother, he writes his own suicide note:

> Once she was dead I no longer had any reason to attune myself to the progress of the superior Life Force (the race, the species). My particularity could never again universalise itself (unless utopically, by writing, whose project henceforth would become the unique goal of my life). From now on I could do no more than await my total, undialectical death. That is what I read in the Winter Garden Photograph.[7]

It is quite clear that art will always enact death because it is the compensation for the creativity which, denied to men, allows women a dialectical relation of both self and other and life and death.

The philosophers to whom Barthes refers sound pretty local – probably Lacanian, with all that junk about the race and the species, the particular and the individual.

It is because they are allowed to get away with such utter banality and abstraction that Barthes can write out such a fantasy which so clearly delineates the uses and abuses of the female pro-creative and maternal body as the hidden centre, the absent structure of phallic surrogate creativities.

I want to talk about death without too many of my own metaphorical delusions.

I want to talk about it in terms of blood, shit, bloating, gas chambers.

I want it to be embodied.

I want to be able to speak and think about my mother, her death, my mourning, my dead babies, those bloodied surgical dishes with the remnants of possible beings, sacs containing almost formed little limbs, who were not my stake in the race, my contribution to the species, but fully formed figurations of my own desire and themselves, real, physical life.

I do not want my body to be the passage through which men may beget themselves and their progeny.

I want it to be the site of a sexually specific and particular sub-jectivity, which is a subject of gestation and of mourning.

Touched as I am by the poignant frankness of Roland Barthes' sharing in public of his feelings about his mother and her death, I see in his text the quintessential forms of the Western masculine narratives which embrace death rather than acknowledge the humanity of women. The female body – as opposed to its femi-nized death as enshrined in our culture – remains a terrifying hybrid, just as shocking those of us who live inside it yet lack a signifying system to speak it. Even to mention my mother in pub-lic lacks, I feel, the validation of the social collective memory which attaches to Barthes' lovely, silent mother to whom he never spoke, in whose presence he admits he never discoursed, for there was just 'the space of love, its music'. I am sure that the term 'my mother' uttered by another woman signifies in our cul-ture someone – or, rather, something – quite different from the image evoked if those words emerge from masculine speech. It risks the decline into sentimentality, autobiography, not philo-sophical reflection on time, history and the text. That is why no image of her, captured in the obvious signifying systems of cul-ture move me to recognize her – my mother. For the relations of woman to woman via the maternal body and imago are sexually specific and, in the words of Kaja Silverman, endemically melan-cholic, that is akin to a state of perpetual mourning. Mourning involves the withdrawal of libidinal investment in an object which is lost or has disappointed and this retraction is complete only when the object is discarded, having been rendered valueless by the success of forces of hatred over those of love which seek to maintain the cathexis. In the formation of feminine subjectivity, Silverman argues for an overlooked Freudian theorization of the negative Œdipal complex – that is, a situation in which the mother is the desired object of the female child as well as the figure of identification in the construction of a gendered positionality in culture. The negative Œdipal attachment must be overcome, but the process will induce melancholia and a kind of mourning in the child because she is asked to devalue that with which she is also identified – in a sense she must lose herself. The cure – devaluation of the object; a detachment from the mother – is not possible or desirable. Femininity is condemned to a permanent and incomplete mourning which perpetually betrays its own ambivalences; these can only be worked out dynamically, in other relations, such as joining the women's movement or having a child – that is, in activity rather than the passivity which masculine narratives impose on women dead or alive.

Seventh deadly tale – a visit to the theatre in 1964

A long time ago, shortly after my mother died, I was taken to the Old Vic theatre in London to see Tom Stoppard's play *Rosencrantz and Guildenstern are Dead*. At the very end of the play, itself a playing out of themes from the margins of Shakespeare's *Hamlet*, The Player declares: 'In our experience most things end in death.' – a truism so banal, yet an ironic sight into patriarchal culture; a comment about the deep structure of narrative, about the ever present death drive. Stories end with death and marriage – much the same thing, traditionally.

Death becomes the figure of stasis, fixity, finality.

It is not.

Stoppard makes Guildenstern say so:

'Death is not anything. Death is not.' It is not in the realm of being; like Woman, it cannot be. It is Other and Thing. But it leaves a trace: 'No one gets up after death – there is no applause – there is only silence and some second-hand clothes ...'

So true – all those poignant remains of daily life. What do we do with someone's recently abandoned clothes, the shell that last hugged their living form?

Wear them, sell them, give them to strangers? Can we bear to part with what once touched the missing body and graced their social presence?

The Player pretends to die, then gets up and takes his bow. He lists the kinds of death he and his players can enact. Guildenstern cannot bear it: 'No ... No ... not for us, not like that. Dying is not romantic, and death is not a game which will soon be over.'

Stoppard gives him the best line:

'Death is not anything ... death is not. *It's the absence of presence, nothing more ... the endless time of never coming back ... a gap you can't see, and when the wind blows through it, it makes no sound...*[8]

The absence of presence,
The absence of presence,

The presence of absence,
The presence of absence,
The endless time of never coming back
The endless time
of never
coming back
of never coming back
of never, never, never,
being there.

Endless neverness is real and constant, and makes a hole in a life that nothing can repair. It makes a gap *you* cannot see but that defines the space around which my subjectivity forever hovers.

When the wind blows through it, it makes no sound.

I wanted to give that gap a sound.

I wanted to speak the endlessness of living with a grief that cannot be assuaged.

Death lives with me and I live in it.

And I have tried to speak it, yet ...

Afterword

However hard I have tried to find aesthetic forms through which to shuffle my pain and grief, to fix death to an image which contains and yet defers it, pacifies it, I cannot in all honesty pretend that the photograph, or any sequence of images I might manipulate and call art, can stop that endless time of someone being missing in daily life as well as in all psychological stagings of my own formation. The millions of people today who are dying are leaving people who are terminally bereaved and there is, in our culture, as yet no adequate narrative which can stay, stop, halt or freeze that process, for me and, I dare to suggest, for most. Why is this?

Notes

1 N. Llewellyn, *The Art of Death: Visual Culture in the English Death Ritual, c. 1500–1800* (London: Reaktion Books, 1991), p. 47.

2 G. Scholem, *Walter Benjamin: The Story of a Friendship* (New York: Shocken Books, 1981), p. 226.

3 T. Adorno, 'After Auschwitz', *Negative Dialectics*, trans. E. B. Ashton (New York: Continuum, 1973), p. 362.

4 R. Barthes, *Camera Lucida* (London: Vintage, 1981). 'Something like an essence of the Photograph floated in this particular picture. I, therefore, decided to "derive" all Photography (its "nature") from the only photograph which assuredly existed for me, and to take it as a guide for my last investigation ... I had understood that henceforth I must interrogate the evidence of Photography, not from the viewpoint of pleasure, but in relation to what we romantically call love and death' (p. 73).

5 Barthes, *Camera Lucida*, p. 72.

6 See N. Segal, 'Reading as feminist: The case of Sarah and Naomi', *University of Leeds Review*, 32 (1989–90), 37–57.

7 Barthes, *Camera Lucida*, p. 72.

8 T. Stoppard, *Rosencrantz and Guildenstern Are Dead* (London: Faber and Faber, 1967), pp. 89–91.

12

To be announced

NICHOLAS ROYLE

To be announced: that is my title and point of departure, the announcement of a departure and the departure of an announcement. What is departure? When will it have begun to depart from everything, or if nothing else to dream of a departing from everything?

> *Departure:* act of departing; a going away from a place; deviation (from a normal course of action, etc); the distance in nautical miles travelled by a ship due east or west; a death (*euphem* [the dictionary uses this abbreviation for 'euphemism', in an act of euphemasia]) ... *the departed:* (*euphem*) a person (or people) who has (or have) died'. (*Chambers Dictionary*)

To be announced, to lie down, as if on your death-bed, with someone listening. Psychoanalysis, in a word, I'm with you, Sigmund, I'm in your dream, I'm holding your hand, or holding your head, I'm trying to hold you in my head as I feel you trying to hold me, your ear in my head, my ear in your voice, my voice in your ear, both of us out to the world. I'm trying to listen to all your death-sentences, first of all to this short but amazing paragraph on 'Symbolism and Dreams' (1916) in the *Introductory Lectures*:

> Departure in dreams means dying. So, too, if a child asks where someone is who has died and whom he [*sic*] misses, it is common nursery usage to reply that he has gone on a journey. Once more I should like to contradict the belief that the dream-symbol [that is, departure] is derived from this evasion. The dramatist is using the same symbolic connection when he speaks of the after-life, as 'the undiscovered country from whose bourn no *traveller* returns'. Even in ordinary life [that's always been one of my favourite Freud jokes, 'even in ordinary

life', as distinguished here, one might be expected to think, from literature and therefore from something like 'the psycho-pathology of literary texts'! – even in ordinary life, you were saying,] it is common to speak of 'the last journey'. Everyone acquainted with ancient rituals [are we still talking about 'ordinary life'? I'm sorry, I'm interrupting you: to repeat: Everyone acquainted with ancient rituals] is aware of how seriously (in the religion of Ancient Egypt, for instance) the idea is taken of a journey to the land of the dead. Many copies have survived of *The Book of the Dead*, which was supplied to the mummy like a Baedeker [or Blue Guide (Norwegian blue: it's not dead, it's resting)] to take with him [*sic*] on the journey. Ever since burial-places have been separated from dwelling-places, the dead person's last journey has indeed become a reality.[1]

'Departure in dreams means dying': what does this mean? Is the statement intelligible or is it such stuff as dreams are made on? Do you mean 'dying' or 'death'? And whose departure and from where? Is there departure? Does departure ever take place as such? Or conversely, when is one not departing in a dream, or when is a dream not a departure? No departures today, I'm sorry, there's a dream-strike. Earlier on in the same lecture you assert: 'Dying is replaced in dreams by departure, [for example,] by a train journey, being dead by various obscure and, as it were, timid hints'.[2] No doubt your comments in the 1916 lecture in some sense go back to the thinking of *The Interpretation of Dreams* (1900) where you speak of '[d]reams of missing a train' as

> dreams of consolation for another kind of anxiety felt in sleep – the fear of dying. 'Departing' on a journey is one of the com-monest and best authenticated symbols of death. These dreams say in a consoling way: 'Don't worry, you won't die (depart).'[3]

I like this last death-sentence especially, where your argument depends on an anthropomorphizing of the dream, where you listen, as it were in a telepathic rapport, to what the dream in its consoling way says to you; but I confess I can't be consoled by this account. In fact, I confess to not being at all clear that there is an 'I' to be consoled, an I to whom dreams speak in a consoling or any other way. In particular, I can't help wondering about this notion of symbols and the claim that there is such a thing as an 'authenticated symbol of death': who's authenticating here?

Not children, it may seem, at least from the way in which you carry on, in the little paragraph in the *Introductory Lectures*. To children, you say, we say, a person who has died has gone on a journey. We do not dream of dying as departure because, for example, of the prevalence of this 'evasion' in so-called 'ordinary life'. Let us just repeat together: 'Once more I should like to contradict the belief that the dream-symbol is derived from this evasion.' In the previous paragraph, concerned with the argument that 'Birth is regularly expressed in dreams by some connection with water', you maintain that learning in childhood that storks bring babies (even if the child does not consider the fact that the stork fetches the baby from a pond or stream) 'contribute[s] nothing to the construction of the symbol'.[4] The evasion as a departure from the truth, departure as 'euphem', a seeming departure for euphemland: this evasion (which can only be 'to be announced', since it is not an evasion of anything imaginable in short) is subordinated to a greater truth, to that great labyrinthine discourse on euphemism called psychoanalysis. *Chambers* defines 'euphemism' as '[1] a figure of rhetoric by which an unpleasant or offensive thing is described or referred to by a milder term; [2] such a term': this split definition ('euphemism' is at once the term itself and the process by which it works) points towards what 'euph' perhaps forgot, that euphemism is always itself euphemistic. No word can escape the law of euphemism, least of all perhaps 'death'. In speaking of death one has to speak well of it. As our telepathic friend Jacques Derrida has said: 'Let us not speak ill of death, not speak badly or unjustly of death. Let us not calumniate it; let us learn not to do so. We would run the risk of wounding, in our memory, those whom it bears.'[5] The context of his remark, the death of Paul de Man, bears on the notion of the limits of death: it is mistaken to speak of the limits of death insofar as such a phrase inevitably tends to imply a logic of surfaces or depths. From everything that one might want to say about death, Derrida suggests, from any and every possible word or sentence, 'nothing collects on the plane of a single surface or in the unity of some depth'.[6] One has to speak well of death and one can only do so thanks to writing, thanks to a logic of repetition that derails every departure while making it possible.

All of this is perhaps to be heard in the concluding sentences of your paragraph:

> Even in ordinary life, it is common to speak of the 'last journey'. Everyone acquainted with ancient rituals is aware of how seriously (in the religion of Ancient Egypt, for instance) the idea is taken of a journey to the land of the dead. Many copies have survived of *The Book of the Dead*, which was supplied to the mummy like a Baedeker to take with him on the journey. Ever since burial-places have been separated from dwelling-places, the dead person's last journey has indeed become a reality.

The labour of authentication is inseparable from the question of writing; the capacity for writing to survive, to endure, to 'travel well', is a crucial reference in an ostensibly historical micro-narrative that moves from 'ordinary life' in the second decade of the twentieth century back to Ancient Egyptian times, back to a time which one might say never existed or exists perhaps only as a fictive point of departure for this history of death in four easy sentences. 'Ever since burial-places have been separated from dwelling-places, the dead person's last journey has indeed become a reality.' What is this supposedly historical time when burial-places became separated from dwelling-places? Did it happen? Can it ever happen? The elegance of this paragraph-ending really makes me want to laugh: 'Ever since burial-places have been separated from dwelling-places, the dead person's last journey has indeed become a reality.' It's so dead neat, this apparently straightforward literalization (what 'has indeed become a reality'). What is 'indeed' this 'reality' of a 'dead person' and of his or her 'last journey'? Where and when? Everything depends on the 'to be announced', the performative pronouncement of being dead, when nothing, perhaps, is less certain. As our mutual friend puts it, in *Spectres of Marx*, to 'pronounce dead' is

> a performative that seeks to reassure but first of all to reassure itself by assuring itself, for nothing is less sure, that what one would like to see dead is indeed dead. It speaks in the name of life, it claims to know what that is.[7]

'To be announced': this aphoristic phrase would be concerned
(like every aphorism: Gk *aphorizein* to define, from *apo* from, and
horos a limit) with limits. However elliptical or cryptic, the phrase
perhaps conveys something of the trembling and hesitation, in
particular regarding the time of death (when is it?) and place
(where is it?) – especially as this is decisively affected by language, by a pronouncement or announcement in language. I think
of a character of perhaps insufficiently recognized importance in
Ibsen's *A Doll's House*, Dr Rank, Medical Practitioner, the one who
has the legal authority to pronounce dead, sending a visiting card
to the lawyer Torvald Helmer and his wife Nora.

> *Torvald:* There's a black cross above his name. Look. What an
> uncanny idea. It's just as if he were announcing his
> own death.
> *Nora:* He is.[8]

The announcement here is undecidably present-futural (to be
announced), and additionally haunted by the dramaturgic context: it is writing (a play), writing about writing (a visiting card, 'a
black cross above [the] name'), a writing characterized by the
'uncanny idea' of an absent character and an annunciative
repeatability that is the condition of theatrical speech. I'll come
back to this theatricality, I promise.

In suggesting that psychoanalysis is a great discourse of
euphemism, I realize that I am contradicting what you say (in the
same lecture, 'Symbolism in Dreams') about its relentlessly non-
euphemistic nature. You declare that only here, in the tenth of
your introductory lectures, are you finally dealing with the subject-matter of sexual life. You claim not to beat about the bush
then, despite having taken nine lectures to get here. I quote:

> Since this is the first time I have spoken of the subject-matter
> of sexual life in one of these lectures, I owe you some account
> of the way in which I propose to treat the topic.[9]

This remark, by the way, makes little apparent sense: even if it
were true, which one might find hard to credit (in the immediately preceding lecture, on 'The Censorship of Dreams', for
example, one can find you getting diverted in a passage about

'love-services' and the satisfaction of 'erotic needs'[10]), but even if one were credulous enough to accept the claim that the first nine lectures of the *Introductory Lectures on Psychoanalysis* say nothing about the subject-matter of sexual life, why should you owe an account or explanation simply because you haven't spoken of it before? Concealing something? A calculated evasion? I'm sorry: you go on:

> Psychoanalysis finds no occasion for concealments and hints, it does not think it necessary to be ashamed of dealing with this important material, it believes it is right and proper to call everything by its correct name, and it hopes that this will be the best way of keeping irrelevant thoughts of a disturbing kind at a distance.[11]

What is the founder of psychoanalysis doing when he evokes 'irrelevant thoughts of a disturbing kind' and the desire to keep them at a distance? What are 'irrelevant thoughts' when it comes to psychoanalysis? I can't help it, I get tangled up in this disturbing thought of disturbing thoughts at a distance. You know what I am talking about: telepathy. Let's not lose touch –

'Departure in dreams means dying ...': what a paragraph! So beautiful and lucid, so seemingly open but strange. (And, in parenthesis – but everything here is that, parenthetical speech on the limits of parenthesis, digression, diversion, departure, the dash – let me just add that what makes the paragraph stand out is that it has nothing ostensibly to do with the so-called subject-matter of sexual life whatsoever: having promised that your lecture will focus on this topic and devoting the rest of the lecture to it, suddenly you seem to forget, your mind goes blank, as if something interposes, you are diverted, as if in a trance, you depart, as if into apparently irrelevant thoughts, into a parenthetical meditation on death, or into a sort of euphemistic meditation on departure itself (if there is such a thing). What is going on? What is passing or being passed by? Close brackets.) For you of course the psychoanalysis of dreams, here as it pertains to the dream-symbol of departure and death (or departure and dying, or departure as death – insuperable difficulties will have marked and complicated all these distinctions in advance, by a sort of uncanny advance-booking), has conceptual and theoretical priority over everything else. This is, as you know, and as you know I know you know, the psychoanalytical gesture *par excellence*: to delimit the boundaries of dreams, and to institute a theory of dreams that works with this delimitation in order to colonize everything, including life, death and literature. But where does a dream begin? For example yours, Sigmund, in this paragraph about departure from which I seem to be having such difficulty departing or not so much departing, perhaps never departing, for in truth there is a part of me, departed or undeparted in me, that never wants to depart from the blithe serenity of this paragraph. We'll be here forever at this rate, I can hear you saying.

In order to corroborate your claim about the priority of psychoanalysis, here as the study of dream-symbols, in order to maintain psychoanalysis as a sort of a Baedeker of life and death, what do you do? You call on literature, and more specifically Shakespeare, or rather you call on 'the dramatist', a term which, in avoiding the name of Shakespeare, might be described as name-dropping with a difference, a contradiction of the earlier commitment to the belief that 'it is right and proper to call everything by its correct name', in short as a euphemism and concealment. You think I am exaggerating, I know; you want to say 'Hey, come on, give me a break, I'm simply saying "the dramatist" rather than "Shakespeare" because I know that everyone knows what I am referring to, everyone knows the provenance of the phrase "the undiscovered country from whose bourn no traveller returns": we all know it, the impossible package holiday, you've said so yourself, it's a euphemism.' But hold on, Sigi: what if we were to adhere as rigorously as possible to the methodological terms of the *Introductory Lectures* themselves, for example, of the first of the three essays on 'Parapraxes' (Lecture 2)? What is at stake there is specifically the business of replying to 'someone who knows nothing of psychoanalysis' and who, in the face of the attempted psychoanalytical explanations of 'such apparent trivialities as the parapraxes of healthy people', comments: 'Oh! That's not worth explaining: they're just small chance events'.[12] All of this will have been enough to give someone a headache. As you go on to remark:

Slips of the tongue do really occur with particular frequency
when one is tired, has a headache or is threatened with
migraine ... Some people are accustomed to recognise the
approach of an attack of migraine when proper names escape
them in this way.

To which the editor of the English translation adds, in a footnote
in square brackets: 'This was a personal experience of Freud's.'[13]
I'm trying to share your headache now, in my mind. My mind?
What mind? Do you mind? Doubtless one's not supposed to mind,
or to pay it any mind, and yet I cannot help myself, I cannot help
being seduced by the perhaps irrelevant thought of a kind of
textual headache, a certain telepathy or suffering-at-a-distance
perhaps, namely, regarding the fact that you don't name Shakespeare: I just want to suggest that this omission of the name, this
evasion, circumlocution, repression, suppression, euphemism,
theoretical parapraxis, this textual absentmindedness or chance
remark if you want ('the dramatist') constitutes an area of
Freudian land-slippage. My concern here is not simply with the
argument that the empire of psychoanalysis is more literary than
you are able or willing to allow[14] but above all with the dream of
another writing, a mutual contamination and reinscription of the
relations between literature and psychoanalysis, dreaming of a
jetty, the jetty of a departure from psychoanalysis *and* literature.

'Bourn' again: does your extraordinary paragraph about departure and death come out of an association-cum-dissociation of
ideas whereby the two paragraphs preceding it, concerned with
birth, give birth to this otherwise apparently digressive meditation on death as the impossible referent of dream-symbolism (for
let's recall, in case anyone was thinking of getting carried away,
that psychoanalysis, for all its apparent pretensions to authenticity and to authority over the empire of dreams, cannot by its own
admission tell us anything about death except on the euphemistic
basis, at best, of 'various obscure and, as it were, timid hints')? Or
is the paragraph set off by a translingual or interlingual pun,
borne into existence by the words 'the undiscovered country
from whose *bourn* no traveller returns'? I have no answer to these
questions, Sigmund, I simply want to elucidate the amazing
dream-thanatography of your writing, to think through the textual

headache, to inhabit otherwise the edges or limits of Freudian *langue*-slippage, to highlight the literary or dramatic *intrigue* of this paragraph as a passage in which, as happens all the time in fact, your voice divides, the logic of your discursive 'place' doubles. What is 'bourn'? *The New Shorter Oxford English Dictionary* specifies:

> 1. A boundary (between fields, etc.); a frontier. 2. A bound, a limit. 3. Destination; a goal. 4. Realm, domain ... Senses 3 and 4 both arise from interpretations of Shakespeare.

And 'interpretations' here (as the fuller text of the *OED* makes clear) means 'misinterpretations': a '*misunderstanding* (my emphasis) of the passage in *Hamlet*'. It's funny: it's as if readers or hearers of Hamlet's words, at least from the eighteenth century, couldn't accept that 'bourn' meant only 'boundary', 'frontier' or 'limit'. 'Bourn' cannot, as such, be 'bourn': it can't be borne. In a sense this may not be surprising: the boundary is always already departed – it is never present; it is the departure 'in' departure as such. In its syntax, Hamlet's 'undiscovered country from whose bourn' would parallel the peculiar possessive in 'the limits of death': the bourn would belong to the undiscovered country as much *and* as little as limits might be thought to belong to death. What is being, perhaps, announced here?

A small detail to begin with: you say that 'the dramatist is using the same symbolic connection [as yourself] when he speaks of the after-life', but it is not Shakespeare who is speaking here, it is Hamlet. Or, simultaneously, it is Shakespeare *and* Hamlet or rather, to employ your own loony terms, Edward de Vere and Hamlet.[15] For the moment, however, let me speak of the phrase simply as Hamlet's, in order to evoke a certain tele-scenario, in which one might be able to start to think at once the theatricality of Hamlet's voice as a voice that haunts and dislocates your discourse (Hamlet as a fictional being irreducible to any psychoanalysis) and the strange radicality of the 'To be or not to be' speech itself:

> To be, or not to be, that is the question:
> Whether 'tis nobler in the mind to suffer

The slings and arrows of outrageous fortune,
Or to take arms against a sea of troubles
And by opposing end them. To die – to sleep,
No more; and by a sleep to say we end
The heart-ache and the thousand natural shocks
That flesh is heir to: 'tis a consummation
Devoutly to be wish'd. To die, to sleep;
To sleep, perchance to dream – ay, there's the rub:
For in that sleep of death what dreams may come,
When we have shuffled off this mortal coil,
Must give us pause ...
For who would bear the whips and scorns of time ... ?
... Who would fardels bear,
To grunt and sweat under a weary life,
But that the dread of something after death,
The undiscover'd country, from whose bourn
No traveller returns, puzzles the will,
And makes us rather bear those ills we have
Than fly to others that we know not of? (III, i, 56–82)

Not to be is not to be borne, but what we bear cannot be
'bourn', can never be the 'bourn', not even with a 'bare bodkin'
(III, i, 76). Harold Bloom has called such speeches examples of
'self-overhearing'. Of Shakespeare's characters he observes:
'Overhearing their own speeches and pondering those expressions, they change and go on to contemplate an otherness in the
self, or the possibility of such otherness.'[16] It is this sort of self-
bugging, this responsiveness within the unfolding of the speech-
act towards an otherness or foreign body within oneself (an
otherness never simply separable from the unimaginable 'reality'
of 'the undiscover'd country'), that illustrates what Bloom attributes to Shakespeare as 'the invention of the human'.[17] A danger
here, as often with Bloom's work, is that this insight be recuperated within the logic of a sort of self-expansiveness or self-
aggrandizement. Bloom, you may be pleased to hear, is something
of a true Freudian in this respect. Less pleasing, I suspect, is his
basic thesis on you and 'the dramatist' – namely, 'Shakespeare is
the inventor of psychoanalysis; Freud, its codifier' or, again,
'Freud is essentially prosified Shakespeare'.[18] But if you don't

mind my saying so, I don't think Bloom goes far enough in acknowledging and exploring the nature and implications of the invention. The speech from Hamlet is one that effectively breaks with all soliloquy (with every sense of an act of talking to oneself), not only because it's being overheard by others (by Claudius and Polonius) or by 'Hamlet himself', but more radically because it's speaking as a being perhaps as much dead as alive, it's a thanato-hypnagogics, 'to be announced'; it is the speech of a dramatic script, waiting to be announced, read, enacted by anyone, the dead, the living and the ghosts of those still to be.

The paragraph from your *Introductory Lectures* in turn belongs to this strange space of the 'to be announced'. On the one hand, there is the more or less acknowledged debt to literature, in particular the works of Shakespeare: you use *Hamlet* to support your claim about the symbolic significance of dreaming of going on a journey and thus to reinforce the proclaimed borders, to bolster the empire of the dream of psychoanalysis as a theory of dreams. On the other hand (and as the very obliqueness of the reference to *Hamlet* may already intimate), the passage from Shakespeare's play at issue here is perhaps less appropriate or appropriable than you are making out. It entails a living-dead recognition of a singular pause, the necessity of trying to respect the aporia or rub of dreams of death, of trying to disentangle the coil of infinitives that moves from 'To die, to sleep; / To sleep, perchance to dream' (III, i, 64–5), while inhabiting the uncertainty of whether one's speech or thoughts are those of the living or the dead, the wakeful or the dreaming. Who speaks here, the subject of this experience of the 'perchance', is *to be announced* – irreducible to Hamlet or to Shakespeare, you or me, to any single speaker alive or dead, awake or dreaming.

Elsewhere too, if not in Elsinore, your thinking of departure, dying and dreams is spectralized by this passage of *Hamlet*: in a section of *The Interpretation of Dreams* entitled 'Dreams of the Death of Persons of Whom the Dreamer is Fond',[19] you talk again about the idea that 'To children ... being "dead" means approximately the same as being "gone"',[20] and then discuss the example of a mother who 'does actually make the journey to that "undiscover'd country, from whose bourn no traveller returns"'.[21] In

effect, it seems to me that you are subscribing to the children's
view and to the notion of death as a journey, but you do it without
really saying so, and specifically by way of this reference (in quotation marks though unattributed) to *Hamlet*. (It is in a footnote to
this passage, added in 1909, that you recall the observation of a
'highly intelligent' ten-year-old boy 'after the sudden death of his
father: "I know father's dead, but what I can't understand is why
he doesn't come home to supper".'[22] I am sorry, I have to ask
myself, I have to ask you, is it possible to read this without recalling in turn Hamlet's apparent euphemism on the subject of the
dead father in answer to the question 'where's Polonius?': 'At
supper'; 'At supper? Where?'; 'Not where he eats, but where he is
eaten' (IV, iii, 16–19).) That Hamlet is the presiding madman of
The Interpretation of Dreams perhaps goes without saying: he is
the point of reference for what you no doubt regard ambivalently
as the pitifully yet thankfully small number of thinkers who
take an approach to dream interpretation similar to your own.
Apparently inadvertently confusing dreams and waking life, you
announce: 'It seems, however, to have dawned on *some* other
writers that the madness of dreams may not be without method
and may even be simulated, like that of the Danish prince on
whom this shrewd judgement was passed.'[23] Goes without saying:
such is the manner in which Shakespeare's *Hamlet* is passed off
here. You go on to talk about some of your precursors, but you
don't mention again, at least by name, the text that has provided
you with the very framework of your account. And yet the ghost
of *Hamlet* returns, almost immediately. For you find yourself
citing the 'sagacious Delbœuf' who writes (in 1885):

> In sleep, all the mental faculties (except for perception) – intel-
> ligence, imagination, memory, will and morality – remain essen-
> tially intact; they are merely applied to imaginary and unstable
> objects. A dreamer is an actor who at his own will plays the
> parts of madmen and philosophers, of executioners and their
> victims, of dwarfs and giants, of demons and angels.[24]

The dreamer is an actor, I would say, but not one who plays
multiple parts 'at his [or her] own will': this dream-acting, this
deathlife, as Hamlet puts it, 'puzzles the will'.

To be or not to be announced: psychoanalysis as a dream of departure from literature, departing from it but by the same token irrevocably altering the bourn of literature and now, here and now, connecting up with the thought of a quite different departure. Jacques Lacan, another telepathic pretender of yours, demonstrates a similar furtiveness and embarrassment around naming Hamlet in his remarks on 'Desire, life and death' when he says:

> All that life is concerned with is seeking repose as much as possible while awaiting death ... [D]ozing off is the most natural of all vital states. Life is concerned solely with dying – *To die, to sleep, perchance to dream*, as a certain gentleman put it, just when what was at issue was exactly that – to be or not to be.[25]

(In parenthesis, let me briefly note the attempt – it does not matter if it is conscious or unconscious, it is the very lucidity of those distinctions that will have been dropping off here – to appropriate Shakespeare's play by speaking of it in the past tense – 'as a certain gentleman put it' – even though, as Lacan immediately proceeds to make clear, it is all about a performativity of language right now, in the strange singularity of a speech act. End of brackets.) The Shakespearean séance continues:

> This *to be or not to be* [says Lacan] is an entirely verbal story. A very funny comedian tried showing how Shakespeare came upon it, scratching his head – *to be or not* ..., and he would start again – *to be or not ... to be*. If that's funny [Lacan no longer seems to be sure, it was a 'very funny comedian' just a moment ago: I'm sorry, there I go, interposing again: If that's funny, says Lacan,] that's because this moment is when the entire dimension of language comes into focus. The dream and the joke emerge on the same level.[26]

Dream, what dream? The dream of 'a certain gentleman', and if so, the dream of Shakespeare or the dream of Hamlet? No: it is the dream rather of psychoanalysis, again. An uncertain psychoanalyst follows you in the violence of his appropriation of Shakespeare's play, most notoriously in the seminar on 'Desire and the Interpretation of Desire in *Hamlet*', where the play is the thing above all insofar as it provides an allegory of the truth of psychoanalysis.[27] Lacan is right, I think, to identify the 'to be or not to be' as a 'verbal story' (even if the 'entirely' begs questions): as I've been trying to suggest, Hamlet's question is at least on one level the equivalent of 'Am I, as a speaking person, alive or dead?'[28] To be or not to be 'announced': for example, starting from the question of what we are doing here, of what is happening, what is going on when one does to, say, Freud and Lacan what they do to Hamlet – in other words, ventriloquize them, letting them speak for themselves while setting them off as comical but thought-provoking characters in a new kind of writing that keeps the memory of psychoanalysis and literature without perhaps returning to either. Something else will always have been interposing: buzz, buzz.

> I heard a fly buzz – when I died –
> The Stillness in the Room
> Was like the Stillness in the Air –
> Between the Heaves of storm –
>
> The Eyes around – had wrung them dry –
> And Breaths were gathering firm
> For that last Onset – when the King
> Be witnessed – in the Room –
>
> I willed my Keepsakes – Signed away
> What portion of me be
> Assignable – and then it was
> There interposed a Fly –
>
> With Blue – uncertain stumbling Buzz –
> Between the light – and me –
> And then the Windows failed – and then
> I could not see to see –
>
> *The Complete Poems of Emily Dickinson*[29]

The blue guide. What interposes through Emily Dickinson's poem: the blue guide in the form of an interposing in interposing itself (the word 'interposed' occurs nowhere else in her poetry: an interposing that occurs, if it occurs, only once), an interring between the light and me, between the remains of the day and the remains of 'me' (having subtracted 'what portion of me be / Assignable'), between one stumbling sibilant and its seemingly stony recitation (you see to see, to see to see to see, you see?). In short, a question of sound and more specifically an experience of voice. It is easy enough, no doubt, to be distracted by the fly and miss the place of the other 'interposing' that is itself the condition of possibility of this fly – in other words, the voice, or a trace in the voice, in a narrative lyrical voice that, initially sounding in around 1862, in a text published posthumously in 1896, interposes as what could be called an irrevocable tear or interring in the history of literature and its others (including literary criticism, philosophy and psychoanalysis). It is an example of prosopopeia, a fiction of the voice from beyond the grave. It calls up what Paul de Man said about Wordsworth: 'Wordsworth', he declared in 'The Rhetoric of Temporality', 'is one of the few poets who can write proleptically about their own death and speak, as it were, from beyond their own graves'.[30] But something else is going on in Dickinson's poem: it sounds a small but dramatic shift, the interposing of a perhaps newly audible kind of foreign body. The voice in the poem is, like any epitaph, an example of prosopopeia, but it also narrates and listens to its own disappearance thanks to a logic that can be described as telepathic. This cryptic text in which the 'I' narrates its own death exemplifies what might be called the telepathic structure *par excellence*: to be able to make contact with yourself as a dead person.

This then would be the final buzz here, the one you knew deep down inside was to be announced: no death without telepathy; no telepathy without death. You felt it all along: telepathy as a bourn of the undiscovered country. I've heard myself and others saying it before, but I am hearing a certain difference in it now: telepathy is a foreign body within the theory of psychoanalysis; you cannot and cannot *not* admit this foreign body, Sigmund; it interposes everywhere and not least where it seems most distant. In the various short texts and other moments where you try to 'treat' telepathy (but there's no 'talking cure' for telepathy), it's invariably in the context of death.[31] Maria Torok goes so far as to assert that, as foreign body, telepathy, for you, is indissociable from the death drive:

Freud's fable of Thanatos becomes justifiable only in relation to an internal and unknown area in Freud himself. In other words, the introduction of a 'death instinct' into psychoanalytic theory makes sense only as a 'foreign body'.[32]

Your secret, Sigmund, but still unimaginable for you: your very own unimaginable, unpossessable secret.[33] Permit me to recall what our mutual friend says, in his *Aporias*:

> *death* is always the name of a secret, since it signs the irreplaceable singularity. It puts forth the public name, the common name of a secret, the common name of the proper name without name. It is therefore always a shibboleth, for the manifest name of a secret is from the beginning a private name, so that language about death is nothing but the long history of a secret society, neither public nor private, semi-private, semi-public, on the border between the two.[34]

The name of death is always on the border between public and private – the limits are here, then, for our telepathic friend – and what 'death' means for you, Sigmund, or for him, or for me, might be figured as an encounter or experience of mind-reading, neither conscious nor unconscious, alive nor dead, awake nor dreaming, in telepathic writing. That's it, that's us. Curtains.

Notes

1 S. Freud, 'Symbolism in Dreams', in *Pelican Freud Library 1: Introductory Lectures on Psychoanalysis*, trans. J. Strachey, ed. J. Strachey and A. Richards (Harmondsworth: Pelican, 1973 [1916]), pp. 182–203 (here p. 195).

2 Freud, 'Symbolism in Dreams', pp. 186–7.

3 S. Freud, *Pelican Freud Library 4: The Interpretation of Dreams*, trans. J. Strachey, ed. Strachey *et al.* (Harmondsworth: Penguin, 1976), p. 507.

4 Freud, 'Symbolism in Dreams', p. 194

5 J. Derrida, *Mémoires: for Paul de Man*, trans. C. Lindsay, J. Culler and E. Cadava (New York: Columbia University Press, 1986), p. 87.

6 *Mémoires*, p. 87. Derrida is commenting on the last letter de Man wrote to him, in which de Man quotes from the final line of Mallarmé's 'Tombeau [de Verlaine]', 'Un peu profond ruisseau calomnié la mort'.

Jonathan Culler's translation, 'this shallow calumniated stream called death', misleadingly makes the 'this' part of the translated phrase and adds what is perhaps not insignificantly elided in the French. Weinfield's translation – 'A shallow stream calumniated death' (Stéphane Mallarmé, *Collected Poems*, trans. and with a commentary by H. Weinfield [Berkeley: University of California Press, 1994], p. 73) – avoids the 'called' and thus perhaps better evokes the trembling force of what is going on here: Mallarmé's poem suggests that any and every calling or naming of 'death' (though in particular in the context of the poet and poetry of Verlaine) is a calumniation. Derrida, on the other hand, evidently wants to avoid the language of calumniation altogether.

7 J. Derrida, *Spectres of Marx: The State of the Debt, the Work of Mourning, and the New International*, trans. P. Kamuf (London: Routledge, 1994), p. 48.

8 *A Doll's House*, in *Henrik Ibsen: Four Major Plays* (Oxford: World's Classics, 1981), p. 74.

9 Freud, 'Symbolism in Dreams', p. 187.

10 Freud, 'The Censorship of Dreams', in *Pelican Freud Library 1: Introductory Lectures on Psychoanalysis*, pp. 170–1.

11 Freud, 'Symbolism in Dreams', p. 187.

12 Freud, 'Parapraxes', in *Pelican Freud Library 1: Introductory Lectures on Psychoanalysis*, p. 53.

13 *Ibid.*, n. 1.

14 As Paul de Man once observed, it is part of your literariness, it is part of the literarity of psychoanalysis, to 'know language's uncanny power to refuse the truth that nonetheless it never stops demanding'. The context of this remark was the occasion of introducing a lecture by Jacques Lacan, in New Haven in 1975. De Man prefaced the observation with a more critical assertion: 'I would say that we have not yet begun to suspect the extent to which this teaching [the teaching of psychoanalysis, what psychoanalysis has to teach] partakes of literature.' Paul de Man, cited by Shoshana Felman, in 'The Lesson of Paul de Man', *Yale French Studies*, 69, 1985, 51.

15 On the so-called 'Bacon-Shakespeare controversy', permit me to refer to my essay, 'The Distraction of "Freud": Literature, Psychoanalysis and the Bacon-Shakespeare Controversy', *Oxford Literary Review*, 12, 1990, 101–38.

16 H. Bloom, *The Western Canon: The Books and School of the Ages* (London: Macmillan, 1995), p. 70.

17 H. Bloom, *Shakespeare: The Invention of the Human* (New York: Riverhead Books, 1998).

18 Bloom, *The Western Canon*, pp. 375, 371.

19 Freud, *The Interpretation of Dreams*, p. 347–74.

20 Freud, *The Interpretation of Dreams*, p. 355.

21 Freud, *The Interpretation of Dreams*, p. 356.

22 Freud, *The Interpretation of Dreams*, p. 355, n. 1.

23 Freud, *The Interpretation of Dreams*, p. 126 (my emphasis).

24 Freud, *The Interpretation of Dreams*, p. 127, n. 1.

25 J. Lacan, 'Desire, Life and Death', in *The Seminar of Jacques Lacan, Book II: The Ego in Freud's Theory and in the Technique of Psychoanalysis, 1954–1955*, ed. J.-A. Miller, trans. S. Tomaselli, with Notes by J. Forrester (Cambridge: Cambridge University Press, 1988), pp. 221–34 (here, p. 233).

26 Lacan, 'Desire, Life and Death', p. 233.

27 'Desire and the Interpretation of Desire in Hamlet', trans. J. Hulbert, *Yale French Studies*, 55/56 (1977), 11–52. (*Literature and Psycho analysis. The Question of Reading: Otherwise*, ed. S. Felman.)

28 Cf. J. R. Lupton and K. Reinhard, *After Oedipus: Shakespeare in Psychoanalysis* (Ithaca: Cornell University Press, 1993), p. 77.

29 *The Complete Poems of Emily Dickinson*, ed. Thomas H. Johnson (London: Faber and Faber, 1975), pp. 223–4.

30 P. de Man, 'The Rhetoric of Temporality', in *Blindness and Insight: Essays in the Rhetoric of Contemporary Criticism*, 2nd edition (London, Methuen, 1983), p. 225.

31 Cf. J. Derrida, 'Telepathy', trans. N. Royle, *Oxford Literary Review*, 10 (1988), 3–41, especially 26–31.

32 M. Torok, 'Afterword: What is Occult in Occultism? Between Sigmund Freud and Sergei Pankeiev Wolf Man', in N. Abraham and M. Torok, *The Wolf Man's Magic Word*, trans. N. Rand (Minneapolis: University of Minnesota Press, 1986), pp. 84–106 (here, p. 91).

33 S. Freud, 'Thoughts for the Times on War and Death' (1915): 'It is indeed impossible to imagine our own death; and whenever we attempt to do so we can perceive that we are in fact still present as spectators.' See *Pelican Freud Library 12: Civilization, Society and Religion, Group Psychology, Civilization and Its Discontents and Other*

Works, trans. J. Strachey, ed. A. Dickson (Harmondsworth: Penguin, 1985), p. 77.

34 J. Derrida, *Aporias: Dying – Awaiting (One Another at) the 'Limits of Truth'*, trans. T. Dutoit (Stanford: Stanford University Press, 1993), p. 74.

Index